REDEFINING BUSINESS MODELS

The world has moved on in the advanced economies where credit-based financial systems coupled with malleable accounting practices disconnect capitalization and wealth accumulation from GDP trajectories and financial surplus. This, the book argues, is the product of economic, financial and cultural imperatives that privilege and encourage financial leverage for wealth accumulation.

This text redefines business models and strategy for a financialized world and presents a distinctive insight into the way in which national, corporate and focal firm business models have adapted and evolved. It also shows how, in the current financial crisis, financial disturbances can be amplified, transmitted and made increasingly porous by accounting systems, threatening economic stability. By making visible the tensions and contradictions embedded in this process of economic development, the authors construct a loose business model conceptual framework that is also grounded in accounting.

This is a valuable resource for practitioners, academics and policy makers with an interest in management, accounting and economic policy.

Colin Haslam is Director of the Finance Accounting Research Unit (FARU) at the University of Hertfordshire, UK.

Tord Andersson is a business broker and financial analyst with Swedbank and is also a visiting research fellow at the University of Hertfordshire, UK.

Nick Tsitsianis is a Principal Lecturer at the University of Hertfordshire, UK and an active researcher in the FARU.

Ya Ping Yin is a Senior Lecturer in Economics at the University of Hertfordshire Business School, UK.

REDEFINING BUSINESS MODELS

Strategies for a financialized world

Colin Haslam, Tord Andersson,
Nick Tsitsianis and Ya Ping Yin

Routledge
Taylor & Francis Group

LONDON AND NEW YORK

First published 2013
by Routledge
2 Park Square, Milton Park, Abingdon, Oxon OX14 4RN

Simultaneously published in the USA and Canada
by Routledge
711 Third Avenue, New York, NY 10017

Routledge is an imprint of the Taylor & Francis Group, an informa business

British Library Cataloguing in Publication Data
A catalogue record for this book is available from the British Library

Library of Congress Cataloging in Publication Data
Redefining business models : strategies for a financialized world /
Colin Haslam . . . [et al.].
p. cm.
Includes bibliographical references and index.
1. Business enterprise—Finance. 2. Capital—Accounting.
3. Surplus (Accounting) I. Haslam, Colin.
HG4026.R388 2012
658.15—dc23
2011052215

ISBN: 978–0–415–67440–9 (hbk)
ISBN: 978–0–203–11250–2 (ebk)

Typeset in Bembo
by Swales & Willis Ltd, Exeter, Devon

MIX
Paper from
responsible sources
FSC
www.fsc.org
FSC® C004839

Printed and bound in Great Britain by the MPG Books Group

CONTENTS

LIST OF FIGURES

LIST OF TABLES

ABOUT THE AUTHORS

Colin Haslam is Professor of Finance and Accounting and Director of the Finance Accounting Research Unit (FARU) at the Business School of the University of Hertfordshire. His research interests span both the public and private sector. He has published a number of reports including *Off-shoring of City Jobs* and *New Technology Firms on the Alternative Investment Market (AIM)* and, most recently, he was joint author of *UK Bio-pharma: Innovation, Re-invention and Capital at Risk* for the Institute of Chartered Accountants Scotland (ICAS). Colin has acted as chair of the Business and Management panel for the Academy of Finland Research Council and is a member of the European Financial Reporting Advisory Group (EFRAG) 'Disclosure Framework Advisory Panel', the aim of whcih project is to improve the disclosure of information in the notes to corporate financial statements.

Tord Andersson runs a management consulting business in Sweden and is a business broker for small and medium enterprises within Swedbank Företagsförmedling. He is also a visiting Senior Lecturer in Finance and an active researcher in the Finance Accounting Research Unit (FARU) at the Business School, University of Hertfordshire. Tord's research interests are concerned with corporate sector and firm-level performance for sustainable wealth accumulation, and with advancing accounting frameworks of analysis within the field of corporate strategy and corporate finance. Previously he worked in the telecommunications industry as product manager before moving into the finance sector as sell-side financial analyst (CEFA/AFA) and then subsequently a buy-side senior investment analyst. He is a member of the Swedish Society of Financial Analysts (SFF) and XBRL Sweden.

Nick Tsitsianis is a Principal Lecturer at the University of Hertfordshire and an active researcher in its Finance Accounting Research Unit (FARU). Prior to joining the university he was a lecturer at Brunel and Kent universities. His specialist research involves the construction of large-scale panel datasets applied to a range of research fields: reference values for gauging income and happiness across Europe, identifying the adopters and non-adopters of broadband, and tracking corporate performance in the S&P 500 and other major stock market indices. Nick has published on corporate financial performance and is joint author of the report *UK Bio-pharma: Innovation, Reinvention and Capital at Risk* for the Institute of Chartered Accountants Scotland (ICAS).

Ya Ping Yin is a Senior Lecturer in Economics in the Business School of the University of Hertfordshire. He was educated as a national economic planner and specialist in national accounting systems in Beijing and was subsequently appointed as an economic systems modeller at Strathclyde University. Dr Yin's main research interests are focused on how we account for productivity and efficiency measurement; market conditions, firm conduct and performance; and multi-sectoral growth models. His recent research cautioned readers about the nature and risk of accumulating consumer debt and questioned the sustainability of a banking-led economic growth trajectory. His published research highlights the structural fragility and increased level of systemic risk generated within the UK national business model.

ACKNOWLEDGEMENTS

This book could not have been written without the support of a number of others and we would like to acknowledge these contributions.

First of all, we would like to thank Jacqueline Curthoys, editor at Routledge, for her initial supportive response, and the anonymous reviewers she commissioned, who took the time and care to respond constructively and critically to our initial proposals.

We are grateful for the support of the University of Hertfordshire Business School, its dean (Julie Newlan and then Jerry Forrester) and its research director, Keith Randle, for providing resources to access datasets, and also the precious resource of 'time' allocated to this team so that they could deliver this project over such a short period. We also wish to express our gratitude to other members of the research team who are not co-authors but have in their different ways helped to make this book possible by their support, by covering for us and by helping to gather data and evidence: George Katechos, Grigorios Theodosoplous and Edward Lee, who has been a joint author on a number of previous articles and whose ideas have helped shape material included in this text

Our thanks also go to the Institute of Chartered Accountants Scotland (ICAS), for its funding of a research project on SME bio-pharma which helped to inform Chapter 10, and to the European Financial Advisory Reporting Group for their observations about the nature of business models and responses in discussion.

Finally, we wish to thank our families who have given their support and encouragement to finish the project we had all started.

ABBREVIATIONS

AIDS	acquired immunodeficiency syndrome
AIG	American International Group
AIM	Alternative Investment Market
ARM	adjustable rate mortgages
BEA	Bureau of Economic Analysis (USA)
BICRA	Banking Industry Country Risk Assessment
BM	business model
CAGR	compound annual growth rate
Cash ROCE	EBITDA as percentage of capital employed, where capital employed is the sum of equity and long-term debt
CDS	credit default swaps
CEO	chief executive officer
CFA	charted financial analysts
CFROI	cash flow return on investment
CIBER	Centre for International Business Education and Research
CII	capital intensity index
DLBM	digital lifestyle business model
EBIT	earnings before interest and tax
EBITDA	earnings before interest, tax, depreciation and amortization
EPS	earnings per share
EVA ™	Economic Value Added
FASB	Financial Accounting Standard Board
FDA	Food and Drugs Administration Agency
FDI	foreign direct investment
FDIC	Federal Deposit Insurance Corporation
FVA	fair value accounting
GAAP	Generally Accepted Accounting Practice

GDP	gross domestic product
GIIPS	Greece, Ireland, Italy, Portugal and Spain
GO	gross output
GOS	gross operating surplus
GSK	GlaxoSmithKline
GVA	gross value added
IAS	International Accounting Standards
IASB	International Accounting Standards Board
IBM	International Business Machines
IC	intermediate consumption
IFRS	International Financial Reporting Standards
IMF	International Monetary Fund
IRR	internal rate of return
LBO	leveraged buy-out
LC	labour costs
MKTVAL	market value at year end
MVA	market value added
NCE	new chemical entities
NETINCPS	net income per share
NOPAT	net operating profit after tax
NPV	net present value
OPEB	other post-employment benefits
OTC	over the counter
PEBM	private equity business model
PEP	private equity partnership
R&D	research and development
RBS	Royal Bank of Scotland
RBT	resource-based theory
ROA	return on assets
ROCE	return on capital employed
ROE	return on equity
ROI	return on investment
S&P	Standard and Poor's
SBB	share buy-backs
SFAS	Statement of Financial Accounting Standards
SME	small and medium enterprise
SPV	special purpose vehicle
SORP	Statement of Recommended Practice
TIPS	Treasury Inflation-Protected Securities
VAR	value added retained
VC	venture capital
WACC	weighted average cost of capital

1

INTRODUCTION

No quality newspaper has recently been complete without a story about the banking crisis and how sovereign governments are finding it increasingly difficult to fund their deficits and refinance their roll-over debt. The current financial crisis is global and interconnected because adjustments are transmitted and amplified by accounting systems that equalize the value of assets and liabilities either up or down. According to a recent Bank for International Settlements report *Rescue Packages and Bank Lending*, recent financial problems are related to the instability of the banking business model.

> The global financial crisis is widely regarded as the worst financial crisis since the Great Depression. While financial distress afflicted the entire financial system, many crisis-related problems crystallised in the banking system, starting with the interbank market freeze in August 2007. Between early 2007 and March 2009, the stock market valuation of the banking sector declined by 79% from peak to trough, losing over 20% relative to the broader equity index (comparing the MSCI World Index and Bank sub index). CDS[1] premia shot up across the board, indicating that the market was pricing in a greater likelihood of bank defaults.
>
> *(Bank for International Settlements, 2011b: 2)*

Liquidity in a credit-based system reconciles timing differences between long-lived assets (loans) and short-term liabilities (deposits). A distinction can be made between liquidity generated by central banks (official) and that which is generated by private corporate financial and non-financial sectors. Private liquidity now far exceeds 'official' liquidity and where asset values (capitalizations) inflate there is a possibility of a 'liquidity disconnect'. That is, capitalizations accelerate ahead of income and surplus driven by factors other than the trajectory of earnings/surplus.

However, when asset valuations reduce the serviceability of capital accumulated under threat, this can compromise the solvency of business models amplifying asset price adjustments, especially where a substantial proportion of 'realizable collateral' is imaginary and based upon intangible goodwill and optimistic assumptions about counterparty viability.

A Bank of England *Financial Stability Report* (December 2011) observes that 'A flight to safety could cause sharp asset price movements . . . Shifts in capital flows as investors seek "safe havens" could cause large and disruptive movements in many asset prices' (Bank of England, 2011: 18). The banking crisis of 2007–2009 reveals how credit losses (loan defaults) were quickly followed by goodwill write-downs that rapidly undermined banking sector capital adequacy, triggering the need for official interventions to sustain balance sheets, capital adequacy and solvency.

> As the crisis proceeded, total credit losses eventually outpaced recapitaliza-
> tions. Combined credit losses of $1,508 billion ($801 billion in North Amer-
> ica) exceeded total recapitalizations of $1,318 billion ($515 billion in North
> America).
>
> *(Bank for International Settlements, 2011b: 4)*

> Banks also increasingly came under capital pressure. The IMF estimates
> that banks' worldwide credit-related write-downs were around $1.6 trillion
> between mid-2007 and end-2009. The national banking systems that have
> tended to cut back lending relatively sharply were the ones that have received
> the largest capital injections from their governments – a proxy for the pres-
> sure on their capital positions.
>
> *(Bank of England, 2010: 7)*

Thus in a credit-based system there is an ongoing tension between cash surplus capacity (liquidity) and ongoing capitalizations (as wealth accumulation for households) where complex global network relations, interconnectedness and financial imbalances have become the norm. When struggling banks were forced to write down goodwill assets in their balance sheets this also triggered a write-down in shareholder equity, threatening the capital adequacy capacity of banks to maintain lending and sustain GDP growth trajectories.[2] The reaction of regulatory authorities has been to try and strengthen global banking business balance sheets (with additional reserves and equity injections) to reduce 'official' exposure to the banking sector, but this may further curtail lending capacity.

> New Basle III capital adequacy will reduce lending capacity going forward
> by as much as 4–5 per cent.
>
> *(IMF, 2011: 3)*

> In normal times and particularly in boom periods, the supply of global
> liquidity will be largely determined by international banks (either directly or

of purpose we borrow from accounting to suggest that this is about securing cash generation and balance sheet capitalizations for liquidity and solvency. In terms of evaluation, accounting numbers can be used to construct alternative critical narratives that describe the development of focal firms, focal firms within their business model and business models relative to more generalized aggregations to assess the nature and extent of financial transformation.

Chapter 5 sets out to describe the global operating context within which advanced economy business models are located. This is one where the resource capacities for generating income growth and that for ongoing capitalization have become unevenly distributed. In terms of share of the global population, numbers economically active and employment costs per hour, the developing and industrializing economies of India and China are capturing a greater share of global GDP and their growth trajectories are far stronger than those of the advanced economies. They are also in receipt of an increased share of foreign direct investment (FDI) by global firms eager to capture cost reduction in the face of competitive price erosion. Furthermore the balance of trade is adjusting, with advanced economies generally in deficit and developing countries in surplus and net exporters of capital. On the other hand capitalization (debt and equity) for wealth accumulation is still the preserve of the advanced economies, and even though the drag on GDP growth has reduced the G7 share of global GDP to 50 per cent, their command of global capitalization (bonds, bank assets, equities) remains at roughly 70 per cent and in recent years capitalization has moved further ahead of GDP. In both Chapters 5 and 6 we reveal that whilst capitalization has been transformed in the advanced economies, there has been no significant adjustment in cost structure and gross operating surplus (cash) in these economies. Capitalization in the advanced economies has become increasingly disconnected from income circuits and surplus-generating capacity, helped, in part, by historically low interest rates but also changes to the nature of business models that facilitate capitalization ahead of liquidity.

In Chapter 7 we establish a bridge into our case studies by considering a number of generic restructuring possibilities that are open to focal firms within their business models. Our focus is on off-shoring and out-sourcing and restructuring through mergers and acquisitions or business combinations where the promise is financial transformation. Using data on US foreign-owned affiliates and their parent companies, we can evaluate the changing geographic location of US affiliate operations. It is clear that they are seeking to take advantage of low labour costs so as to maintain competitiveness against price erosion. However, we argue that a distinction needs to be drawn between price competitiveness and generating a higher return on capital invested. US affiliates tend to out-source more of their financial value chain, reducing their value retention rates, and so even after deducting employee costs, the cash surplus margin is no higher than that generated by US parents and, moreover, cash return on assets is also not significantly transformed by shifting production off-shore. We also find that corporate restructuring in the USA, through merger and business combinations, tends to inflate balance sheet capitalizations of the acquiring company as the market value of these deals is absorbed. In the S&P 500 group of firms the value of balance sheet capitalization moved ahead of cash earnings, reducing the cash return on capital employed (ROCE) from 27 to 17 per cent over the past fifteen years. The purpose of this chapter is to reveal how the accounting numbers can be used to challenge assumptions and reveal how contradictory forces operating in the information genotype can frustrate financial outcomes.

In the final third of this text we construct five cases that employ a business model framework of analysis to consider the viability of business models. Our first case considers the evolution of the US banking business model and how this adapts over time. First, restructuring has resulted in fewer larger banks and the difference between the market and book value of these deals accounted for as goodwill in the acquiring bank's balance sheet. Second, a process of asset securitization changed US banks from a 'retain and hold' to 'buy and sell on' business model, serving also to decouple loans outstanding from deposits and hence also GDP. Banks leveraged returns for equity investors where profits on assets, in a good year (before the banking crisis in 2007), were just 2 per cent. To convert this 2 per cent return on assets into a 25 per cent return on shareholder equity means that equity should be equivalent to 8 per cent of total assets. This equity to assets cover ratio not only leverages the return to equity investors but also doubles as the capital adequacy ratio which is set by Basle II and Basle III banking regulations. In 2009, household loans written off reached 2.8 per cent of bank loans outstanding, leading to a 60–70 per cent write-down in the market value of US banks. This then also triggered goodwill impairments in US banks. The combination of loan losses and goodwill write-downs reduced shareholder equity to a point where exposed banks (Lehman Brothers, Wachovia and 412 other banks since 2008) were no longer solvent.

The private equity business model described in Chapter 9 also depends on leveraging debt on behalf of equity investors. In a leveraged buyout, private equity investors have tended to mix debt funding with their own equity in the ratio 70:30 on the basis that acquired firms can be turned around and then sold on for a higher price than when acquired. Thus after paying repayments of debt, the funds remaining represent the return to the providers of equity funding (after payments have also been deducted for private equity partners – often 20 per cent of profits). In a leveraged buy-out, unlike a venture capital investment, the private equity partnership takes *de facto* ownership and management control with the purpose of improving financial performance and market value. Our analysis reveals that private equity partnerships have drawn down more funding than they have returned to equity investors. Moreover, this business model depends upon transforming acquired firms, a buoyant stock market, ease of access to debt finance, favourable loan covenants and maintaining a high debt to equity funding ratio.

In Chapter 10 we consider how the US big-pharma business model has evolved and adapted. We reveal that this is a business model that spends a significant proportion of income on R&D, but double this sum on marketing and distribution and even more on corporate acquisitions. As new chemical entities (NCEs) are developed, fewer are finding their way on to the market after obtaining US Food and Drug Administration (FDA) approval. Revenues in big-pharma are exposed to a patents 'cliff' as blockbusters move out of patent and generic manufacturers offer the same product at a significant discount. This business model has evolved to now include also biotechnology firms, but after a relatively short period of time the financial operating ratios of these firms converged to levels generated by big-pharmas. This business model is restructuring through acquisitions and out-sourcing of R&D. We argue that, as the business model consolidates into fewer firms, this is accelerating capitalization ahead of cash earnings capacity as the market value of acquired firms is absorbed on to the acquiring firm accounts. We also explore the way in which out-sourcing of R&D by big-pharma is designed to spread financial risk but also create opportunities for establishing small and medium enterprises (SMEs). These bio-pharma SMEs list to raise funds from equity investors and then burn these cash funds to develop NCEs, but they also require frequent refinancing events to keep it all going. It is all a gamble on new product development where innovation and reinvention might generate substantial financial returns to equity investors. The stakeholder networks within which these SMEs are subtended are complex and fragile and include universities, medical schools, business angels, venture capitalists, private and institutional investors, big-pharma partnerships and government. Our argument is that as the big-pharma business model has evolved, it has become increasingly capitalized and leveraged.

Chapter 11 is about the Digital Lifestyle Business Model (DLBM) which we construct by amalgamating computer hardware and peripherals, software and applications, internet and software services and communications technologies. Our argument for doing so is that the products of these 'industries' share many similar stakeholder network characteristics and thus it is sensible to combine their financials. In any case as firms evolve and adapt, they may organically migrate or be absorbed (by acquisition) into other industry sectors or provide outputs which are used as inputs by other sectors, such that a 'business model' might best be described as a loose matrix of activities that share relatively similar stakeholder and information networks. The financial characteristics of this business model contrast with those of the big-pharma business model in terms of the exceptionally high cash returns generated on capital. The composition of this business model (in terms of cash surplus generation) is shifting from computers and peripherals to software, applications and communications technology. During the 1990s this business model captured a greater share of S&P 500 sales, cash surplus and market value, but there are signs that the trajectory is maturing and stabilizing.

Our final case is on UK hospices (Chapter 12) which are part of the voluntary sector, dependent for most of their income on charitable donations, and provide palliative care for terminally ill patients young and old. The case is used to demonstrate how we can apply a business model approach to a range of activities that need liquidity and solvency to stay viable. Hospices are subtended in a complex information genotype that defines the nature of the business model in which they operate. This includes regulatory bodies, the National Health Service (NHS), local funding bodies and their influence over the delivery of care services, and a complex set of financial arrangements that generate income, such as shops, lotteries, legacies, donations and income from investments. Income streams into this business model are complex and often volatile; for example, legacies will change in terms of their market value whilst income from shops is relatively stable; more shops are required to boost income and this adds additional expenditure. Surpluses are accumulated in reserves which are invested and have in recent years generated holding gains, which can help to accelerate much-needed development projects as more of us live longer and require care. Unstable income and lower returns on invested capital threaten the viability of this business model and its capacity to provide additional palliative care going forward.

In summary, our aim in this book is to reconceptualize economic development within a loose business models conceptual framework that is grounded in accounting, not economics, where liquidity and solvency matter. We employ accounting numbers to construct alternative critical narratives about economic development and transformation in a financialized world.

2

ACCOUNTING FOR THE FIRM AS A BUSINESS MODEL

Introduction

In economic theory the nature and boundary of the firm are determined by managerial decisions about what productive activities are to be carried out within and outside the firm. These make-or-buy decisions and firm boundary conditions are informed, according to Ronald Coase (1937), by the need to minimize transaction costs with other market transactors. In this transaction cost approach to economic organization, markets and the firm are viewed as alternative modes of organizing productive activities and the yardstick for selecting whichever mode or combination of modes leads to the optimal minimization of transaction costs. The concept of transaction costs was referred to by Coase as 'the cost of using the price mechanism' (Coase, 1988: 38) or 'the cost of carrying out a transaction by means of an exchange on the open market' (Coase, 1961). Although much controversy still exists over the precise definition and measurement of transaction costs, such costs typically include searching and information costs attached to identifying other potential market transactors, their terms and conditions of transacting, costs of contractual negotiations with other transactors, and expense of enforcing contracts and settling any disputes. Coase's emphasis on transaction costs in economic analysis was motivated by the omnipresence of such costs in market-based transactions and his dissatisfaction with the implicit counterfactual assumption of frictionless or costless market exchanges in the orthodox economic theories. If, within the firm, an appropriate form of organizational structure under managerial direction can reduce transactions costs relative to the market mechanism for conducting the same activities, then it becomes financially attractive to carry out these activities within the firm. The transaction cost theory thus establishes a framework within which to construct business models using transactions cost minimization to discriminate between productive activities carried on within or outside the firm. The nature of firms' activities are, however, narrowly defined within a 'productionist' framework that is purported to explain why firms exist, and are more or less vertically integrated in the input and output value chain for specific goods and services. The object is to understand why firms modify their productive scope in terms of vertical integration and how this depends upon the costs of contracting with market agents versus internalizing activity within the firm's managerial control. Among the managerial tools used to inform agents about costs are accounting numbers, where the purpose and function of accounting is to report on economizing transactions and provide information to agents to enable modifications in a firm's strategic behaviour in terms of whether to extend or restrict the scope of the firm within its value/supply chain.

However, what happens between the purchase of the factors of production and the sale of goods that are produced by these factors is an area largely ignored in traditional economic theories according to Coase (1990). Troubled by the almost exclusive role in resource allocation and coordination of activities that economists had assigned to market prices, Coase was also interested in the role of intra-firm allocation mechanisms such as direct cooperation or managerial direction. In his words 'we had a factor of production, management, whose function was to coordinate. Why was it needed if the pricing system provided all the coordination necessary?' (ibid.: 715). This comment is important as Coase and others have contributed to the view of the firm as a set of interrelated contracts among a host of stakeholders ranging from various suppliers of input factors to the purchasers of the final product (Cornell and Shapiro, 1987).

The seminal work by Coase (1937) seeks to reconcile the gap between the way in which economists treat the price mechanism as a coordinating *instrument* and the coordinating *function* of the entrepreneur. In so doing Coase is trying to answer the question of why there are firms and under what conditions it is possible to organize or consolidate transactions within a firm (subject to variable governance arrangements) so as to economize on corporate resources and capabilities (for example, negotiation, renegotiation and administration of contracts with stakeholders) relative to the cost of organizing market-based transactions. If the costs of organizing/governance of contractual transactions are lower in the firm, then it is assumed that transactions will congeal within the boundaries of the firm (Coase, 1937: 392).

> Our task is to attempt to discover why a firm emerges at all in a specialized exchange economy. The price mechanism (considered purely from the side of the direction of resources) might be superseded if the relationship which replaced it was desired for its own sake.
>
> *(Coase, 1937: 390)*

Oliver Williamson (1975) consolidates the theory of the firm based upon a finer micro-analytic view of the different modes of economic organization and corresponding transaction costs, and identifies a number of characteristics associated with transactions and how these determine governance arrangements and hence also the boundary of the firm. Governance will vary according to the extent to which a firm's output depends upon investments in assets specific for the firm's outputs/ services and frequency/uncertainty attached to these transactions, as well as the nature of incomplete contracts and the 'unprogrammed' adaptations by contracting parties to significant contractual disturbances. The combination of incomplete contracts, high bilateral dependency (contingent on asset specificity) and defection from the norm of coordinated adaptation in the presence of significant contractual disturbances and substantial stakes provides the usual rationale for the firm to vertically integrate. For Williamson (1971), vertical integration is not about capturing more of the financial value chain, reducing costs or increasing balance sheet capitalization. Vertical integration is a response to market failure where transactions, as a result, are captured within the boundaries of the firm at lower cost.

> In more numerous respects than are commonly appreciated, the substitution of internal organization for market exchange is attractive less on account of technological economies associated with production but because of what may be referred to broadly as 'transactions failures'.
>
> *(Williamson , 1971: 112)*

Ghoshal and Moran note that the 'attempt to create a model of organizations based on the logic that creates the first set of behaviours (*markets*) destroys the context that is necessary for the second set (organizations)' (1996: 41). If we abandon the logics of the market and price mechanism as the *a priori* organizing force determining the location of a transaction, it is possible to argue that other logics and contextual conditions are shaping the emergence and evolution of the firm. For example, it is possible for firms competing in a similar market to produce components in-house (Ford) or out-source (Toyota) for considerable periods of time and still remain financially viable. This, according to Ghoshal and Moran (1996), reveals that 'there is no systematic evidence that for any given kind of transaction the inherent superiority of one governance mode has effectively weeded out the other, even in highly competitive contexts' (ibid.: 32).

In a reflective article on 'The Nature of the Firm', Coase (1988) reveals that the struggle for economists has been that they 'have tended to neglect the main activity of a firm, running a business'(ibid.: 38). Significantly, Coase observes that this involves an understanding of the process by which resources are (re)organized.

> In the 'Nature of the Firm' I said that a firm would tend to extend the range of its control as long as its costs were less than the costs of achieving the same result by market transactions or by means of operations within some other firms. But in that article I emphasized the comparison of the costs of transacting with the cost of organizing and did not investigate the factors that would make the costs of organizing lower for some firms than others.
>
> *(Coase, 1988: 47)*

Madhok further observes that 'the firm as an institution enjoys an organizational advantage which enables it to organize economic activity in a manner that markets simply cannot' (Madhok, 2002: 536) and Johanson and Mattsson. (1987) note that firms are dependent on one another as they divide the work among themselves in a network of firms. As a result, 'coordination takes place through interaction among firms where price is just one of several influencing conditions' (ibid.: 34). Even if firms are free to choose counterparts in the marketplace, exchange relationships are often established over time to gain access to external resources as well as to sell products. As a result, 'there are specific inter-firm dependence relations that are different in nature from the general dependence relationship to the market in the traditional market model' (ibid.: 35). This implies 'that a firm's activities in industrial markets are cumulative processes' as relationships are constantly being renegotiated to gain short-term economic returns and long-term (strategic) market positions, where an important assumption in the network model 'is that the individual firm is dependent on resources controlled by other firms' (ibid.: 36).

Cheung (1983) reinforces these observations, particularly emphasizing the limitations of Coase's distinction between the firm and the market, arguing that when a firm vertically integrates (internalizes market-based transactions) this does not supersede the market. Rather, a new set of intra-firm market transactions is replacing those that were previously externalized. Bringing external component manufacture or services in-house requires that one set of market transactions be replaced with another and this is then just a matter of choice over stakeholder contracts. Klein *et al.* (1978) observe that the conventional sharp distinction between markets and firms may have little general analytical importance. The pertinent economic question we are faced with is, 'what kinds of contracts are used for what kinds of activities, and why'?

Stakeholder management for residual claims

From this perspective of contracts the firm's claimants include shareholders, bondholders, customers, suppliers, providers of complementary services and products, distributors and employees. Preston (1990) states that stakeholder theories originated in the USA during the early 1930s, when General Electric identified four major interest groups, namely customers, employees, shareholders and the general public. Freeman (1984: 46) defines stakeholders in much broader terms as 'any group or individual who can affect or who is affected by the achievement of the company's objectives'. Donaldson and Preston (1995: 68) also argue that stakeholders are 'all persons or groups with legitimate interest participating in an enterprise [that] do so to obtain benefits and that there is no prima facie priority of one set of interests and benefits over another'. This stakeholder model contrasts explicitly with the 'primary stakeholders' (customers, employees, suppliers and investors) of the input–output model 'in all its variations' (Donaldson and Preston 1995: 68). Rather Freeman (1984) identifies 'primary stakeholders' as those who have 'a formal, official, or contractual relationship with the firm' and all other stakeholder(s) are labeled 'secondary stakeholders' (see Carroll, 1989); as such the categorization of primary stakeholders as used in the input-output model is rarely used. Clarkson (1995) also defines stakeholders as primary and secondary, where primary stakeholders are defined as shareholders, employees, customers and those with regulatory authority, which are essential to the survival and well-being of the organization. Secondary stakeholders are defined as those who are not essential for the survival of the organization but interact with it.

According to Freeman (2000), stakeholder theory is about management in a broad sense:

> It does not simply describe existing situations or predict cause-effect relationships; it also recommends attitudes, structures, and practices that, taken together, constitute stakeholder management. Stakeholder management requires, as its key attribute, simultaneous attention to the legitimate interest of all appropriate stakeholders, both in the establishment of organizational structures and general policies and in the case-by-case decision making. This requirement holds for anyone managing or affecting corporate policies, including not only professional managers, but shareowners, the government and others. Stakeholder theory does not necessarily presume that managers are the only rightful locus of corporate control and governance.
>
> *(ibid.: 175–176)*

Freeman (2000) argues that the work of managers is crucial because it is about mediating firm objectives towards value creation and trade within a network of stakeholders.

> If 'stakeholder theory' is to join the mainstream conversation about business and capitalism it will be because theorists are able to understand both practical management problems and offer narratives or stories that enable managers and stakeholders to enact a better, more useful version of value creation and trade.
>
> *(ibid.: 174)*

Freeman (2000: 177) constructs the notion of continuous value creation whereby business, as an institution, cooperating with stakeholders and motivated by values, is continuously creating new sources of value. This continuous cycle of value creation in business is justified because it also contributes to raising the general 'well-being' of society. In the strategic stakeholder approach managers take the role of achieving a balance between the interest of all stakeholders to ensure survival of the firm and the attainment of other performance goals. Here the normative condition 'is that managers must provide returns (economic or otherwise) to stakeholders in order to continue in wealth creating activities by virtue of the critical resources stakeholder provide to the firm' (Shankman, 1999: 322). The importance of stakeholders lies as such in the decision-making process of agents in organizations (Hill and Jones, 1992), whilst it is Cornell and Shapiro's (1987) belief that stakeholders other than investors as the principal and managers as agents play an important role in financial policy and constitute a vital link between corporate strategy and corporate finance. The traditional emphasis in corporate finance has been on the central role of a firm's investors, and their evaluation of managerial responses to the firm's changing economic circumstances. Jensen and Meckling (1976, 1990) argue that the boundary of the firm does not matter because the firm is a nexus of contracts, with internal and external stakeholders, where the objective of managers is to reconcile competing stakeholder claims in the interest of generating a return on capital for investors (see also Asher *et al.*, 2005; Blair, 2005).

For Jensen and Meckling (1976):

> It is important to recognize that most organizations are simply legal fictions which serve as a nexus for a set of contracting relationships among individuals. This includes firms, non-profit institutions such as universities, hospitals, and foundations, mutual organizations such as mutual savings banks and insurance companies and co-operatives, some private clubs, and even governmental bodies such as cities, states, and the federal government, government enterprises such as TVA, the Post Office, transit systems, and so forth.
>
> *(Jensen and Meckling 1976: 8)*

From this perspective the firm is a bundle of contracts and thus a locus of contractual claims and obligations where significantly there are 'divisible residual claims on the assets and cash flows of the organization' (ibid.: 9).

> Viewed this way, it makes little or no sense to try to distinguish those things that are 'inside' the firm (or any other organization) from those things that are 'outside' of it. There is in a very real sense only a multitude of complex relationships (i.e., contracts) between the legal fiction (the firm) and the owners of labor, material and capital inputs and the consumers of output.
>
> *(ibid.: 9)*

Within this framework of analysis the firm is treated as a locus of contracts with both internal and external stakeholders where competing financial claims need to be both satisfied and moderated. These competing claims are reducible, it is argued, to those between the principal (contractor/investor) and the agent (the contracted party/management). According to Jensen and Meckling (1976), such competing claims will give rise to a gap between what managers wish to do and what investors require to generate a surplus return on capital invested. In the specific case of owner-investors (as principals) and managers (as agents), the 'agency gap' (Ross, 1973) that arises from a potential divergence of interests between the principal and the agent cannot be easily or perfectly reconciled through formal or informal mechanisms (e.g. contractual agreements). Managers may, for example, invest in projects where the net present value (NPV)[1] of projects is negative, i.e. below the cost of capital.

Free cash flow is cash flow in excess of that required to fund all projects that have positive net present values when discounted at the relevant cost of capital. Conflicts of interest between shareholders and managers over payout policies are especially severe when the organization generates substantial free cash flow. The problem is how to motivate managers to disgorge the cash rather than investing it at below the cost of capital or wasting it on organization inefficiencies.

(Jensen, 1986: 325)

Jensen suggests that, to close the agency gap, debt finance is helpful because it contractually forces managers as agents to deliver expected returns on investment. Specifically he encourages the use of leveraged finance arrangements (high debt to equity) because 'Debt creation, without retention of the proceeds of the issue, enables managers to effectively bond their promise to pay out future cash flows' (ibid.: 329). Managers should thus be encouraged to pursue strategies that generate returns above the cost of capital or 'disgorge' free cash to equity investors as dividends and share buy-backs. The ensuing contest for residual control rights of the corporate firm between the principal and the agent entails rising agency costs and, in situations where a significant amount of free cash is generated, the agency costs are, it is argued, particularly substantial. Where the calculations of managers diverge from those of investors, appropriate incentives and penalties are needed to modify behaviour and align the interests of the principal and the agent, and thus monitoring through the publication of budgets/forecasts and financial statement is required. Reconciling the interests of the investors with the motivations of managers introduces the practical importance of financial recording for management control and monitoring returns on invested capital for investors in contrast to the more abstract concepts of economic profit.

Decision making and control for residual income

In an earlier period Chandler (1962) revealed how firm structures evolve in the USA from a functional form to the M-form or multi-divisional structure, which decentralizes considerations of operational management from strategic policy making and what General Motors described as 'formation policies'. These policies include issues of scope, product market expansion, horizontal/vertical integration, and the deployment of capital funding into the business divisions and the division of profits as between retained profits and distributed dividends.

Within the framework of central policy, the duties of a division head were quite comparable to those of a senior executive of a single-product yet multi-function enterprise. Divisional performance was appraised by the financial success (return on investment) and to a lesser extent by the share of the market which the division chiefs could conquer or maintain. From these units, data flowed continuously to the headquarters in the form of statistics, charts, reports, etc.,

> supplemented by oral communications during visits, both of the unit heads to
> headquarters and of the central office executives to the operating units.
>
> *(General Motors, 1937: 37)*

According to Chandler, it is the emergence of the M-form organization that also
establishes the possibilities for a separation of administrative from strategic management, where the latter involves goal determination, planning and budgeting. It is
senior management's responsibility, as agents, to manage resources and capabilities
towards generating profit and return on capital.

> Stockholders have only negative (veto) power not a positive one. They can
> direct the top team not to do certain things, but they cannot force it to do others.
> Only in very special cases can they overturn a particular 'top management'.
>
> *(Chandler, 1962: 27)*

The divisional structure of organization not only precipitated a separation of strategy
from operations through a process of decentralization, it also facilitated the deployment of financial control mechanisms such as budgeting and financial reporting which
focused divisional managers' attention on profit and return on investment (ROI).

> Decentralization occurs when corporate management assigns decision rights to
> lower-level managers. We operationalize decentralization as the extent to which
> decision-making authority over key investment decisions is vested with divi-
> sional managers (compared with their superiors). Divisional summary perform-
> ance measures (DSMs) have two defining characteristics. First, they summarize
> the action choices of divisional managers into one performance metric (e.g.,
> profit, ROI) and, second, they measure performance at the divisional level.
>
> *(Abernathy et al., 2004: 546)*

Hayek (1945) observes that decentralization is of significance because it locates
problem solving with those most able to carry out decisions using their local knowledge and expertise. Decentralization therefore provides a mechanism by which the
knowledge of those closest to the problem to be solved or overcome can be appropriated by the firm.

> If we . . . agree that the economic problem of society is mainly one of rapid
> adaptation to changes in the particular circumstances of time and place . . .
> decisions must be left to the people who are familiar with these circum-
> stances, who know directly of the relevant changes and of the resources
> immediately available to meet them. We cannot expect that this problem
> will be solved by first communicating all this knowledge to a central board
> which, after integrating all knowledge, issues its orders. We must solve it by
> some form of decentralization.
>
> *(Hayek, 1945: 524)*

Solomons (1965) is clear that although non-monetary measures of divisional performance are plausible (see Kaplan and Norton, 1996; Mouritsen *et al.*, 2005; Norreklit, 2000), they have generally not been introduced because of the difficulty in comparing different functions and for that matter products and services with variable physical qualities.

> Since its scope is narrower than corporate accounting, we might suppose that divisional accounting would have developed and brought into widespread use a broad range of nonmonetary measures of divisional performance. The fact is, however, that little has been achieved in this area: but it has to be recognised that the supremacy of money as a measure of business largely reflects the interconnection of the various parts of a business concern into a system. Only in money terms can we bring the results of several different functions together to see if the success of each of them has contributed to the success of the firm.
>
> *(Solomons, 1965: 44–45)*

The objective of the management of divisions within the firm should, according to Solomons, be the maximization of 'residual income' which is the difference between the annual net earnings and the cost of using capital. In Table 2.1 the profit (earnings) generated is $1,000 and this represents a 20 per cent return on capital invested. Deducting the cost of capital (10 per cent of $5,000) from the earnings reveals the 'residual income', $500 or 10 per cent of capital invested. This can also be found using the so-called spread which is the difference between the rate of return on capital and the cost of capital as a percentage.

Thus accounting measures are designed to focus managerial attention on financial performance and specifically to ensure that the return on capital is in excess of the cost of using the capital. Marshall (1920), in an earlier period, also observed that 'the gross earnings of management which a man is getting can only be found after making up a careful account of the true profits of his business, and deducting interest on his capital' (Marshall, 1920: VI.VII.28). And as Veblen (1904) also observed, 'gain and loss is a question of accounting'.

TABLE 2.1 Exhibit for rate of return, residual income and spread

Capital invested	$5,000
Net annual return	$1,000
Rate of return on capital invested	20%
Cost of capital	10%
Residual income	$1,000–$500 = $500
Spread (rate of return − cost of capital)	10%

Source: The authors.

Accounting for the nature of the firm

Our argument from the preceding review is that managers are manipulating the stakeholder network for the purpose of generating surplus earnings for value creation, where the outcomes are reported by firms in annual budgets and translated into summary annual financial statements as profit and balance sheet capitalization. Such disclosures in these financial statements (and their accompanying notes) are used by stakeholders to decipher the extent to which managerial interventions have delivered positive growth, higher margins, lower capital binding and thus a higher return on capital employed. Immediately issues arise when we locate a framework of analysis within accounting and focus specifically on bottom line outcomes. At one level, it is not clear what a bottom line ratio reveals or explains and so, we argue, there is a need to deconstruct the ratio (both numerator and denominator) to capture the story about how we arrive at the bottom line.

The DuPont pyramid of ratios presents the bottom line ratio as a per cent return on capital, but this is progressively deconstructed on the right-hand side of Figure 2.1 into its elements: income–sales percentage (profit margin) and sales to investment (capital turnover) ratios which can be further broken down into the ratios of cost and capital elements. The importance of the pyramid structure of ratios is not that it provides predictive capacity or relevance for costing (Kaplan, 1988) and

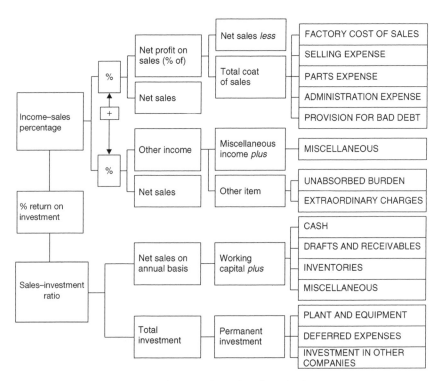

FIGURE 2.1   DuPont pyramid of ratios (after Chandler, 1977)

pricing, but that it reveals how various factors of production contribute to the bottom line and how these may align or not to support or frustrate financial outcomes.

To illustrate this idea let us focus, for example, on the cash return on capital employed where we can comment on movements in the ratio from one time period to the next. However, we are not able to discern what has contributed to changes in the ratio:

cash from operating activities / capital employed

To obtain further information about movements in the aggregate ratio it is necessary for us to deconstruct the numerator and denominator. Cash from operating activities, or earnings before interest, taxes, depreciation and amortization (EBITDA), is effectively:

Revenue less expenses (+ depreciation and amortization added back)

However, most firms' annual reports show expenses by their function, that is sales revenue less cost of goods sold, selling, general, administration, and research and development expenses. The DuPont pyramid of ratios reveals how these functional cost elements contribute to establishing a bottom line as cost of sales, administration expenses and so forth. To illustrate this functional accounting format of reporting, we have summarized the financial results for Johnson & Johnson (J&J) Inc., a US firm involved in the broad provision of health-care services and products.

Table 2.2 is constructed using the conventional presentation of financial statement items disclosed in the annual report and accounts, that is, total sales less expenses by their function: cost of goods sold, selling, general and administrative (SGA) and R&D expenses. Although most firms disclose expenses by 'function', we would point out that it is possible for managers to have some discretion over the allocation of expenses into these categories, for example, increasing R&D expenses which may have previously been categorized as selling, and that it is difficult to align financial numbers with resources used. Finally, it is not possible to discern, from a function of expenses approach, the firm's share of the financial value chain as 'value added or value retained' after paying all external costs to suppliers. This is because the line item 'cost of goods sold' includes a mix of external costs (materials and services) and internal expenses such as employee compensation.

An alternative approach to formatting the financial statements is to use the nature of expenses and thereby construct a value added statement (ASSC, 1975; Cox, 1979; Gillchrist, 1971; Riahi-Belkaoui, 1992) which has much to commend it, because financially 'it is the only technique which clearly separates product or service costs into those produced or controlled by the firm and those provided by others outside of their immediate control' (Bryant, 1989: 42). Our preference is to reformat financial statements into the value added/retained format because this reveals the total influence that a firm has over its product markets and contribution

TABLE 2.2 Johnson & Johnson: income and expenses by function

$ billion	2010	2009	2008	2007	2006	2005	2004	2003	2002	2001	2000
Total sales	61.6	61.9	63.7	61.1	53.3	50.5	47.3	41.9	36.3	32.3	29.2
Cost of products sold	18.8	18.4	18.5	17.8	15.1	14.0	13.5	12.2	10.5	9.6	9.0
Selling, marketing and administrative	19.4	19.8	21.5	20.5	17.4	17.2	16.2	14.5	12.5	11.5	10.7
Research & development	6.8	7.0	7.6	7.7	7.1	6.5	5.3	4.8	4.1	3.7	3.2
Total expenses	45.1	45.2	47.6	45.9	39.6	37.7	35.0	31.5	27.1	24.8	22.8
Earnings before interest and tax	16.5	16.7	16.2	15.2	13.7	12.8	12.4	10.3	9.2	7.5	6.3

Source: Edgar datasets, Securities Exchange Commission, 10K annual report and accounts, available at www.sec.gov/Archives/edgar/data/200406/000095012311018128/y86310kexv13.htm.

3

STRATEGY

Arbitrage for financial leverage

Introduction

The strategy literature borrows many of its elements from economics and the theory of the firm for its organization and development, specifically firms as belonging to industries and utilizing resources to sustain competitiveness. In this way the firm satisfies the 'rents' of the various contracted stakeholders and also generates an appropriable surplus for those investing in the firm as residual claimants. Our argument in this chapter is that strategy is concerned with arbitraging, in its broadest sense, stakeholder relations where new information informs adaptation where the purpose is to sustain operational and financial leverage for liquidity and recapitalization for solvency. With this in mind we argue that firm-based strategy, focused on manipulating resources and global value chains, can be viewed as leveraging financial returns to generate additional earnings capacity. In an era of shareholder value where managerial and investor interests align, this cultural purpose is amplified because product and service development, the sale of output and manipulation of corporation finance are all directed towards sustaining liquidity and capitalization. In this respect strategy is not simply a 'productionist' venture, that is, extracting earnings out of product and services sold for immediate consumption, but 'financialized', when, in a credit-based economy, ongoing asset trading and the extraction of holding gains are a substitute for cash surplus earned from selling goods and services.

Strategy as manipulation of value chains

Porter (1980) is concerned with how managers assess their external environment in terms of the attractiveness of industries and the extent to which it is possible to extract a competitive advantage over industry peers to gain 'excess rents'. Specifically this involves managers assessing the 'competitive forces' operating in their industry sector, namely bargaining power of suppliers, bargaining power of buyers, threat of new entrants, substitutes and the extent of intra-industry rivalry. Borrowing from economics concepts such as economies of scale and barriers to entry, these forces are employed to describe the industry environment and thereby inform agents about the competitive position of the firm and thus strategic alternatives. If competitors can exploit scale economies for low price competition, then it may be best to focus on differentiating output to obtain a share of the product market at a profit. The force of this framework is that it is concerned not only with an assessment of the external industry environment of the firm, but also introduces the notion of a competitive position with bargaining power. Strategy is thus concerned with a focal firm's bargaining power in contractual negotiation with a range of market participants and the extent to which this is sufficiently strong to capture profit and generate a surplus on invested funds. Moreover, strategy is formulated with reference to the bargaining power and competitive position of the focal firm along the physical value chain that traces the entire process from the procurement of various productive inputs to the sale of the products/services. Porter (1980) locates the firm in an essentially productionist-defined industry space, where firms share common technologies and thereby also produce similar products and services. Firms are thus prisoners of a value chain where physical inputs are transformed into physical outputs in a value chain rather than financially adding value. In *Competitive Advantage* Porter (1985) observed that:

> An analysis of the value chain rather than value added is the appropriate way of examine competitive advantage. Value added (selling prices less the cost of purchased raw materials) has sometimes been used as the focal point for cost analysis because it was viewed as the area in which a firm can control costs. Value added is not a sound basis for cost analysis, however, because it incorrectly distinguishes raw material from the many other purchased inputs used in a firm's activities. Also, the cost behavior of activities cannot be understood without simultaneously examining the costs of the inputs used to perform them. Moreover, value added fails to highlight the linkages between a firm and its suppliers that can reduce costs or enhance differentiation.
>
> *(Porter, 1985: 39)*

The value chain described by Porter (1985) depicts the firm as a collection of value-creating activities, such as production and sales, as physical goods move along the value chain and money moves the other way. He distinguishes between five primary activities (inbound logistics, production operations, outbound logistics, marketing and sales as well as service) and four support services (firm infrastructure, human resources, technology development and procurement). The financial dimension to the physical value chain is essentially characterized as a series of functionally specified expenses that do not lend themselves to the discrimination between intra- and extra-firm expenses. Thus the value added financial accounting format which aligns with the notion of a physical input-output relation is missing and its contribution to formulating strategy and assessing outcome is lost (Besanko *et al.*, 2000; Vilen, 1991). Where a firm concentrates only on the internal value creation process it will lose sight of the strategic opportunities emerging in its environment (Vilen, 1991). Analysing competitive advantage involves not only the firm's own value chain, but also the entire vertical chain of production where value created depends on judicious make-or-buy decisions that are sensitive to conditions of technology and transaction costs (Besanko *et al.*, 2000).

Although Porter dismissed the value added financial framework, this accounting format is, as we have argued in Chapter 1, a useful investigative framework which permits the discrimination between internal and external costs and the extent to which vertical integration/disintegration transforms operating financials from firm level restructuring within a financial value chain. Consider the case of the Ford Model T and Henry Ford's decision to double wages in 1914 to $5, significantly above the going rate within the local manufacturing sector. This was not simply a social experiment ahead of its time. It was also economically and financially sensible. Control over labour and flexibility in terms of the reorganization of work and tasks significantly reduced the number of hours taken to build the average Model T even though labour costs per hour were increasing.

> In 1909 when hourly labour costs were 28 cents and there were 400 hours of labour in a T, Ford's in-house labour costs were $100 for each car produced. By 1915, earnings had doubled to 55 cents but, with just 125 hours of labour in a T, the in-house payroll cost was just $64 for each car produced.
>
> *(Williams et al., 1992: 526)*

The Ford factory producing the Model T was flexible and the model produced in 1909 was not the same as that produced in 1914. Both the product itself and the production process were continually reconfigured to consolidate tasks, remove indirect labour (moving parts around the factory) and improve production flow, thus securing a reduction in labour hours embodied in each Model T. Internal cost reduction was then passed on in lower prices, thus reducing the average price of a Model T from $850 in 1909 to $360 in 1916. Ford executives also realized that if productive reorganization could be achieved for their existing activities, accounting for just 30 per cent of the financial value chain, it would make sense to vertically integrate (either through original investment or acquisition) and employ similar productive interventions to reduce costs further than was then possible through putting pressure on external suppliers. Ford thus captured greater financial share of the overall value chain of the Model T, increasing production in-house from 30 per cent to 50 per cent over the period 1909 to 1916 and employing principles of 'progressive manufacture'. Not only did Ford capture more of the value chain, the company reduced labour costs across a greater span of the value chain to lever price reduction but also boost overall earnings capacity. In the case of Ford and the Model T, external purchase costs were driven down by a process of internalizing the value chain which was also made subject to Ford's process of progressive manufacture and further labour cost reduction. The value added accounting format reveals the modifications to the Ford Model T cost structure as a fall in external purchases and internal labour costs per unit jointly explaining the price cut of $490 over the period 1909–1916.

In a later period the superiority of Japanese car manufacturers relative to their US competitors is put down to their ability to organize a vertically disintegrated value chain (Womack *et al.*, 1990). In the case of companies like Toyota, with just a 20 per cent share of the financial value chain, pressure on suppliers and accessing a steep wage gradient within their domestic economy made sense when suppliers account for 80 per cent of total cost. When Japanese manufacturers like Honda and Toyota transferred production off-shore into the USA, after yen appreciation in the mid-1980s, the financial advantage relative to home producers like Ford and GM was lost because the wage gradient between assemblers and suppliers in the USA was less steep (Williams *et al.*, 1994), generating less pronounced financial leverage.

A central feature of the latest development in the global rationalization of the value chain is compartmentalization of the firm's value chain and standardization (or digitization) of individual components (either products or processes) in conjunction with the adoption of effective sourcing models to achieve financial leverage. Gupta (2006) discusses a prominent recent development in the policies of financial and non-financial firms which is to increasingly componentize their business value chain and then out-source and off-shore these business process elements. There are obvious benefits from unbundling and relocating the value chain into low labour cost economies such as India or China where such costs are one-sixth of those in the USA. In Chapter 7 we argue that a significant factor forcing the restructuring of global value chains is price erosion in competitive markets and the need to reduce labour costs. However, we also note in this chapter that cost reduction for competitiveness is often incorrectly conflated with boosting return on capital for shareholder value.

Strategy as resource deployment and exploiting core competence

What goes on inside the firm in terms of the mobilization of resources and capabilities is the focus of resource-based theory (RBT) where resources are deemed to be both tangible and intangible and the capabilities, skills/knowledge and creativity of employees are viewed as underpinning a firm's ability to generate above-average profit and return on capital (Conner and Prahalad, 1996; Barney, 1986, 2001).

> A historical review of strategy research suggests that a resource-based perspective long has been central to the field. Influential literature, including, for example, Barnard (1938), Selznick (1957), Sloan (1963), Chandler (1966, 77) and Rumelt (1974), connects performance with a firm's special competences in deploying and combining its human, physical and reputational capital.
>
> *(Conner, 1991: 122)*

In RBT it is the firm's unique capabilities and contribution of both tangible and intangible assets that serve to leverage profit and maintain competitiveness. The capacity of the firm to appropriate capabilities and exploit intangible assets for profit is subject to a range of conditions that limit the firm's capacity to simply appropriate knowledge and exploit capabilities embedded in intangible assets and its workforce.

> The issue of appropriability concerns the allocation of rents where property rights are not fully defined. Once we go beyond the financial and physical assets valued in a company's balance sheet, ownership becomes ambiguous. The firm owns intangible assets such as patents, copyrights, brand names, and trade secrets, but the scope of property rights may lack precise definition.
>
> *(Grant, 1991: 128)*

According to the resource-based (Almor and Hashai, 2004) or dynamic capability-based view of the firm (Easterby-Smith and Prieto, 2008), it is of critical importance for corporate firms to identify and create strategic assets and core competitive capabilities, as well as to devise strategies and systems for mobilizing, utilizing, maintaining and renewing such key resources to achieve competitive advantage in the marketplace. The literature has generally defined strategic assets and core capabilities to be those that command economic or quasi-economic rents. Economic rent, in turn, is generally defined to be the excess return to the owner of an asset when deployed for a particular use over and above the opportunity cost of the asset used in a competitive market (Tollison, 1982).[1] Traditionally, strategic assets and core capabilities comprise mainly tangible assets such as strategic natural resources, patents and royalties, and in-house R&D capabilities. Possession of such assets would put the firm in a favourable bargaining position vis-à-vis the market transactors and enable the firm to derive the excess return. However, over recent decades the domain of strategic assets and core capabilities has increasingly extended to also cover intangibles like databases, brand image, incumbent market position, relational networks (including licensing and regulatory agreements), distribution channels, marketing and advertising capabilities, and proprietary asset pricing formula and trading platforms.[2] In Table 3.1 the

TABLE 3.1 Tangible and intangible investments by UK firms (£ billion)

Year	1990	1995	2000	2007
All tangibles	67	62	87	95
Intangibles				
Software development	6	10	16	20
R&D	8	8	11	15
Design[a]	9	12	18	22
Mineral exploration and copyrights	3	3	2	4
Branding	5	7	12	14
Training	13	16	24	32
Organizational	9	12	17	26
All intangibles	53	68	100	133

Source: UK ONS Business Structure Database.

Note:
a 'Design' refers to architectural and engineering design, and financial product development.

UK Office for National Statistics has recalibrated the national accounts to reveal the growth of 'intangibles' relative to tangible assets and uses this to explain productivity growth.

Strategy as manipulation of corporation finance

Industry structure, value chain and RBT approaches share a common purpose which is to recalibrate the financial span of the value chain and deployment of resources to generate financial leverage in terms of surplus generating capacity on assets and capital employed. They also share a productionist framework in that tangible or intangible assets are configured and reconfigured to extract a surplus from the production and sale of services/products which are consumed to recover costs and generate a return on assets. However, a considerable amount of corporate effort is directed to what we might term managing 'corporation finance', that is, the manipulation of financial flows and value of assets within capital markets where cash deployment, asset churn and price inflation combine to generate financial leverage from ongoing transactions that, in turn, release holding gains to further inflate capitalizations. This manipulation of corporation finance and ongoing process of trading and engagement within a credit-based economy is an additional source of financial leverage beyond that generated out of products and services sold and consumed. We illustrate the strategy of leveraging financial resources through the capital market using three examples: cash and share buybacks; cash used to buy and sell marketable securities and asset 'carve outs'.

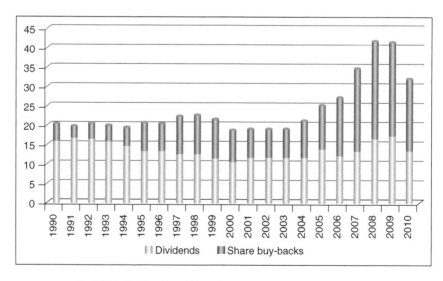

FIGURE 3.1 S&P 500 dividends and share buy-backs as % of cash. EBITDA is earnings before interest, taxes, depreciation and amortization.

Source: ThomsonOneBanker.

Over the period 1990 to 2010 the Standard and Poor's 500 group of companies distributed $3.3 trillion of cash as dividends and $3.1 trillion of share buy-backs, a sum equivalent to 26 per cent of their outstanding market value as at the end of 2010. During the past two decades the balance of cash distributed to shareholders as dividends and share buy-backs has changed significantly, with share buy-backs (SBBs) accounting for a higher share of cash distributed. From 1990 to 2000 the share of cash appropriated to dividends fell from 15 to 10 per cent, but the growth in SBB operated to compensate and this maintained cash distribution to shareholders at 20 per cent. During the past decade the share of cash surplus resources distributed to shareholders as dividends gently increased back to 15 per cent of cash, but there was a significant jump in SBBs, pushing total cash surplus distributed to shareholders to 40 per cent in 2009 before falling back to 30 per cent in 2010.

The motivation for using cash surplus for share buy-backs rather than dividends is that shares repurchased have a different quality from dividends paid. Shares repurchased as treasury stock reside on the firm's balance sheet, and in a period when stock markets are inflating there is the possibility that shares repurchased in an earlier period for treasury stock will yield holding gains when they are used to finance transactions such as a business combination. SBBs are a bet on the firm's share price appreciating into the future whereby using treasury stock, to part-finance an acquisition, will release holding gains and leverage cash resources deployed in an earlier period. Consider the case of Merck which has used one-quarter of its cash surplus from operations to repurchase share capital since 1990, a sum 15 per cent greater than capital expenditure.

In Table 3.2 we estimate the cost of repurchased treasury shares using the disclosed cost of accumulated treasury stock divided by treasury stock outstanding and compare this with the average share price quoted on the stock market to estimate the possible holding gain if all treasury stock were to be exchanged at

TABLE 3.2 Merck: implicit holding gains from cash invested in treasury stock

	Treasury stock (million shares)	SBB average cost ($ per share)	Share price ($ per share)	Holding gain ($ billion)
2000	660.8	28.5	80.7	34.5
2001	703.4	31.8	70.2	27.0
2002	731.2	33.0	53.2	14.8
2003	754.4	33.9	50.0	12.1
2004	767.6	34.1	35.7	1.2
2005	794.3	33.9	30.9	−2.4
2006	808.4	34.1	43.4	7.5
2007	811	34.6	74.7	32.5
2008	875.8	35.1	28.4	−5.8
2009	454.3	46.2	36.7	−4.3
2010	494.8	45.3	36.0	−4.6

Source: Merck 10K annual report and accounts, various years, available at www.sec.gov/edgar/searchedgar/companysearch.html.

this market price. In 2000 we estimate that had all treasury stock been used in, for example, the purchase consideration for a corporate acquisition the holding gain would have been $35bn. As the price of Merck's stock falls during the period 2001 to 2005 so its ability to extract holding gains from repurchased shares is also reduced.

Not only are firms deploying cash to repurchase their own share capital to extract holding gains, they are also using cash funds in the form of deposits and marketable securities, that is, investing in other firms' share capital, fixed interest securities and treasuries which are bought and sold to skim a margin. In Table 3.3 we show some extracts from Apple Inc.'s balance sheet and cash flow statements that reveal the scale and extent of dealing in marketable securities and cash held in financial instrument investments.

In the balance sheet financial assets held were approximately $50 billion in 2010 and ten times greater than the value of investment in tangible assets – property plant and equipment. Moreover, in the cash flow statement we can also gauge the extent to which these liquid investments are being churned relative to cash from operations. In 2010 Apple churned the equivalent of $100 billion of cash resources buying and selling marketable securities, a sum four to five times that generated as cash from operations in that same year. Firms like Apple and Merck are actively churning cash resources into and out of the capital market to skim a margin from asset trading, whether this is in share buy-backs or marketable securities.

It is also possible for firms to set up subsidiary companies that contain specific aspects of the business, for example Royal Bank of Scotland's spin-out of its payment processing division WorldPay. These 'carve out' deals often include the parent company selling all or a share of one or more of its operating subsidiaries to raise additional cash resources beyond that from simply operating these subsidiaries. Consultancy companies, such as Accenture, sell a service supporting firms that are looking to disaggregate their assets to extract additional cash and value for shareholders.

TABLE 3.3 Extracts from Apple Inc.'s balance sheet and cash flow statement, 2010 ($ billion)

	2010	2009
Balance sheet		
Property plant and equipment	4.8	2.9
Cash and equivalents	11.3	5.2
Short-term marketable securities	14.4	18.2
Long-term marketable securities	25.4	10.5
Cash flow statement		
Cash from operations	18.6	10.2
Purchase of marketable securities	57.8	46.7
Proceeds from maturity of marketable securities	24.9	19.8
Proceeds from sale of marketable securities	21.8	10.8

Source: Apple Inc., 10K Edgar datasets, available at www.sec.gov/edgar/searchedgar/companysearch.html.

Our framework includes a comprehensive methodology and assets that help companies plan, set-up and execute the separation or carve-out of business units from parent companies.

> *(http://www.accenture.com/us-en/Pages/service-carve-out-strategy-divesture-summary.aspx)*

Firms are, on a regular basis, deploying resources to leverage returns from capital market interventions that include share buy-backs, dealing in financial instruments and breaking up and selling on assets held in subsidiaries. The pressure to lever return on capital from interventions in the value chain, exploit intangible assets and execute interventions in financial markets is fundamentally driven by the need to generate liquidity and solvency to maintain a going concern.

Strategy: managing for shareholder value and financial leverage

In their 1932 text *The Modern Corporation and Private Property* Berle and Means noted how, in an earlier period, the ownership of corporate capital had become concentrated in the hands of a few owner-managers. Veblen (1904) also observed how the development of modern corporation finance resulted in a more complex network of business relations where contractual negotiation and shrewd manipulation are important. This mediation is conducted through pecuniary transactions carried out for business ends rather than from simply a narrow efficiency of industry perspective. Veblen's observation on pecuniary negotiation separates the businessmen from the rest of society because they are able to exert discretion and position to exploit change and disturbances in and across markets to (possibly) boost earnings capacity and increase the probability of wealth accumulation for owner-managers.

> In proportion as the machine industry gained ground, and as the modern concatenation of industrial processes and of markets developed, the conjunctures of business grew more varied and of larger scope at the same time that they became more amenable to shrewd manipulation . . .
>
> The adjustments of industry take place through the mediation of pecuniary transactions, and these transactions take place at the hands of the business men and are carried on by them for business ends, not for industrial ends in the narrower meaning of the phrase.
>
> *(Veblen, 1904: 17–18)*

As the US corporate sector expanded its requirement for capital, beyond that available from a narrow group of owners, this also served to dilute ownership and ceded control to appointed managers. A great deal of attention has thus been focused on the impact of this separation of ownership and control, the so-called 'agency gap' (see Chapter 2) where the management of corporate resources and financial outcomes may not align with the financial interest of owner-shareholders. The dispersion of stock ownership prevalent during the 1950s and 1960s only served to dilute the power of shareholders to influence the way in which corporation finance and resources were deployed. Jensen's 1986 paper on the agency cost of free cash is concerned with how to close down the conflict of interest between managers and investors. Jensen addresses the problem of trying to reconcile management behaviour, in terms of managing corporation finance, and demands of investors. Focusing on free cash flow he notes that:

> Free cash flow is cash flow in excess of that required to fund all projects that have positive net present values when discounted at the relevant cost of capital. Conflicts of interest between shareholders and managers over payout policies are especially severe when the organization generates substantial free cash flow. The problem is how to motivate managers to disgorge the cash rather than investing it at below the cost of capital or wasting it on organization inefficiencies.
>
> *(Jensen, 1986: 3)*

To reconcile the conflict of interest, Jensen argues that debt finance can play a role in 'motivating organizational efficiency' because they (managers) are subject to a contractual obligation to generate a return on capital that covers the cost of serving debt capital (interest payments). Jensen observes that with dividends or share buy-backs managers can vary these payments and, as such, the commitment to shareholders is both malleable and weak.

> Managers with substantial free cash flow can increase dividends or repurchase stock and thereby pay out current cash that would otherwise be invested in low-return projects or wasted. This leaves managers with control over the use of future free cash flows, but they can promise to pay out future cash flows by announcing a 'permanent' increase in the dividend. Such promises are weak because dividends can be reduced in the future.
>
> *(Jensen, 1986: 4)*

In the decade after Jensen bemoaned the extent of managerial control over cash distributions, the concentration of assets under management (securities and equities) within institutional investors – insurance, mutual and pension funds – steadily increased in the advanced economies, moving up from $22 trillion to $60 trillion and from a position where these funds were equivalent to GDP to where they were 1.7 times GDP (see Table 3.4 and Figure 3.2). This concentration of share equity held by institutional investors rather than households modifies the governance relationship between investors and managers.

In 2009 the global value of corporate equities under management within these main institutional sectors amounted to roughly $25 trillion, equivalent to two-thirds of the main economy stock market capitalizations in that year. A similar pattern of increased institutional management of equity capital can be observed in the USA, the most significant by market capitalization. By the mid-1980s the share of US corporate equities held by households had fallen to roughly 40 per cent

TABLE 3.4 Institutional investors: funds under management ($ trillion and per cent of GDP)

	1995	2000 ($ trillion)	2009	1995	2000 (% GDP)	2009
Institutional investors	21.9	33.5	60.3	103	147.6	173.7
Investment funds	6.3	12.1	24	29.8	53.4	69.2
Insurance companies	8	10.4	20	37.7	45.6	57.7
Autonomous pension funds	7.2	10.8	15.9	33.8	47.4	45.9
Other institutional investors	0.5	0.5	0.7	2.5	2.2	2.0

Sources: OECD and IMF estimates, available at www.imf.org/external/pubs/ft/gfsr/2011/02/pdf/ch2.pdf.

Note: Data based on the assets under management by institutional investors in seventeen OECD countries.

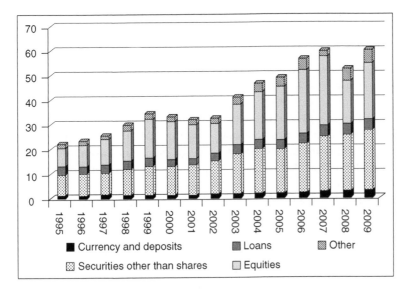

FIGURE 3.2 Institutional investors: assets allocations ($ trillion). Data based on the assets under management by institutional investors in seventeen OECD countries. 'Other' includes commercial loans and credits; financial derivatives; short-term investments; investments in hedge funds, private equities, and commodities; and miscellaneous assets.

Sources: OECD and IMF estimates, available at http://www.imf.org/external/pubs/ft/gfsr/2011/ 02/pdf/ch2.pdf.

from a level close to 100 per cent in 1945. This progressive shift and consolidation of equities managed by institutions on behalf of households throughout the past two decades was such that by 2008 two-thirds of corporate equities were managed by institutions (investment banks, insurance companies and the like) (see Figure 3.3). This shift from households to institutions modifies the relationship between owners and managers, ushering in the era of shareholder value. For agency theorists the concentration of equity in the hands of institutional investors activated a market for corporate control and for Lazonick and O'Sullivan, 'The transfer of

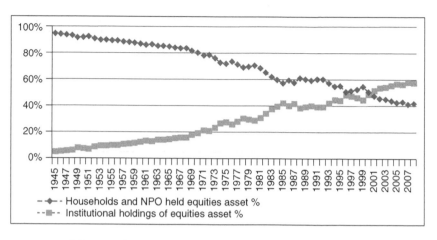

FIGURE 3.3   US equity holdings: households and institutions.

Source: US Federal Reserve Board, Flow of Funds Z1, available at http://www.federalreserve.gov/releases/z1/current/.

stockholding from individual households to institutions such as mutual funds, pension funds and life insurance companies made possible the takeovers advocated by agency theorists and gave shareholders much more collective power to influence the yields and market values of corporate stocks they held' (Lazonick and O'Sullivan, 2000: 16).

In this era of shareholder value there is increased pressure on managers as agents to extract a higher return on capital invested. Many senior executives have remuneration packages that stress meeting certain financial targets such as earnings per share (EPS), cash and profit return on assets/capital employed, and Economic Value Added (EVA™) *relative* to a selected peer group or stock market index (Worthington and West, 2001). All of these performance metrics combine earnings (as profit or cash) and a measure of capital employed where the general objective is to boost earnings capacity (profit or cash generated per financial unit of capital employed) relative to other firms in a competition of all against all.

> EVA is based upon something we have known for a long time: What we call profits, the money left to service equity, is usually not profit at all. Until a business returns a profit that is greater than its cost of capital, it operates at a loss. Never mind that it pays taxes as if it had a genuine profit. The enterprise still returns less to the economy than it devours in resources . . . Until then it does not create wealth; it destroys it.
>
> *(Drucker, 1995: 59)*

EVA™ is trade marked by Stern Stewart and is part of their suite of consultancy products that they will install into organizations for a fee! And to quote Drucker again:

Taking advantage of these developments and the growing demand for new 'value-based' management practices that could better align the interests of managers with those of shareholders, the consulting firm Stern Stewart & Company, in the 1980s and 1990s, revived the notion of residual income. Stern Stewart developed this notion into a broader, EVA-based management control system, implemented at dozens of large, publicly traded companies including AT&T, Coca-Cola, and Quaker Oats.

(Drucker, 1995: 2)

The computation of EVA™ is described in the 'intellectual property'[3] tab on the Stern Stewart website as net operating profit after Tax (NOPAT) minus a capital charge (capital invested multiplied by the weighted average cost of capital – WACC). Stern Stewart suggest that firms that are boosting their EVA™ over time will also increase the probability of accelerating their market value added (MVA) which is the firm's market value of equity less the book value of equity. In this way Stern Stewart suggest that managers who generate higher levels of EVA™ one year to the next will also generate higher MVA for their shareholders. Shareholder value metrics such as EVA™ (and for example, CFROI, earnings per share (EPS) and cash/profit ROCE) are commonly installed into the remuneration packages of senior executives. Salaries, cash bonuses and stock options allocated are generally tied to one or more of these key shareholder value metrics. For example, Tesco plc in the UK pays directors a basic salary and bonuses based on short-term performance (boosting earnings per share (EPS) and group return on capital employed) and long-term performance (sustained EPS and return on capital targets). These remuneration components can significantly inflate a director's basic salary.

The agency gap that Jensen draws our attention to is now essentially closed because the force of financial incentives aligns management calculation with institutional investor interests. Institutional investors look to managers to boost financial performance: earnings per share (EPS), EVA™ and return on capital employed (ROCE). These financial metrics are also those employed by analysts to estimate a firm's share price and hence overall market value. In addition financial institutions are in receipt of corporate cash transfers that take the form of cash distributed as dividends, share buy-backs and payments for acquisitions which serve to further inflate the pool of funding in equity and debt markets.

Our general argument in this chapter is that firms will manipulate their financial value chains, adjusting the balance between domestic and overseas supply and

TABLE 3.5 Tesco plc directors' remuneration and bonuses

Basic salaries (£ million)	Benefits (£ million)	Short-term bonuses (£ million)	Short-term shares (£ million)	Long-term share options (million)
6.2	0.8	6.6	5.5	8.6

Source: Tesco plc remuneration report, available at www.tescoplc.com/media/417/tesco_annual_report_2011.pdf.

production and what is done in-house and what is out-sourced. They will deploy intangible assets and unique resources to generate financial leverage where it is possible to stretch margins, until competitors enter the market and erode price structures such as happened with the mobile phone and portable computer technology product markets. And they will engage in a whole host of capital and financial market interventions to extract additional margin from the manipulation of corporation finance. Milberg (2008) argues that US firms have recalibrated their global organization of production, and that out-sourcing and off-shoring have delivered a boost to the operating margins of these firms as they arbitraged global labour markets, noting also that this motivation to off-shore, out-source and reduce the scope of corporate activity coincided with consultancy and academic recommendations about the benefits of organization focus around core competences. Milberg observes that the extra surplus extracted from this restructuring process is being reinvested into financial assets rather than productive assets for growth and competitiveness.

> We find that the expansion of global production networks has served a dual purpose in the evolving corporate strategy. Cost reductions from the globalisation of production have supported the financialisation of the non-financial corporate sector, both by raising profits and by reducing the need for domestic reinvestment of those profits, freeing earnings for the purchase of financial assets and raising shareholder returns. The emphasis on maximising shareholder value and aligning management interests with those of shareholders emerged around the same time that management experts advised corporations to reduce the scope of corporate activity to focus on 'core competence'.
>
> (*Milberg* et al. *2010: 276*)

Strange (2009) also notes that the motivation for outsourcing primary activities of the firm has less to do with maintaining resource capabilities and more to do with extracting financial leverage: 'It is argued that certain firms choose to outsource primary activities within their production chains to independent suppliers, not because of relative capability considerations, but because they are able to leverage their resources to appropriate the rents from the chain whilst reducing their asset base' (Strange, 2009: 3).

Pisano and Shih (2009) take this argument further and argue that the drive to off-shore and out-source is now undermining US competitiveness because innovative capacity is being lost.

> Companies operating in the US were steadily outsourcing development and manufacturing work to specialists abroad and cutting their spending on basic research. In making their decisions executives were heeding the advice *du jour* of business gurus and Wall Street: Focus on your core competences, off-load your low value added activities and redeploy your savings into innovation . . . But in reality, the outsourcing has not stopped with low value

tasks like simple assembly or circuit board stuffing. Sophisticated engineering and manufacturing capabilities that underpin innovation in a wide range of products have been rapidly leaving too.

(Pisano and Shih, 2009: 3)

The additional cash/profit margin extracted by US firms from these global supply chain manipulations have been distributed to shareholders as dividends and share buy-backs rather than being recycled back into 'productive' investment. Lazonick (2007) refers to this as a process of 'downsize and distribute' where US corporations are:

> Engaging in what can be called a '*downsize-and-distribute*' allocation regime, these companies downsized their labor forces and increased the distribution of corporate revenues to shareholders. This allocation regime represented a reversal of the '*retain-and-reinvest*' regime that had characterized these companies in the post-World War II decades; they had retained corporate revenues for reinvestment in organization and technology, expanding their labor forces in the process.

> *(Lazonick, 2007: 988)*

Figure 3.4 does indicate, in line with Milberg's (2008) and Lazonick and O'Sullivan's (2000) argument, that the share of capital investment expenditure in GDP (value retained) has followed a downward trend in the major developed economies from an unweighted average of 25 per cent to 17 per cent in 2010.

Figure 3.5 also reveals that the amount of cash resources distributed to shareholders in the S&P 500 group of companies has increased relative to capital expenditure

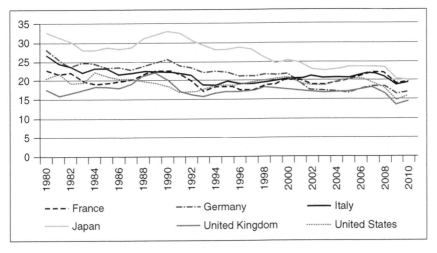

FIGURE 3.4   Investment in GDP: advanced economics (%).

Source: IMF World Economic Outlook Database (October 2010).

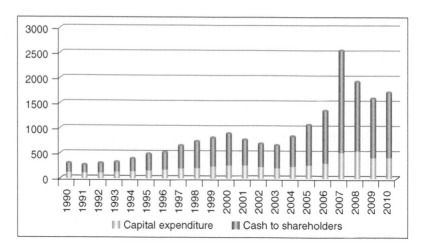

FIGURE 3.5   S&P 500 capital expenditure and cash to shareholders ($ trillion). Cash to shareholders is dividends, share buy-backs and cash acquisitions.

Source: ThomsonOneBanker.

over the past two decades. One of the main components driving up the share of cash distributed to shareholders is that used to finance share buy-backs and acquisitions. In the case of share buy-backs these may be used, as we have argued, to lever financial holding gains if they can be used to finance acquisitions when the implicit value of treasury stock has inflated. Cash can be deployed for a variety of purposes: productive resource investment motivated by a need to modify cost structures and improve cost recovery, the financial span of operations or extract holding gains from investments in financial assets. We do not make the case that one type of cash deployment is superior to another, rather that strategy is about how corporation finance can be directed in a multiplicity of ways towards generating liquidity and financial leverage on capital employed, all of which are legitimate.

Strategy: intervention(s) for financial leverage

The previous discussion nominates strategy, in an era of shareholder value, with a given purpose, namely that of generating higher financial returns on capital or financial leverage for investors. With this purpose in mind the firm, as a financial reporting entity, can deploy a range of strategic interventions to lever financial returns and these broadly include manipulating the financial boundary of the firm, resources embedded in products and services, and corporation finance. The nature and range of strategic interventions available to exert financial leverage on capital employed raise a number of issues. The first of these relates to the nature and identity of the firm as the subject of investigation. It is not possible to identify a singular productionist firm located in a supply chain where profit is extracted out of

TABLE 3.6 Johnson & Johnson: cost structure (share of sales revenue) and return on capital

	1990	2008
Sales	100	100
Purchases	(50)	(47)
Value retained	50	53
Labour costs	(29)	(23)
Cash surplus (EBITDA)	21	30
Capital intensity	0.55	0.8
Cash ROCE	38.2	37.5

Source: SEC Edgar database, available at www.sec.gov/edgar.shtml.

Notes: Financial information converted into a percentage of total sales revenue. Capital intensity is capital employed (long-term debt plus equity) as per cent of total sales. Value retained is sales revenue minus purchases. Cash is value added retained minus labour costs. The capital to intensity index is sales revenue divided into capital employed (long-term debt plus shareholder equity). The cash ROCE is found by dividing cash share of sales by the capital intensity index.

managing input–output relations. Second, it is not possible to clearly establish how the firm's core resources and capabilities straightforwardly translate into generating financial leverage when other corporation finance initiatives are blended into the reported financials. To illustrate these issues we consider the case of Johnson & Johnson and utilize the financial framework outlined in Chapter 2 to consider these anomalies and contradictions.

Johnson & Johnson (J&J) has been expanding its overseas manufacturing capacity during the past few decades and reconfiguring its value chain. During the period 1988–1999 non-US manufacturing capacity increased by 20 per cent and in the following period (1999–2007) the cumulative increase was significantly higher at 40 per cent. This shift to overseas production was coincident with a reduction in external costs as a share of sales from 50 to 47 per cent. In addition, the switch into overseas markets for production may also have contributed to a reduction in the share of internal labour costs from 29 to 23 per cent of sales revenue as low labour costs were accessed. However, the reduction in labour costs might also be

TABLE 3.7 Johnson & Johnson: balance sheet asset structure

	1992		2010	
	$bn	*%*	*$bn*	*%*
Property plant and equipment	4.1	34	14.5	14
Intangible assets	1.0	8	16.7	16
Goodwill	0.0	0.0	15.3	15
Marketable securities	0.5	5	8.3	8
Cash	0.4	4	19.3	19
Current assets	6.0	49	28.8	28
Total assets	12.2	100	102.9	100

Source: SEC Edgar database, available at www.sec.gov/edgar.shtml.

explained as resulting from the introduction of new innovative products with less labour cost congealed in their manufacture. The combination of lower external costs and also internal labour costs increases the share of cash extracted from sales revenues from 21 to 30 per cent. (See Table 3.6.)

As we have noted it is not an easy matter to identify the distinct contribution that may have come from modifying the geographic configuration of the business and that which arises from exploiting core competences and knowledge-based capabilities. And practically, although the cash surplus margin has been transformed from 21 to 30 per cent, this did not translate into a higher return on capital employed because capital intensity has also increased, acting to put a brake on the cash ROCE.

There have also been significant changes in the composition of assets in the balance sheet, with tangible and intangible assets (patents, etc.) accounting for 42 per cent of total assets in 1992 and 30 per cent in 2010 (see Table 3.7). By way of contrast cash, marketable securities and goodwill arising from acquisitions are up from 1 per cent of assets in 1992 to 42 per cent in 2010. The compositional adjustment in assets structure of the balance sheet would suggest a shift in strategic priority from leveraging financial gain from product development and final consumption towards ongoing capital market interventions and asset trades to inflate balance sheet capitalization and generate opportunities to extract holding gains that also boost earnings capacity (see Chapter 2). The nature of these arbitrage moves carried out to generate financial leverage are complex; for example, firms undertake development activities using current financial resources to generate future cash flow, but are also selling products and services for consumption to recover costs and generate a margin, whilst also manipulating corporation finance to extract holding gains and lever up existing cash resources. The outcomes of these complex interventions are recorded and congeal within reported financials, modifying cost structures, margins and capitalization in the balance sheet.

The strategy literature shares a common underlying element, which is to isolate how specific forms of intervention can stretch margins in an era of shareholder value, where managerial and investor interests align. Where generating higher returns on capital employed for value creation will increase the probability of wealth accumulation for shareholders. Strategic interventions, the purpose of which is to deliver this financial leverage, operate through the prism of complex stakeholder relations both within and outside of the firm (Laplume et al., 2008). Freeman (1984) observes that the introduction of 'stakeholders' into the framework of analysis can help rework our understanding of the nature of the firm.

> Just as the separation of the owner-manager-employee required a rethinking of the concept of control and private property as analyzed by Berle and Means (1932), so does the emergence of numerous stakeholder groups and new strategic issues require a rethinking of our traditional picture of the firm . . . We must redraw the picture in a way that accounts for the changes.
>
> *(Freeman, 1984: 24)*

Freeman (1984) and Freeman *et al.* (2004) observe that the primary concern of management within the firm is with aligning stakeholder interests. On the one hand, the firm is a normative locus for reconciling stakeholder interests and on the other, there is an instrumental purpose which is to generate 'outstanding' performance. According to Freeman, stakeholder theory 'encourages managers to articulate the shared sense of the value they create, and what brings its core stakeholders together. This propels the firm forward and allows it to generate outstanding performance, determined both in terms of its purpose and marketplace financial metrics' (Freeman *et al.*, 2004: 364).

Donaldson and Preston (1995) note that stakeholders are those from whom the firm (managers) need to induce support in order to accomplish their desired outcomes.

> The much-quoted Stanford Research Institute's (SRI) definition of stakeholders as 'those groups without whose support the organization would cease to exist' (SRI, 1963; quoted in Freeman, 1984: 31) clearly implies that corporate managers must induce constructive contributions from their stakeholders to accomplish their own desired results (e.g., perpetuation of the organization, profitability, stability, growth).
>
> *(Donaldson and Preston, 1995: 72)*

There is no doubt that the firm is interacting with a range of stakeholders (Kaler, 2006) and that a process of ongoing negotiation and adaptation is required as these relations change over a period of time (see Figure 3.6). This, in turn, introduces the notion of the firm as running a set of negotiations and contracts with stakeholders (Coase, 1937; Williamson, 1991). According to Freeman and Evan (1990: 352), 'Managers administer contracts among employees, owners, suppliers, customers, and the community. Since each of these groups can invest in asset specific

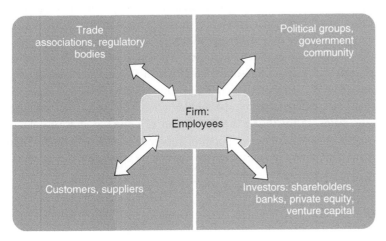

FIGURE 3.6 Stakeholder interactions.

Source: The authors.

transactions which affect the other groups, methods of conflict resolution, or safeguards must be found.'

Donaldson and Preston on Evan and Freeman (1993) note that 'management has a duty of safeguarding the welfare of the abstract entity that is the corporation and of balancing the conflicting claims of multiple stakeholders to achieve this goal', further declaring that 'a stakeholder theory of the firm must redefine the purpose of the firm . . . The very purpose of the firm is, in our view, to serve as a vehicle for coordinating stakeholder interests' (Evan and Freeman 1993: 102–103).

Summary

In this text our purpose is not to construct a stakeholder theory of the firm but to argue the point that stakeholder interactions do congeal into the financial numbers as reported by firms (see Chapter 2), and that it is possible to construct a financial format that reveals the contribution and influence of these stakeholder interactions over income, expenses and capitalization. As the relation with stakeholders evolves, this would be reflected in the financial numbers upon which critically engaged narratives about success and failure can be constructed. Where, we suggest, the purpose of the firm, as a reporting entity, is to try and generate liquidity and leverage from capital employed within the constraints of its stakeholder network, these stakeholder constraints are not stable but rather malleable, and this prompts opportunistic responses: adaptation to global value chains (Kogut, 1984, 1985), innovative resource deployments, exploitation of capabilities (Prahalad and Hamel, 1990) and manipulation of corporation finance where success and failure are possible.

In the following chapter we argue a case for reworking a business model framework of analysis, one founded upon a loose conceptual framework that captures focal firms within similar stakeholder relations and information genotype. In constructing a business model framework of analysis, we suggest it is possible to classify and locate business models (and their focal firms) in terms of their capacity to generate earnings and secure ongoing recapitalization(s). For this purpose the underlying accounting framework outlined in Chapter 2 is significant because it is from these numbers that we generate a resource upon which to construct critically engaged narratives about the extent to which business models are robust and viable. That is to say, about the extent to which stakeholder interactions are capable of transforming value chains, restructuring the articulation of resources and capabilities, and sustaining the manipulation of corporation finance to secure a surplus (for liquidity) and sustain ongoing recapitalizations (solvency) for a going concern.

4

BUSINESS MODELS

Reworked for a financialized world

Introduction

Why use the term 'business model' (henceforth BM), especially when there has been substantial disappointment and disillusion with its use and its association with the tech stock bubble, Enron, World.com and the failure of the banking business model (see Chapter 8)? Although the term business model is associated with 'disappointment and disillusion', we argue in this chapter that there are strong reasons why a reworked BM conceptual framework can support innovative and insightful critical reflection(s) about the possibilities and limitations of economic transformation. There are many definitions of 'shareholder value' and so it is also with business models. Business models have become a short-hand for the way in which products, services, business processes and organization functions such as information systems, marketing and distribution might be reworked to transform firm, industry and national economic performance. In the literature the terminology used to construct BMs varies across academic disciplines such as information systems, strategy, innovation studies and entrepreneurship. The result is that there are substantial differences in scope and purpose attached to the BM concept because it is applied in many different contexts. In an extensive review of the BM concept, Osterwalder *et al.* (2005) usefully classify the existing definitions into three broad generic approaches according to level of application and abstraction. Thus a BM can be viewed as:

i) an overarching conceptual framework for describing all real world businesses at the most abstract level;
ii) a classification scheme for describing different types of generic business models with common business characteristics, such as the banking, pharma, e-business and no-frills air-travel business models; or
iii) specific operational business models in the real world, such as the Dell or Amazon business models.

In this text we argue that a loose BM conceptual framework should provide an overarching abstraction about the real world, generate a system of classification and reveal the specific activity characteristics of focal firms in their business model. The loose conceptual framework developed in this text incorporates three elements: *structure, purpose* and *evaluation*. In terms of structuring business models we first draw upon the notion of a BM located in an information genotype where focal firms share a similar stakeholder information network.

> One of the first definitions that became popular was proposed by Timmers (1998). He defined a business model as 'an architecture for the product, service and information flows, including a description of the various business actors and their roles; and a description of the potential benefits for the various business actors; and a description of the sources of revenues.' This definition has also influenced the definition of Weill and Vitale (2001) and is also very similar to the definition of Mahadevan (2000). These conceptualizations see the business model as an architecture and address the business network with a focus on the different roles of the actors and their interactions. A network approach is also very explicit in Tapscott's definition (2001) and his work on business webs (Tapscott, Lowy, & Ticoll, 2000).
>
> *(http://www.smartservicescrc.com.au/PDF/Business%20Service %20Management%20Volume%203.pdf)*

Second, we argue that business models should be granted a sense of strategic purpose which Chesbrough suggests is one of value creation and value capture.

> Chesbrough (2006) states that a business model performs two important functions: value creation and value capture. First, it defines a series of activities that will yield a new product or service in such a way that there is net value created throughout the various activities.
>
> *(http://eprints.qut.edu.au/41609/1/Business_Service_Management_ Volume_3_Mar2011_Understanding_Business_Models_Final.pdf)*

In this text, we argue, that the general purpose of a business model is to sustain a financial surplus from operations (for liquidity) and generate ongoing (re)capitalization (for solvency) for focal firms located within its boundary (although we also accept that there will be exceptions to this, for example, the small and medium enterprise (SME) bio-pharma business model is about cash burn rather than augmenting cash surpluses and capitalization although this may not be sustained indefinitely (Haslam *et al.*, 2011)). Third, we incorporate Magretta's (2002) view about evaluation, whether the story about a business model makes sense and how financial numbers provide a useful resource upon which to construct alternative critical narratives (Froud *et al.*, 2006). Magretta refers to 'tying narrative to numbers' and states that there are two tests for a business model: the narrative test ('the story doesn't make sense') and the numbers test (the profit and loss doesn't add up).

Thus our business model conceptual framework is about providing a loose overarching conceptual framework informed by a need for structure, purpose and evaluation. Distinct from elaborating a conceptual framework for business models, we are also concerned with locating business models in a 'financialized' context. The literature on financialization has developed over the past two decades and now incorporates a number of perspectives. At a macro-economy level Krippner (2005) argues that there has been a shift in the composition of investment away from productive towards financial and intangible asset structures. This leads to profits increasingly accrued from the accumulation of financial assets rather than productive assets used for trade and commodity production.

> I define financialization as a pattern of accumulation in which profits accrue primarily through financial channels rather than through trade and commodity production . . . 'Financial' here refers to activities relating to the provision (or transfer) of liquid capital in expectation of future interest, dividends and capital gains.
>
> *(Krippner, 2005: 174, 175)*

Lazonick and O'Sullivan (2000) and Lazonick (2010) observe that, in the USA, financialization modifies corporate governance towards managing for shareholder value and the distribution of profits and earnings to shareholders at the expense of reinvestment of financial resources into innovation and productive renewal. The main thrust of Lazonick's perspective on financialization is that managerial remuneration packages and financial incentives have modified the distribution of cash surpluses at the cost of innovation and competitiveness.

> By financialization, I mean the evaluation of the performance of a company by a financial measure such as earnings per share. The manifestation of the financialization of the US economy is the obsession of corporate executives with distributing 'value' to shareholders, especially in the form of stock repurchases, even if it is at the expense of investment in innovation and the creation of US employment opportunities.
>
> *(Lazonick, 2010: 6)*

Milberg (2008) argues that there has been a tendency for US firms to disintegrate and off-shore their value chains as they pursued strategies to narrow their productive scope and focus on their core competences. This has served to boost profit margins which were then made subject to modified corporate governance where the priority was to distribute funds to shareholders rather than reinvest in productive assets.

> Financialization has encouraged a restructuring of production, with firms narrowing their scope to 'core competence.' And the rising ability of firms to disintegrate production vertically and internationally has allowed firms to

maintain cost markups – and thus profits and shareholder value – even in a context of slower economic growth. The argument put forth here is not that globalized production triggered financialization, but that global production strategies have helped to sustain financialization.

(Milberg, 2008: 35)

Erturk *et al.* (forthcoming) employ the case of Apple Inc. and its relation to Chinese overseas operations to reveal the cost and margin differences of assembly in China compared with the USA. This, the authors argue, provides a 'narrative and numbers' platform upon which to secure favourable analysts' opinions about the Apple business model, which combines cost reduction across its global value chain with strong cost recovery conditions because branded 'must-have' lock-in products are then sold off into high income markets. Erturk *et al.* (forthcoming) argue that the Apple case illustrates that there is no one best way to run a financialized firm, by which they suggest that a multiplicity of interventions are possible.

So how do we understand what's going on at Apple in the context of financialisation? This is not downsize and distribute (Lazonick and O'Sullivan, 2000) nor the increased propensity for merger and acquisition activity (Stockhammer 2004; Epstein 2005). The one best way social science models of how to run a financialised firm are irrelevant here.

(Erturk et al. (forthcoming))

In this text we would agree with this general position on there being no 'one best way' and that this can best be understood within a loose business model conceptual framework that accommodates variability. That is, a business model captures focal firms that share a similar information genotype, but accommodates variability in terms of how firms act and respond to generate a financial surplus and secure ongoing recapitalization(s). Thus the mechanics of how focal firms in a business model adapt around restructuring global value chains, the deployment of capabilities, restructuring resources and the manipulation of corporation finance are variable and contingent. Within a business model framework we can make sense of Apple Inc.'s moves as value chain manipulation to access low labour costs, the deployment of intellectual and intangible capabilities to generate new product to evade price erosion, and manipulation of corporation finance for additional financial leverage and capitalization. In this text we take the view that stakeholder interactions generate information genotypes which capture focal firms within loosely described business models. Business models contain focal firms/reporting entities that are executing adaptive responses where the purpose is to generate financial surplus for liquidity and ongoing recapitalization to remain solvent. The financial numbers can be used to construct alternative critical narratives about the nature of specific business models in terms of their capacity to generate economic and financial transformation.

Structuring business models

A business model contains organizations/firms that share similar stakeholder networks and information genotypes, for example, product market coverage, services provided, and institutional and regulatory conditions. For example, retail banks, investment banks, private equity partnerships, big-pharma/bio-pharmaceuticals, hospices and auto manufacture/assembly belong to industries by virtue of the share of sales revenue or profit generated from product and service provided. However, in structuring a business model our concern is with how similar stakeholder interactions define the information genotype and the nature of a business model within which focal firms are subtended. Within the context of a relatively stable macrofinancial ecosystem, business models are still emerging, maturing and decaying and this acts to redistribute resources. New innovative business models emerge or are reinvented in circumstances where stakeholder relations and the information genotype can be restructured or institutional and regulatory change can be exploited to generate new opportunities for financial accumulation. Often the latest 'new or modified' business model is canvassed to stakeholders (and specifically investors) with a supportive rhetoric that promises considerable economic and financial transformation (Feng et al., 2001). Yet business models also degrade in circumstances where stakeholder networks, regulatory frameworks and the institutional environment are no longer capable of underwriting the conditions for financial viability. Business models are thus a useful organizing concept because they reveal how physical and financial resources are redeployed, redistributed and accumulated as business models emerge, mature or degrade.

Our starting point is the way in which business models are structured and constituted, and our argument is that they are conditioned by the information resources arising from stakeholder interactions in the general econosphere. This information may derive from knowledge about the needs of consumers and households and how this transmits into development expenses and products and services sold. But it may also include information about different types of financial products and how these might be deployed within the firm so as to reduce financial risk, for example, hedge products and derivatives. Moreover, information from regulatory institutions may impact on the business model in terms of how physical and financial resources are managed. In broad terms a business models exists where information attributes congeal to establish a broad boundary within which focal firms can be situated: for example, investment banking, mixed retail, bio-pharma and digital lifestyle, to name a few.

In Table 4.1 we describe some of the elements of the intelligence arising from stakeholder interactions in the general econsphere, which provide the informational basis for structuring a business model genotype. The nature of the business model depends upon its relation to households or other final consumers in the value chain, what products and services are located within the business model and how relations to other stakeholders are structured (see Figure 4.1).

TABLE 4.1 Information content within the econosphere

Stakeholders	Information
Households and other customers	Number of households, active and retired and size, products and services consumed and expenditure trends. Patterns of income distribution and employment, savings.
Suppliers	Capital equipment, information and communications technology, materials, consultancy and general business services.
Employees	Age distribution, population, workforce, educational attainments, wages, salaries, social charges and hours worked.
Investors	Retail banks, business angels, venture capital, private equity, investment banks, government agencies, households.
Institutional and regulatory	Corporate governance arrangements, rules and routines, accounting standards, financial regulations, health and safety, legal frameworks. Government regulatory agencies and institutions.

Source: The authors.

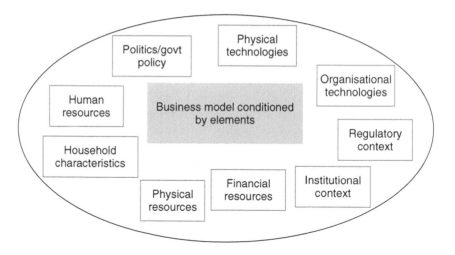

FIGURE 4.1 Business model within the econosphere.

Source: The authors.

The purpose of a business model

Our presumption is that focal firms and business models have a central purpose – that of generating a financial surplus from which ongoing capitalization(s) can be augmented. Although we accept that there are focal firms (and also business models) that, for a period of time, may not generate surplus and inflate capitalization(s), our argument for taking this general position is grounded in accounting and the notion that the reporting entity fundamentally needs to be a 'going concern', that is, generate surplus earnings (liquidity) and inflate capitalization and net worth (solvency).

The financial viability of a business model thus reflects the aggregate position of focal firms contained within its boundary where some, but not all, focal firms may be generating surplus and inflating capitalizations. In this respect a business model is also the sum of its focal firm parts and their aggregated financial numbers, which allows us to say something about the relative viability of one business model compared with another.

If we assume that the purpose of reporting entities, in their business model, is to generate financial surplus and inflate capitalization, this also suggests, as we have argued in Chapter 2, that the purpose of strategy is to extract financial leverage. To extract financial leverage a focal firm will arbitrage stakeholders that constitute its business model genotype and operating architecture. Our use of the term arbitrage is far broader than its narrow use in financial markets, where similar financial instruments are traded to extract a margin on the difference between their bid–ask price spread. Rather, we use the term 'arbitrage' to reflect how business intelligence and information gathered about stakeholders is employed to renegotiate and adjust existing arrangements. This would include, for example, not simply modification to a global value chain to access low labour costs, but how this might need to be passed on as lower prices to consumers, or how the additional cash extracted is remitted to shareholders as either dividends or share buy-backs for holding gains. This notion of arbitrage is not simply about how individuated stakeholder relations are manipulated, but about how the financial numbers are the product of complex ongoing simultaneous manipulations.

Thus focal firms within their business model are actively collecting and deciphering information from a variety of sources and interventions, and this information is utilized to arbitrage stakeholder arrangements (see Figure 4.2). In Figure 4.3 we summarize the financial purpose of focal firms in a business model in terms of a capital augmented financial framework (see Chapter 2) where cash surplus generation (for liquidity) and capitalization (for solvency) matter. It is an account of income received and how this is deployed to satisfy external and internal financial claims before a residual cash margin is determined. The balance sheet of focal firms in a business model reveals the extent to which capitalization is contracting, holding or expanding relative to cash resources. On the equity and liability side of the balance sheet we have accumulated shareholder funds (original shares issues at par value plus accumulated gains and losses carried forward in the year adjusted for treasury stock) and liabilities as long-term debt, post-employment benefits, trade payables, etc. On the asset side of the balance sheet we are concerned with how the balance between fixed assets (financial, tangible and intangible including goodwill) and current assets (inventory, receivables and cash) adapts and evolves over a period of time. The financial purpose of firms in a business model can thus be described as a tension between flows (income, expenditure and cash surpluses) and stock (capitalization of the balance sheet). This tension is a nexus of wealth at risk where contradictory forces embedded in a business model's information genotype play out in a focal firm's financial numbers, promoting or frustrating the return on capital. A few examples will serve to illustrate and expand upon Figure 4.3.

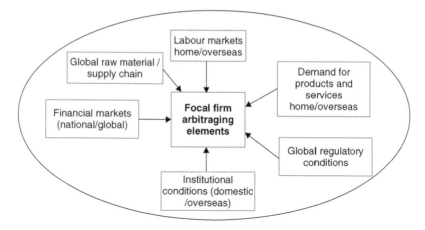

FIGURE 4.2 The focal firm in a business model.

Source: The authors.

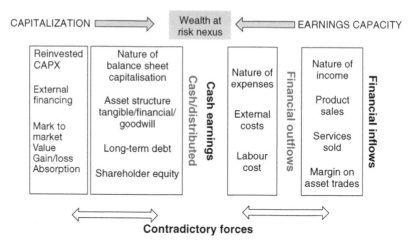

FIGURE 4.3 Financial purpose of a focal firm in its business model.

Source: The authors.

Wealth at risk: a financial nexus

Modifying value chains

To boost cash surplus margins focal firms in a business model might recalibrate their share of the financial value chain, increasing or reducing out-sourcing. Depending on the wage gradient this could substitute lower cost suppliers (increase external purchases) for high internal labour costs (lowering internal labour costs) to boost cash margins. However, if all of this adjustment is taking place in a competitive market where price erosion is the norm we may not observe a transformed cash surplus margin.

Pensions: market to market

Focal firms in a business model are required to make pension provisions and these are assessed on the basis of the estimated market value of assets and liabilities undertaken by actuaries called in to provide expert advice. Where stock markets are inflating and the value of assets exceeds liabilities, focal firms in a business model might not need to provide cash resources and take a so-called 'pension holiday'. Inflated capital market values are, in this circumstance, releasing cash resources, but where capital market conditions deteriorate and liabilities exceed assets real cash is required to fill the gap.

Share buy-backs as holding gains

Buying back shares for treasury stock differs from paying shareholders straightforward dividends because repurchased shares can, when the firms share price inflates, accrue implicit holding gains which can be realized when used to finance a corporate acquisition or pay salaries and bonuses. Adobe's acquisition of Flash Macromedia was paid for with treasury stock of 103 million shares that had been repurchased at an average cost of $22.60. At the time Adobe announced its objective to acquire Macromedia (15 April 2005), its share price on the open market was $30.33, one-third higher that the average cost of treasury shares repurchased, thereby leveraging previously allocated cash resources (see Table 4.2).

Business combinations and capitalization

When the acquiring firm purchases another business, this has to be accounted for at market value rather than pooling or simply aggregating the two sets of company accounts. The acquiring firm has to absorb the market value of the company plus any premium paid above market value into its accounts, and depending on the scale of the acquisition this could easily inflate balance sheet capitalization ahead of cash earnings capacity. Absorbing the market value (rather than book value) of significant acquisitions will often mechanically reduce the reported cash surplus return on capital employed (cash ROCE). To improve the reported cash ROCE there will

TABLE 4.2 Adobe treasury stock, 31 March 2005

Treasury stock outstanding (units)	102.8 million
Total value of repurchased stock	$2.324 billion
Average stock repurchase price	$22.60
Adobe share price at acquisition date	$30.33

Source: Securities and Exchange Commission, 10K annual return.

be additional pressure to reduce costs to boost cash and/or reduce balance sheet capitalization. Share buy-backs now make sense because treasury stock repurchases are accounted for as reducing shareholder equity (capital employed) and thus help to restore the cash ROCE.

Asset structure and impairments

The asset structure of US firms has adjusted to include more intangible and financial assets relative to tangible assets (Krippner, 2005). The growth in marketable financial assets and ongoing trade in these assets can be an important financial supplement to that generated from selling products and services to be consumed. In addition a large component of the S&P asset side balance sheet is represented by goodwill arising from acquisitions and the difference between the market and book value of businesses acquired. Thus accounting regulations have a variable impact on assets valuation(s) and these are also exposed to changes in market value, for example, marketable securities and goodwill are periodically tested by auditors to establish whether valuations are impaired. This may be the case where current market values are below that recorded as the carrying value in the balance sheet or because their cash earnings capacity going forward is not sufficient to recover goodwill (excess paid above book value for an asset).

> If there is objective evidence that an impairment loss on financial assets measured at amortised cost has been incurred, the amount of the loss is measured as the difference between the asset's carrying amount and the present value of estimated future cash flows (excluding future credit losses that have not been incurred) discounted at the financial asset's original effective interest rate (i.e. the effective interest rate computed at initial recognition). The carrying amount of the asset shall be reduced either directly or through use of an allowance account. The amount of the loss shall be recognised in profit or loss.
>
> *(IAS 39: para 63)*

The significance of goodwill is revealed in Figure 4.4 where we assess the exposure of S&P 500 companies to goodwill impairments. If goodwill is to be written down because it is impaired this will be recorded as a reduction in profit (earnings) and in turn will carry forward reducing the value of shareholder equity. In 2010 a total of eighty-nine companies listed in the S&P 500 recorded goodwill equivalent to 75 per cent or more of reported shareholder equity exposing one-fifth of S&P 500 market value to the possibility of leveraged goodwill impairments.

In the USA the financial and non-financial institutional sectors are accumulating goodwill in their balance sheets which could possibly be written off in very large 'lumpy' adjustments, undermining the value of reported shareholder equity which is a key solvency test. If a firm's equity is damaged by goodwill write-offs, the auditors may consider that this is threatening solvency. Consider, for example,

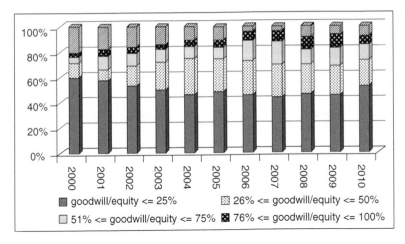

FIGURE 4.4 US S&P 500 market value and goodwill to equity exposure (%). Goodwill is that arising from corporate acquisitions and is the difference between market value and book value of assets purchased.

Source: ThomsonOneBanker.

the case of the Royal Bank of Scotland (RBS) where goodwill impairment tests are carried out each year to assess the extent to which the balance sheet (carry) value of goodwill is aligned with the fair market value.

> For the purposes of impairment testing, goodwill acquired in a business combination is allocated to each of the Group's cash-generating units or groups of cash-generating units expected to benefit from the combination. Goodwill impairment testing involves the comparison of the carrying value of a cash-generating unit or group of cash generating units with its recoverable amount. The recoverable amount is the higher of the unit's fair value and its value in use. Value in use is the present value of expected future cash flows from the cash-generating unit or group of cash-generating units. Fair value is the amount obtainable for the sale of the cash-generating unit in an arm's length transaction between knowledgeable, willing parties.
> *(www.rbs.com/microsites/gra2008/downloads/RBS_Annual_Report_08.pdf)*

Table 4.3 reveals that in 2008 RBS had made provisions for loan losses (impairments of assets) of £8 billion but the goodwill impairment charges against profit for the same year amounted to £32.5 billion – some four times greater than loan losses. The negative leverage exerted from the write-down of goodwill capitalized in the balance sheet was substantial and equivalent to reducing shareholder equity by one-third in 2008 and forcing an equity cure to maintain capital adequacy under Basle II banking regulations. This equity cure had to then be provided by the UK government because private shareholders were, at that time, unwilling to fund the additional capital because RBS's share price was so uncertain and volatile.

TABLE 4.3 Royal Bank of Scotland: income statement, December 2008 (£ million)

Net interest	18,675
Non-interest income	7,193
Total income	25,868
Staff costs	10,241
Premises	2,593
Other admin expenses	5,464
Depreciation and amortization	3,154
Write down of goodwill	32,581
Operating expenses	54,033
Loss before impairments	−28,165
Insurance	−4,430
Impairment	−8,072
Pre-tax loss	−40,667
Tax	2,323
Profit from other operations	3,971
Loss for year	−34,373

Source: www.rbs.com/microsites/gra2008/downloads/RBS_Annual_Report_08.pdf

Note: Data extracted and summarized from the income statement.

If the purpose of business models is to generate cash surplus (for liquidity) and secure recapitalization (for solvency), then this is subject to a range of contradictory forces because different stakeholders install their imprint upon the business model information genotype and hence reported financials. There is no guarantee that the stakeholder interactions that constitute a business model will deliver the promised financial transformation and viability.

Business model evaluation: performance, numbers and levels of analysis

Business models are structured by the information genotype that arises from stakeholder interactions and settled in-contractual and non-contractual arrangements which, as we have argued, are captured within the prism of reported financial numbers. The strategic purpose of focal firms and their respective business models is one of generating a cash surplus for liquidity and ongoing capitalization for solvency. We have described how the financial prism congeals complex and often contradictory outcomes such that the accounting system transmits financial adjustments via the process of double entry bookkeeping. That is, financial transmissions work their way through the income, expense and cash flow accounts to register positive or negative adjustments to assets and liabilities. Changes in financial levels, trajectory and ratios are thus a significant and valuable resource for conducting business analysis because they can be used to construct narratives about strategic endeavour, performance and outcome. To construct these evaluative narratives it is necessary, we argue, to simultaneously conduct different levels of analysis: focal firm (micro-level), business model (meso-level) and aggregate (macro-level). Focal firm financials can inform us about trajectories, operating ratios and financial leverage and how these have changed over a period of time. However, we suggest that it is also important to set the focal firm's financials against all other firms located in its business model and thereby construct narratives about relative performance before then turning to comment on the focal firm and business model relative to the macro financial picture. To construct an illustrative performance evaluation framework we employ, for illustrative purposes, the case of Pfizer, which we locate within the big-pharma business model, and Apple, which we locate in the digital lifestyle business model (see also Chapters 10 and 11).

Apple Inc. Products and services include Macintosh (Mac) computers, iPhone, iPad, iPod, Apple TV, Xserve, a portfolio of consumer and professional software applications, the Mac OS X and iOS operating systems, third-party digital content and applications through the iTunes Store, and a range of accessory, service and support offerings.	**Pfizer Inc.** Products include the research and development of new chemical entities (NCEs) for regulatory approval and use in primary and speciality care. Also produces animal and consumer health-care products. Blockbuster drugs: Lipitor (reduces LDL cholesterol), Enbrel (rheumatoid arthritis), Lyrica (epilepsy).

Our analysis starts with a firm-level profile and a description about the performance of these two companies over the period 1990–2010. We then turn to consider the financials of both firms relative to all firms in their respective business models before aggregating focal firm financials to construct a business model assessment. That is, we consider the performance of Pfizer and Apple Inc. relative to the big-pharma and digital lifestyle business model (DLBM) respectively and their respective business models relative to the S&P 500 as a whole.

The focal firm

We start with a consideration of Pfizer's and Apple Inc.'s cash surplus margin and cash return on capital employed,[1] where the cash surplus margin is found by subtracting all external costs and internal labour costs from total revenues and is a measure of the extent to which an individual firm is able to manipulate product markets, supply chain and employment costs to stretch the share of cash extracted from operations. For Pfizer the share of cash surplus extracted from income gently increased from 1990 to 2008, before the recent financial crisis (see Figure 4.5). However, there is a turning point with the cash ROCE, which dropped after the

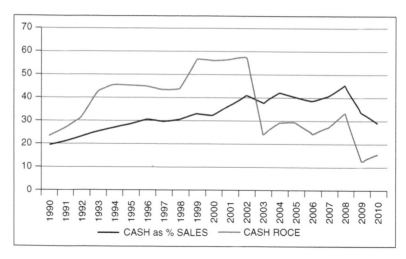

FIGURE 4.5 Pfizer: cash margin and cash ROCE (%).
Source: ThomsonOneBanker.

year 2001 when a series of corporate acquisitions, accounted for at their market value, inflated balance sheet capitalization and reduced the cash ROCE from more than 50 per cent to 15 per cent in 2010.

The financial profile for Apple reveals a phoenix rising from the ashes with the cash surplus margin and cash ROCE falling for most of the 1990s but thereafter recovering as a new generation of products recovers the financial position of the company (see Figure 4.6). By 2010 the cash surplus margin is above 20 per cent and cash ROCE approaching 40 per cent as Apple extracts an increased share of cash from income to reverse the decline in reported cash ROCE.

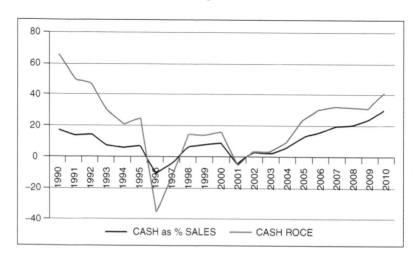

FIGURE 4.6 Apple Inc.: cash margin and cash ROCE (%)
Source: ThomsonOneBanker.

It is apparent from Table 4.4 that whilst Pfizer has generated more than four times as much accumulated cash resources over the period 1990–2010 compared with Apple Inc., there are also significant differences in the deployment of EBITDA. Both firms have set aside roughly the same share of their cash surplus for the purpose of capital expenditure, but this is where the similarities end. During this period Pfizer has been actively restructuring using one-quarter of its cash surplus resources to help finance corporate acquisitions, and 27 per cent of cash surplus resources have been spent on share buy-backs with roughly the same share spent on dividends. Pfizer's restructuring, through acquisition, has inflated balance sheet capitalization and the response has been to try to reduce this by deploying £60 billion of cash to finance share buy-backs, which incidentally reduce shareholder equity and hence capital employed. With Apple, cash surplus resources distributed as dividends, share buy-backs and cash acquisitions are a much smaller share of cash at 7 per cent, leaving a significant lump of free cash (on average 77 per cent of EBITDA) which had been accumulated in the balance sheet as cash, short- and long-term marketable securities, earning interest and dividends. In both companies reconfiguring the value chain, resource deployment for new product and higher margin, and manipulation of corporation finance are variably acting upon their respective reported financials.

Focal firms in their business model

On the one hand, it is possible to construct narratives about the financial performance of individual firms around their financial trajectory, costs structure, margins and how they are manipulating corporation finance. However, it is also necessary, to contextualize specific firm-level financials relative to all focal firms in their business model. While we accept this involves making judgements about which firms to include in a business model for the purpose of its financial construction, it is worth noting that over time firms migrate into or out of business models. In the case of the S&P 500 food and staples business model over the period 1990–2010, the number of firms drops from 22 to 9, real estate increases from 1 to 8, big-pharma business drops from 13 down to 11 and the digital lifestyle business model (DLBM)[2] moves from 27 firms in 1990 to a peak of 64 firms in 2002 before dropping back to 53 firms.

TABLE 4.4 Pfizer and Apple: cash application, 1990–2010

	EBITDA	Capital expenditure	Cash acquisitions	Share buy-backs	Dividends	Residual free cash
Pfizer ($ billion)	220.1	30.1	52.0	59.8	65.0	13.2
Apple ($ billion)	50.1	8.1	1.3	1.9	0.4	38.4
Share of EBITDA (%)						
Pfizer		13.7	23.6	27.2	29.5	6.0
Apple		16.2	2.6	3.8	0.7	76.7

Source: Thomson One Banker.

Once we have the main financial variables for all firms within their respective business models, it is possible to aggregate this information and compare a focal firm (Pfizer/Apple) with the average for their respective business model. This 'average' financial profile of a business model is constructed from the financials for all focal firms contained in a business model. This now provides a reference point against which to construct alternative narratives which would otherwise not be possible. In Figure 4.7 we show Apple Inc.'s cash surplus margin relative to the average generated by all focal firms in its business model. This reveals how Apple drops out of the frame from the early 1990s before its steady recovery as new innovative products come on line and cost structures also transform, but that it has only been in recent years that its margin out-runs the business model average.

Apple Inc.'s improved cash surplus margin and income trajectory are also associated with an increase in balance sheet capitalization throughout the 1990s bringing the company into line with the average for the DLBM (see Figure 4.8). The combination of improved cash surplus margin and lower rates of capitalization operate to boost the reported cash ROCE where the cash ROCE is:

(cash surplus/sales) / (capital employed/sales)

or   cash surplus margin/capital intensity.

Apple Inc.'s renaissance after reappointing Steve Jobs in 1996 (after Apple's acquisition of neXT brought him back into the company as CEO) was a substantial marketing and productive achievement, but financially it was all about restoring Apple back to the average ROCE for all firms in the DLMB (see Figure 4.9). Let

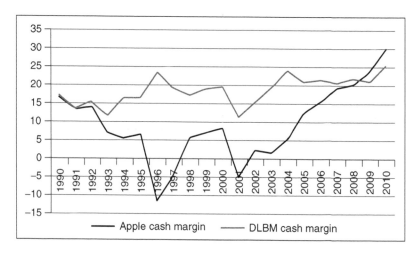

FIGURE 4.7 Apple Inc. and DLBM: cash margin (%).

Source: ThomsonOneBanker.

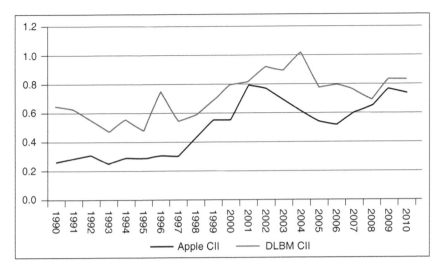

FIGURE 4.8 Apple Inc. and DLBM: capital intensity (CII). Capital intensity is capital employed divided by total sales.

Source: ThomsonOneBanker.

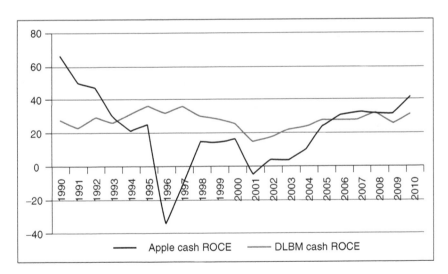

FIGURE 4.9 Apple Inc. and DLBM: cash ROCE (%).

Source: ThomsonOneBanker.

us now turn to the position of Pfizer relative to all other firms in its business model, starting with the cash margin which is revealed in Figure 4.10 and shows that Pfizer manages to shift its operations from a 20 per cent cash surplus margin to nearer 40 per cent by the mid-2000s. Likewise the average cash surplus margin for all firms in the business model also gently tracks up from 25 to 30 per cent by the mid-2000s.

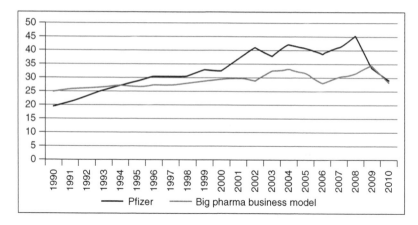

FIGURE 4.10 Pfizer relative to big-pharma business model: cash margin (%).
Source: ThomsonOneBanker.

Although focal firms within the big-pharma business model are generally extracting a greater share of cash surplus from their operations, this, as we can see in Figure 4.11, is associated with a significant increase in balance sheet capitalization in the business model. The period 2000–2010 is one where there is significant corporate restructuring with firms merging and acquiring other companies. These deals have to be accounted for at their fair or market value under accounting rules introduced in the USA after the year 2000 and this change serves to inflate balance sheets when the market value of acquisitions are absorbed on to balance sheets (Andersson et al., 2009).

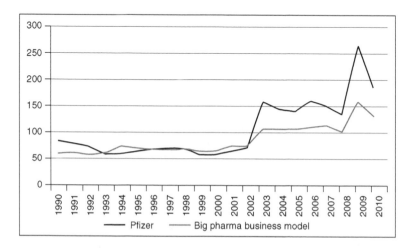

FIGURE 4.11 Pfizer relative to big-pharma business model: capital intensity. Capital intensity is capital employed divided into sales revenues.
Source: ThomsonOneBanker.

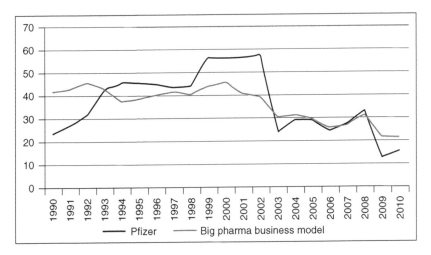

FIGURE 4.12   Pfizer relative to big-pharma business model: cash ROCE (%).
Source: ThomsonOneBanker.

Thus we find that the big-pharma business model generates a strong and steady 40 per cent cash surplus return on capital employed over the period 1990–2000 with Pfizer significantly out-performing its business model peers. After the year 2000 the return on capital extracted from this business model is undermined by its need to restructure, which also coincides with a change in accounting standards, whereby business combinations should be accounted for at market value. The big-pharma business model is adjusting the calibration of its value chain and delivering ongoing product innovation and reinvention to leverage higher cash surplus margins out of revenues. However, the balance sheets of focal firms in this business model inflate ahead of cash earnings, forcing the reported ROCE down from 40 to 20 per cent (see Figure 4.12).

We next outline how we might classify the financial nature of business models by locating these models along a financial spectrum in terms of how they can migrate from relatively unleveraged to leveraged balance sheet positions and vice versa. It is also the case that business models emerge, mature and degrade and we consider a number of emergent and mature business models within the S&P 500. In the final section of this chapter we observe that within business models the performance of focal firms modifies over a period of time such that there are winners and losers as firms succeed or fail to financially adapt to changes in the information pool within which they are subtended.

Business models: a financial typology

In Figure 4.13 we identify a spectrum that describes a range of possible business models in terms of their financial operating characteristics, although we also admit that these typologies would not exist in a clear and precise way. Rather this set of

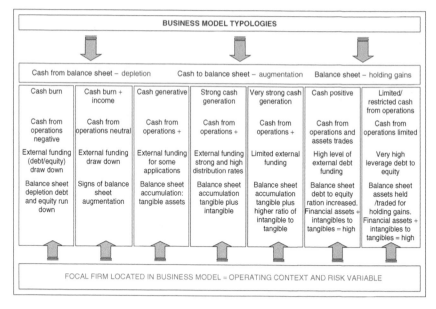

FIGURE 4.13 Business model financial typology.
Source: The authors.

typologies is a useful means by which to characterize the 'dominant' financial characteristics of a business model whilst accepting that business models will contain a mixture of these financial attributes.

On the extreme left-hand side of our spectrum we locate business models that might be purely cash burn, that is, they raise funds from investors and then draw down these funds to cover the expenses of an activity, such as product development. As time elapses, the product or service under development may (or may not) be transferable to a market and generate revenues and cash surplus. As we move to the right out of the cash burn territory, we encounter business models that are operating with some cash burn activities but are also generating income and slim cash margins from operations. For example, the food and staples business model within the S&P 500 has undergone a significant degree of restructuring down from 22 to 9 firms in 1990–2010. This business model is located towards the left-hand side of the financial spectrum in Figure 4.13 and generates slim cash margins out of total income. This is because food retail involves a high level of external purchases (often 80 per cent of sales) which are then sold on to customers, for example, in Walmart stores. Thus the value retained by firms is approximately 20 per cent of sales and then we still have to deduct employee compensation to leave a slim residual cash margin (see Figure 4.14). This business model generates a steady, but thin, average cash surplus margin from total income of 6–7 per cent and a market leader such as Walmart cannot easily break out from this constraint.

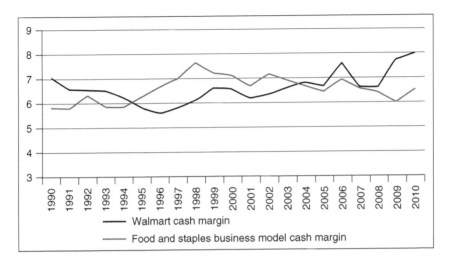

FIGURE 4.14   S&P 500 food and staples: cash margin (%).
Source: ThomsonOneBanker.

This means that firms within this business model must economize on capital (capital intensity) if they are to generate a strong cash return on capital employed. Figure 4.15 reveals that the capital intensity of this business model is gently falling from 30 to 25 per cent (capital as a percentage of total sales) and this helps to bring the cash ROCE up towards 25 per cent, whilst the average for the S&P 500 group of firms is drifting down from 25 per cent in 1997 to 17 per cent in 2010.

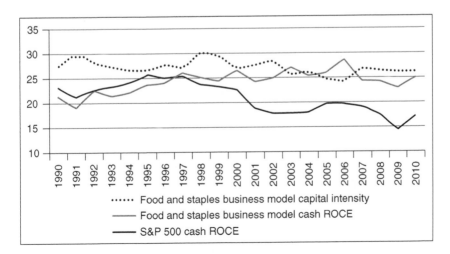

FIGURE 4.15   S&P 500 food and staples: capital intensity and cash ROCE (%).
Source: ThomsonOneBanker.

Moving now towards the centre of Figure 4.13 we encounter business models which are selling products and services which command higher cash surplus margins and are able to service the cost of debt and accumulate shareholder equity in their balance sheets. On the asset side of the balance sheet a mix of tangible and intangible asset accumulation is being recorded. Beyond the central point we find business models that are generating very high cash surplus margins relative to other business models and are able to maintain a relatively clean (i.e. debt and goodwill free) balance sheet. Progressing now further to the right, we start to encounter business models where balance sheet capitalization has increased relative to cash margin, that is, we observe business models that are increasingly leveraged and capitalized. Towards the extreme right-hand side we encounter business models that to a significant extent rely on the manipulation and trade in assets whereby margins, commissions and holding gains on asset deals sustain the payment of expenses attached to running the business model. We might include here banking and private equity business models which are highly leveraged and depend upon inflated balance sheet values to extract margins and holding gains from capital market asset exchanges (see Chapters 8 and 9).

Consider, for example, the real estate business model subsumed within the S&P 500. This is a business model which is generating a high and increasingly strong cash margin from total income rising from 20 to 50 per cent by 2010. However, the capital intensity of this business model is very high because the motivation is to add real estate and commercially rented office space to the business model. Capital intensity starts off from just 10 per cent of total income to a level, in 2010, that is five times total income. The impact of this increased capital intensity is to reduce the cash ROCE from 20 per cent to 10 per cent (see Figure 4.16). The real estate business model is highly leveraged with, at peak, debt finance accounting for

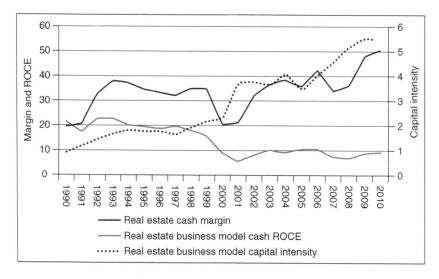

FIGURE 4.16 S&P 500 real estate business model.

Source: ThomsonOneBanker.

roughly 70 per cent of total capital employed. This is also a volatile business model because it depends upon extracting holding gains from inflated property prices and using this 'equity' to lever additional debt finance. In 2011 US real estate prices were 30 per cent down on their peak in 2006. The combination of lower real estate prices and difficulties in raising debt finance, in the current financial crisis, are severely testing the viability of this business model.

The business model financial typology we construct in Figure 4.13 is useful because we can track how business models change over time in terms of their financial evolution and adaptation. An example will serve to illustrate: the US biotech business model. In 1990 just two firms were listed in the S&P 500 within the biotech business model and by 2010 this had growth to ten firms as the viability of the business model evolved. In the early phase of development the cash surplus margin (for three listed firms) increases from 10 to 30 per cent and the cash ROCE from 25 to 45 per cent. The business model financially evolves and the cash surplus margin reaches a plateau of roughly 30 per cent by the year 2000, more or less equivalent to the average for the big-pharma business model (see Chapter 10). Capital funds flow into this relatively new business model, in expectation of high returns from the development of new chemical entities (NCEs), and this inflates capital employed. The biotech business model is becoming increasingly leveraged as the capital employed to sales ratio jumps to a level 2.5 times greater than sales revenue and well above the big-pharma business model capital intensity ratio of 1.5:1.

After a period of rapid expansion and recapitalization, the US biotech business model, contained within the S&P 500, becomes more like the big-pharma business model in terms of its capital intensity, cash surplus margin and cash ROCE. The financial condition of this business model changes as capital funding inflates ahead of the business model's capacity to generate cash surplus, thus reducing the reported cash ROCE from a peak of 45 per cent to 20 per cent in 2010 (see Figure 4.17).

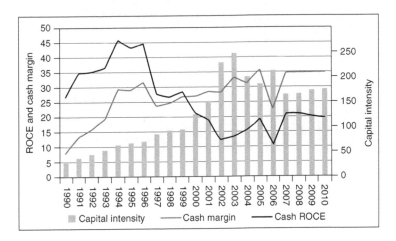

FIGURE 4.17   US biotech business model.

Source: ThomsonOneBanker.

Distribution of firm performance within a business model

The evolution of a business model involves changes in the number of focal firms located within that business model where focal firms also experience different rates of migration in terms of their share of sales, cash surplus and market value within their respective business models. The drivers of these changes in a focal firm's share of the financial space occupied by their respective business models are varied but fundamentally explained by a focal firm's ability or inability to exploit and arbitrage relevant information content from stakeholder interactions, some of which information relates to product market conditions, access to new resources and technology, capital markets and limits to corporate restructuring. Bristol Myers Squibb has seen its share of market value accounted for by the S&P 500 big-pharma business model drop from 18 to 7 per cent. In the meantime Merck, having lost share from 20 to 10 per cent, regained its share in recent years, whilst Johnson & Johnson, having maintained a steady market value share at 12–14 per cent from 1990 to 2001, has increased this to 27 per cent (Figure 4.18).

Turning to the digital lifestyle business model (DLBM) and focal firm share of market value, we observe that International Business Machines (IBM) loses its dominant share of market value as the business model becomes increasingly fragmented with new firms entering. IBM's share of the S&P 500 DLBM market value stood at 63 per cent in 1990 and just 10 per cent in 2010. Apple Computers' share of the DLBM market value was small at 4 per cent in the mid- to late 1990s, falling to 1 per cent, before a rapid and significant increase to 15 per cent over the period 2004–2010. During this period, Apple accounts for more than half of DLBM market value growth (see Figure 4.19 and also Chapter 11).

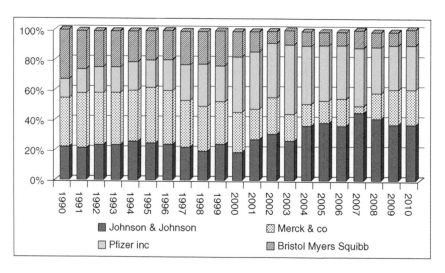

FIGURE 4.18   Share of big-pharma market value.

Source: ThomsonOneBanker S&P 500 data.

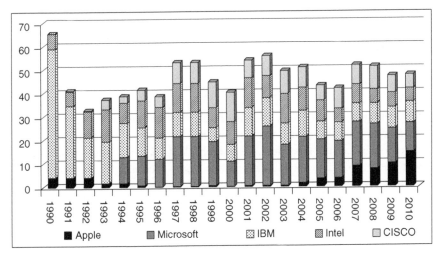

FIGURE 4.19   Share of DLBM market value: Apple, Microsoft, IBM, Intel and Cisco.
Source: ThomsonOneBanker S&P 500 data.

Summary

In this chapter we have argued the case for structuring analysis around a loose business model conceptual framework where focal firms share a similar information genotype arising from stakeholder interactions. We suggest that this information is not simply the product of transactions and official contracts between stakeholders. More broadly a business model consolidates information arising from stakeholder interactions which congeal into and modify reported financial numbers. In response to changing patterns of information, business model genotypes are constituted, evolve and adapt over a period of time, and this is captured in the prism of financial numbers which reflect the viability and sustainability of business models in terms of 'liquidity' and 'solvency' .

The purpose of a business model, we argue, is to generate a financial surplus (for liquidity) and maintain ongoing recapitalizations (for solvency), although we accept that under certain circumstances a business model may generate negative cash flows and run down balance sheet capitalization. Within business models we would expect focal firms to modify their financials, adapting their relation to a physical and financial value chain, variably deploying resources and capabilities and manipulating corporation finance to inflate surplus and capitalization. We argue that the information content extracted by a focal firm from its business model stakeholder network becomes congealed into, and affects, the financial numbers reported by focal firms. Thus the role and nature of accounting now takes on added significance in terms of how the financial numbers can be used to construct narratives about purpose and outcomes.

Within a financialized context, business models extract financial return from leveraging balance sheets, modify the distribution of surplus towards shareholders and are a source of narratives about the possibilities for financial transformation and economic development. Within a framework of analysis, grounded in accounting, we are able to assess the extent to which business models are becoming financialized. At a basic level business models can generate surplus from selling products and services for final consumption or from the manipulation of corporate finance, and both, we argue, are equally legitimate. However, there are significant qualitative differences between investing and selling into goods markets for final consumption and generating surplus from ongoing recapitalizations from the manipulation of corporation finance in capital markets, and other secondary markets. The latter may induct greater volatility into business models now increasingly dependent upon realizing leveraged holding gains from asset appreciation.

Specifically, in financialized business models, asset-liability risk (financial instability) is amplified when holding gains and ongoing recapitalizations are subject to capital market volatility. Additionally we have in mind the way in which accounting processes also contribute to this volatility and the specific requirement to adjust valuations to 'mark to market'. Accounting processes import capital market volatility into reported corporate financials and this works its way through to affect stakeholder arrangements, forcing business models to adapt and respond.

5

BUSINESS MODELS

Global context

Introduction

In this chapter our concern is with broadly outlining the financial development of the key advanced and developing economies within the global economy in terms of income growth, distribution of income, surpluses, deficits and capitalization. Although the global economy is expanding, in terms of income generated as gross domestic product (GDP), it is clear that some economies are expanding at a faster or slower rate. The prolonged differential in GDP growth rates between emerging economic powers such as India and China and the developed economies has led to significant changes in distributional shares of global GDP. This process modifies not only shares of global economic activity but also trade balances where surplus generating economies have moved into deficit as the pattern of their consumption switches from domestic to foreign sourced goods and services. These adjustments in the pattern and trajectory of GDP have a variable impact on both the developing and advanced economies in terms of growth in employment, income and wages per capita. Headline news will generally focus on the extent to which GDP growth has increased from one quarter to the next or the degree to which the advanced economies are falling behind India and China. In recent years our attention has been drawn to the growth of national debt and equity outstanding and the ability of banks or governments to maintain credit ratings and secure financial viability. Banks and governments are finding it increasingly difficult to sustain higher levels of aggregate debt rollover at a time when further recapitalizations are required to bridge funding gaps.

The challenge of sustaining wealth accumulation and recapitalization is also the subject of this chapter, that is, to what extent is it possible to inflate the stock of debt and equity outstanding within the boundaries of the advanced economies? Our analysis reveals the extent to which GDP and capitalization are moving on different trajectories and on what basis these aspects of economic development are, or have become, decoupled. The argument we develop in this chapter is that wealth accumulation matters because it provides the financial foundation upon which to secure income for ageing populations where the ratio of economically active to inactive is falling. It also matters because wealth extraction, in the form of holding gains and equity withdrawal, has provided useful additional financial leverage for households and the corporate sector, and a boost to GDP as accumulated wealth leaks into GDP to boost income, consumption and leverage cash resources.

Advanced economy national business models are being stress tested because debt and equity are accumulating ahead of GDP growth in circumstances where there has also been a lack of transformation of earnings capacity (gross operating surplus – GOS). If we treat the aggregate business model of advanced national economies as a set of activities which generate value added (GDP) and surpluses (GOS) after paying employee compensation, then, in the absence of a transformation in the share of GOS in GDP, capitalization (debt and equity) should generally track GDP. The disconnection between GDP and balance sheet debt and equity values outstanding might be explained by historically lower interest rates that have helped reduce the cost of financing capital accumulations. However, in a credit-based economy, where trading in capital markets is brisk and asset values are inflated, capital can become its own self-fulfilling collateral in an ongoing process of recapitalizations. In these circumstances the recapitalization and inflation of debt and equity values outstanding bears only a distant relation to underlying earnings capacity of assets and the cost of financing capital. Within the national business models of the advanced economies there are also subsidiary business models that play their part in amplifying the process of recapitalization and leverage. The financial condition of these subsidiary business models is also critical to our understanding of why, even when interest rates are low, they (leveraged business models) cannot withstand significant deteriorations in the quality of their balance sheet assets and credit rating before they are insolvent.

This chapter is split into four sections, the first of which describes and captures the salient characteristics of GDP growth in the advanced economies relative to the developing economies of India and China. A clear finding is that growth rates in GDP have been sluggish in the advanced G7 economies and, for example, the US share of global GDP is down from 30 per cent to nearer 20 per cent over the period 2000–2010. In the USA recent low levels of real economic GDP growth have contributed to a flat-lining of employment growth and no real wage increases in the private sector for a number of years. The second section reviews the extent to which national economic business models have been transformed in terms of their operating cost structure and earnings capacity. Specifically, after deducting external expenses and employment costs from gross output (GO), the residual surplus (GOS) out of which putative capitalizations are funded has increased such that it now accounts for a higher share of gross output. Our analysis reveals that, for the advanced economies, the GOS earnings capacity of national business models is relatively untransformed. Although the trajectory of GDP is subdued and transformation of cost structures in GDP of the advanced economies is limited, this is not the case when we consider national balance sheets and capitalization in section three of this chapter. Most of the action and transformation is in the balance sheets of the G7, not their income and expenditure GDP accounts. The gap between balance sheet capitalization and GDP across the advanced economies has risen to a ratio of 5:1 in 2010. Using long-run data for the USA, we observe how capitalization moves ahead of GDP, starting in the 1980s, and that the compound annual growth rate of balance sheet capitalization is double that of GDP over the period 1980–2010. The final section considers how the process of inflated capital and asset stocks generates holding gains which leak back into GDP, both in the corporate and household sectors, where, in the advanced economies, we have become accustomed to extracting holding gains from capital accumulations.

GDP: growth in advanced and developing economies

Our focus is on describing the structural changes in GDP shares and income distribution in the advanced economies (the G7) and comparing this with the two developing economies of India and China. Our objective is to reveal the extent to which the shares of global GDP and trajectories of economic growth in terms of employment and income levels are variable between these two groups of economies. We start with population growth in the G7 group of economies and compare this with growth in India and China (see Table 5.1). During the period 1980–2010 the global population increased by 2.4 billion and of this increase just over one-third is accounted for by changes in the populations of India and China.

The economic development of both India and China has been fuelled by an abundant supply of labour where the size of the economically active population

TABLE 5.1 Population growth (in millions)

Country	1980	1985	1990	1995	2000	2005	2010	Increase	Share of Increase (%)
World	4,453	4,858	5,289	5,700	6,090	6,470	6,852	2,399	
China	987	1,059	1,143	1,211	1,267	1,308	1,341	354	14.8
India	693	775	862	953	1,043	1,131	1,216	523	21.8
Canada	24	26	28	29	31	32	34	10	0.4
France	54	55	57	58	59	61	63	9	0.4
Germany	77	76	79	82	82	82	82	5	0.2
Italy	56	57	57	57	57	58	60	4	0.2
Japan	117	121	123	125	127	128	127	10	0.4
United Kingdom	56	57	57	58	59	60	62	6	0.2
United States	228	238	250	266	282	296	310	82	3.4

Source: International Monetary Fund, World Economic Outlook Database, October 2010, available at www.census.gov/ipc/www/idb/worldpoptotal.php.

has increased significantly. In both countries the economically active population has roughly doubled from 1 billion to just over 2 billion, and in the developed countries as a whole there has been an increase of roughly one-quarter from 800 million to approximately 1 billion. In the USA it is estimated there will be a 50 per cent increase in the economically active share of the population, rising from 230 to 350 million by 2020, but this is modest when compared with China and India (see Figure 5.1).

The developing economies of both China and India thus have available a substantial pool of economically active labour where the average number of hours worked per week per employee exceeds that in the USA by one-fifth and employment costs per hour are $1.5–2 in the manufacturing sectors (see Table 5.2).

The combination of economic deregulation, a large pool of economically active labour and labour costs roughly one-tenth of those in the USA has fuelled GDP growth in India and China in recent decades. A consequence is a

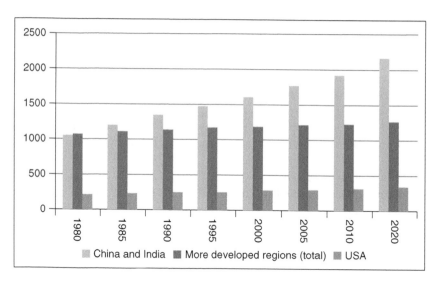

FIGURE 5.1 Economically active population (millions).

Source: ILO.

TABLE 5.2 Manufacturing labour costs per hour in the USA, China and India ($)

	USA 2008	China 2008	India 2006
Hours worked	40.8	47.9	46.9
Earnings per week ($)	723.8	73.6	77.6
Earnings per hour ($)	17.7	1.5	1.7

Source: http://laborsta.ilo.org/.

Note: Exchange rates used are for the end of 2008 and 2006 to convert yuan and rupees into US dollars.

progressively rising share of global GDP for the two countries. The trajectory of GDP growth in both China and India has moved substantially ahead of that of the G7 group of countries over the period 1980–2010 as Figure 5.2 reveals. This overall period can be split into two distinct sub-periods. The first is 1980–1995, when the compound average growth rate (CAGR) of GDP, in current prices, was 7 per cent in the G7 and 6.8 per cent for China and India. In the second period, 1995–2010, the CAGRs diverge, with the G7 averaging 5.2 per cent and China and India now averaging 10 per cent.

In addition, we also observe that in the G7 group of nations, the average growth rate in real GDP per capita, adjusting for price level, has also slowed in recent years and is generally below rates achieved in an earlier period (see Table 5.3). So, for example, in the USA real per capital growth rates in GDP have run at 1.4 per cent compared with 1.8 per cent in an earlier period.

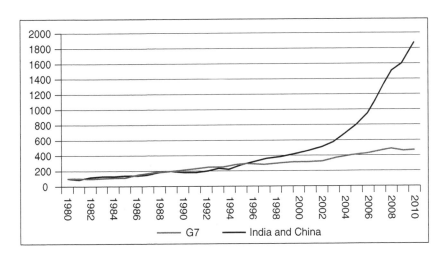

FIGURE 5.2   GDP: G7, India and China in nominal prices expressed as an index. Base year 1980 =100.

Source: IMF.

TABLE 5.3 G7: real GDP per capita, 1980–2010 (constant prices)

	1980–2010	*1980–1995*	*1995–2010*
Canada	1.4	1.2	1.5
France	1.3	1.4	1.1
Germany	1.5	1.7	1.1
Italy	1.1	1.8	0.4
Japan	1.8	2.9	0.6
United Kingdom	1.8	2.0	1.5
United States	1.7	1.8	1.4

Source: International Monetary Fund, World Economic Outlook Database, October 2010.

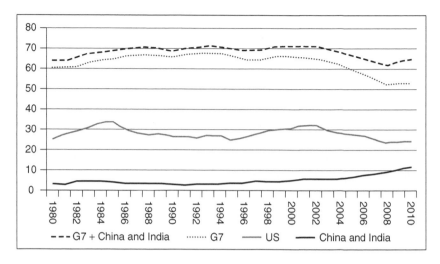

FIGURE 5.3 Share of global GDP (%).

Source: International Monetary Fund, World Economic Outlook Database, October 2010.

Focusing on the US economy and G7 group in a little more detail, we note that the USA has taken a relatively stable share of global GDP (expressed in US dollars) over the period 1980–2000 (Figure 5.3). During the more recent period 2000–2010, the US share of global GDP fell from 30 per cent towards 20 per cent and the G7 group including the USA from 65 per cent towards 50 per cent as the shares of both India and China moved up from 4 per cent to more than 10 per cent.

US nominal GDP increases at a CAGR of 5.5 per cent over the period 1980–2010 and real GDP averaged 2.7 per cent (see Table 5.4). However, real economic growth slows in the second period (1995–2010) relative to the earlier period and is down from 2.8 per cent to 1.2 per cent.

In the earlier sub-period, 1980–1995, GDP growth was the platform upon which the US economy was able to generate additional employment, for example, in the US private industry sector levels increased from 75 million to 100 million. However, during this same sub-period the real weekly earnings of employees across the private sector did not increase, on average, holding steady at around $300 (see Figure 5.4).

In the USA, what growth there has been in GDP did not transmit into an increase in median real weekly earnings. Instead it delivered higher levels of employment in

TABLE 5.4 USA: nominal and real GDP growth rates (%)

CAGR %	1980–2010	1980–1995	1995–2010
Nominal GDP	5.5	4.7	4.3
Real GDP	2.7	2.8	1.2

Source: International Monetary Fund, World Economic Outlook Database, October 2010.

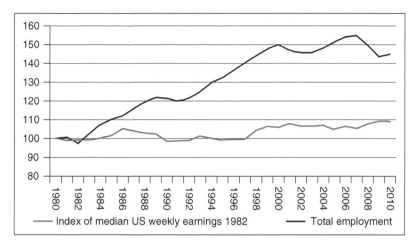

FIGURE 5.4   USA: all private industry: median real earnings and employment index. 1980=100.

Source: US Bureau of Labor Statistics: median usual weekly earnings – in constant (1982–84) dollars series ID: LEU0252881600. Total Private Sector Employment series ID: CES0500000001, available at www.bls.gov/data/.

private sector industries, supporting 50 per cent more employees over the period 1980–2000. Thereafter, both the level of employment and growth in real weekly earnings in the US private industry sector flat-lined. In the UK the picture is slightly different, with a 40 per cent increase in real average monthly earnings (1990–2010) but only an 8 per cent increase in total employment. Although the mix between employment growth and real wage increases is variable between the USA and UK in an earlier period, both countries share a similar pattern in more recent times. That is, after the year 2000 employment growth and real average earnings have both levelled off.[1]

India and China have emerged as newly industrializing countries which have at their disposal a significantly large share of the global economically active population. Moreover, their cumulative growth rates significantly exceed that of the G7 group where, in recent years, real wages and employment increases have become progressively difficult to secure. We now turn to consider the pattern of trade flows and balances between the G7 and India and China.

Trade flows and balances

The current UK government has tasked itself with rebalancing the economy, that is, shifting the emphasis away from financial services towards manufacturing, not just because of the employment that manufacturing establishes but also because of the contribution manufacturing output could make towards reducing the trade deficit. The emergence of both India and China as an employment resource at low cost per hour has helped to alter the pattern of foreign direct investment (FDI) flows and exports (see Figure 5.5). In the late 1970s the G7 group of countries accounted for roughly two-thirds of global FDI flows, but over the next three decades its share of global FDI flows reduced to just one-third. China and India have emerged to take a 10 per cent share of global FDI as overseas manufacturers and service providers access these countries' low labour costs and their growing domestic markets, the latter a result of income levels (GDP per capita) in these countries also increasing.

Within the G7 group of countries, the general trend in terms of trade balances has been one in which Japan and Germany managed to sustain a trade surplus whilst Italy, France, the UK, USA and Canada operated with trade deficits throughout the 1980s. The emergence of China and India as major trading nations in the late 1980s and early 1990s complicates matters, with India running a small deficit whilst China accumulated a significant trade surplus, predominantly at the expense of accelerating the US trade deficit (see Figure 5.6).

There is a general tendency for countries that operate with a trade surplus to also export capital funds, and in terms of the global share of exported capital China now accounts for one-fifth of capital exports, followed by Japan and Germany with 12 per cent shares respectively. The major importers of capital funds are the USA, taking a 40 per cent share, followed closely by the UK, Italy, Spain and Canada at roughly 5–6 per cent of global imported capital (see Table 5.6).

Central government finances

At a national level the advanced economies also share another common underlying trend which is that central government deficits are increasing as expenditures drift ahead of income received from taxes. In the euro area (seventeen countries)

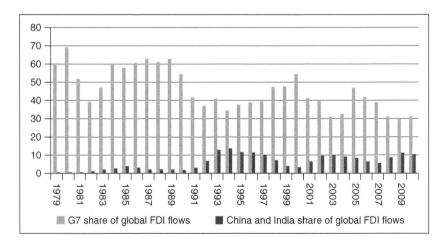

FIGURE 5.5 G7, China and India: share of global FDI flows (%).

Source: UNCTAD.

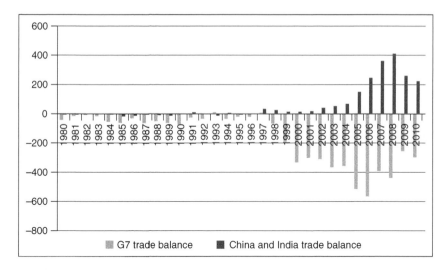

FIGURE 5.6 G7 and China/India: trade balances ($ billion).

Source: IMF World Economic Database.

TABLE 5.6 Shares of global imports and exports of capital (%)

	Economies that export capital		Economies that import capital
China	20.1	United States	39.7
Japan	12.9	United Kingdom	6.0
Germany	12.3	Italy	5.7
Switzerland	5.5	Spain	5.4
Russia	4.7	Canada	4.2
Saudi Arabia	4.4	Turkey	4.1
Netherlands	3.7	Brazil	4.0
Norway	3.4	Other economies	30.9
Singapore	3.3		
Taiwan Province of China	2.6		
Kuwait	2.4		
Qatar	2.1		
Sweden	1.9		
Other economies	20.7		

Source: IMF.

aggregate annual deficits as a share of government revenues increased from 4 to 13 per cent and in the USA and UK the annual deficit is a much higher share of total government revenues at 33 and 35 per cent respectively. In Japan central government revenues remain flat whilst borrowing has gently drifted up to 26 per cent of total income. Although government deficits have moved substantially ahead of total income in the advanced economies, the share of interest paid out of revenues

TABLE 5.7 Central government finances

	2000	2005	2010
Euro area			
Total revenue (€ billion)	3,214	3,654	4,092
Deficit	−133.9	−207.6	−549.8
(Share of total revenue %)	(4.2)	(5.7)	(13.4)
Interest	−268.8	−243.9	−254.5
(Share of total revenue %)	(8.4)	(6.7)	(6.2)
USA			
Total revenue ($ billion)	3,524	4,160	4,598
Deficit	−53.4	−402.9	−1,536.20
(Share of total revenue %)	(1.5)	(9.7)	(33.4)
Interest	−329.7	−331.9	−377.6
(Share of total revenue %)	(9.4)	(8.0)	(8.2)
UK			
Total revenue (£ billion)	415.3	510.4	587.4
Deficit	4.9	−42.9	−148.1
(Share of total revenue %)	(1.2)	(8.4)	(25.2)
Interest	−23.7	−26.3	−42.1
(Share of total revenue %)	(5.7)	(5.2)	(7.2)
Japan			
Total revenue (trillion yen)	160.5	159.1	156.8
Deficit	−31.3	−33.6	−41.1
(Share of total revenue %)	(19.5)	(21.1)	(26.2)
Interest	−15.9	−12.1	−12.2
(Share of total revenue %)	(9.9)	(7.6)	(7.8)

Source: http://puck.sourceoecd.org/vl=37966599/cl=13/nw=1/rpsv/oecd_database.htm.

has remained relatively stable in the range 6–10 per cent of total revenues (see Table 5.7). Central governments in the advanced economies have, for a number of years, financed their deficits by borrowing at favourable low interest rates. During the period 1980–2010 the long-term average interest rate within the euro area and US economy progressively dropped from highs of 14 per cent to lows of 1–2 per cent by 2011. However, there are signs that interest rates will not remain as low as they have been in recent decades. In the euro area the deterioration in sovereign government credit ratings running into 2011 is pushing up the cost of debt refinancing and further stressing central government finances.

Investment in GDP

Although interest rates have been falling since 1980 (see Figure 5.7), this did not encourage the advanced economies to adjust their share of investment in GDP. The proportion of GDP allocated to investment has progressively fallen in the G7 group from a level averaging 25 per cent of GDP in 1980 to approximately 18 per cent in 2010. In contrast India and China are investing at a rate which is running

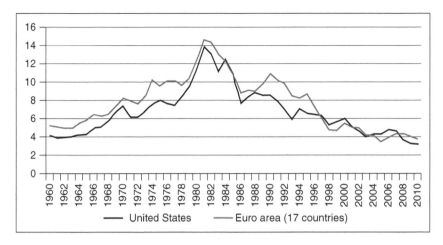

FIGURE 5.7   Long-term interest rates, 1960–2010. Euro area (17 countries) from 1970 on; prior to this we have averaged the European country data available. Long-term interest rates are for ten-year bonds.

Source: OECD.

ahead of GDP and hence the share of investment in GDP has also moved up over the period 2002–2010. Table 5.8 reveals the share of GDP allocated as investment (and also savings) in China and India relative to the G7 group over the period 2002–2010, and it shows that the rate of investment in GDP in India and China is roughly double that of the G7 group.

Our analysis so far in this chapter suggests that the advanced economy business models are financially boxed in and operating with weaker GDP trajectories, low rates of investment in GDP, higher relative labour costs, trade imbalances and

TABLE 5.8   Investment in GDP (%)

	China	India	G7
2002	37.9	25.2	20.1
2003	41.2	28.0	19.4
2004	43.3	31.5	19.3
2005	43.3	33.8	19.7
2006	43.0	35.7	20.1
2007	41.7	38.1	20.7
2008	44.0	34.5	20.4
2009	44.2	36.5	17.9
2010	50.7	37.0	18.3
Average	43.3	33.4	19.5

Source: Asian Development Outlook, various years for China and India, www.adb.org/documents/books/ado/2011/ado2011.pdf; International Monetary Fund, World Economic Outlook Database, October 2010, for G7.

significant central government deficits, whilst the developing economies are exploiting a plentiful supply of labour at relatively low labour costs, expanding GDP, running trade surpluses and exporting capital. We now turn to a consideration of the cost structure of GDP in the G7 advanced economies. The framework of analysis we employ focuses on total national aggregates for gross output (GO), gross value added (GVA), labour costs (LC) and the residual of gross operating surplus (GOS). Our purpose is to consider the extent to which, at a national level, cost structures have been modified within the advanced economies.

National business models and financial transformation

Using the financial framework outlined in Chapter 2, we now turn to consider the extent to which the structure of GDP has been transformed in recent decades. Our financial analysis deconstructs national GDP into its broad constituent components to establish the extent to which the share of GOS in GDP has increased in the advanced economies. We start by deducting intermediate consumption and then total employment costs from gross output to determine the gross operating margin.

Intermediate consumption in gross output

$$(GO-GVA)/GO \tag{1}$$

where GO = gross output
GVA = gross value added

Labour costs in gross output

$$LC/GO \tag{2}$$

where LC = labour costs
GO = gross output

Gross operating surplus[2] in gross output

$$GOS/GO \tag{3}$$

where GOS = GVA − LC

The first ratio reveals the proportion of total economic output which is intermediate consumption within an economy, whilst ratio (2) describes the share of gross output which is distributed to cover total employee compensation and ratio (3) the share of gross output which is retained as GOS. If national business models are being financially transformed, our expectation would be that the share of GOS in total gross output will have increased over a period of time. That is, the share of intermediate consumption and employment costs deducted from gross output are reducing to transform the residual GOS extracted from total output.

In Figure 5.8 we have computed the share of intermediate (external) costs in total gross output for a range of advanced economies for the period 1970–2007.

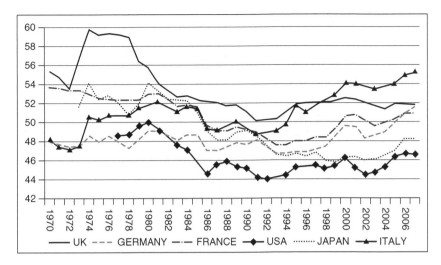

FIGURE 5.8 Intermediate costs in gross output (%).

Source: www.euklems.net/.

This figure reveals two distinct periods. The first is 1970–1990 when, in general, the advanced economies are reducing intermediate consumption in total gross output. Thereafter there is a general upwards drift in the share of intermediate consumption in gross output such that by 2007 the range is 46–55 per cent of gross output.

Figure 5.9 reveals that the share of employment costs in total gross output for the six advanced economies remains steady (apart from Italy) and in the range 26–34 per cent. Moreover, apart from some cyclicality, there is no overall structural trend to indicate, for example, falling shares of employment costs in total gross output across the advanced economies. Adding together intermediate consumption/external costs plus total employee compensation gives a total cost figure which, when deducted from gross output, is equivalent to GOS and a proxy for 'cash surplus generated from national economic activity'.

If the advanced economies had reduced the share of intermediate consumption (IC) or total employment compensation in GO, this would lead to an increase in the share of GOS in GO. That is, the national economic business models of the advanced economies are generating additional earnings capacity out of GO upon which putative balance sheet capitalizations could be inflated and sustained.

In the advanced economies the combination of external costs and internal employee compensation in gross output delivers a general increase in operating surplus in gross output from 1970 into the mid–1980s (see Figure 5.10). Thereafter the share of GOS in GO for individual countries stabilizes over the period 1985–2007 and settles in the range 18–26 per cent of gross output, with Germany, France and the USA clustered in the 20–22 per cent range. This pattern of relative stability is reinforced when we aggregate the financial data for all fifteen European Union nations (as of 1995), shown in Figure 5.11. This reveals a surprising level of stability in the key operating cost

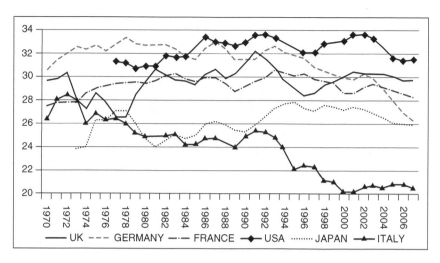

FIGURE 5.9 Labour costs in gross output.

Source: www.euklems.net/.

structure ratios for the main European economies, with the GOS, after deducting intermediate and employee compensation, steady at 20 per cent for many decades.

Although the national economic business model(s) of the advanced economies have experienced significant demographic, technological, regulatory and institutional change, something is lost in the financial translation when GOS is not

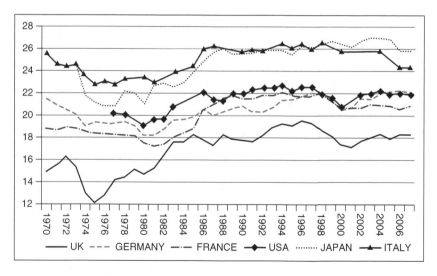

FIGURE 5.10 Operating surplus as a percentage of gross output in the advanced economies.

Source: www.euklems.net/.

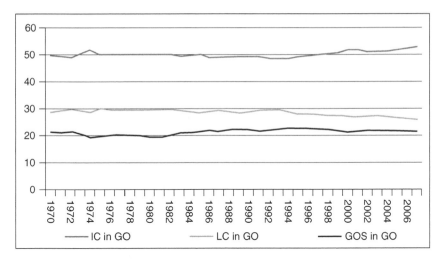

FIGURE 5.11 Europe: intermediate, labour costs and gross operating surplus for the fifteen European Union member states as of 1 January 1995 (Austria, Belgium, Denmark, Finland, France, Germany, Greece, Ireland, Italy, Luxembourg, the Netherlands, Portugal, Spain, Sweden and the UK).

Source: www.euklems.net/.

significantly transformed over an extended period of time, 1970–2007. In contrast to this stability and lack of transformation we turn our attention to the national balance sheets of the advanced economies.

Global business models: the recapitalization cycle

In a credit-based economy when ongoing asset trades are brisk, and market prices inflating, it is possible to extract holding gains from financially leveraged positions which act as a substitute for generating cash and accumulated capital from the trade in goods and services for final consumption.

> Trading under the old régime was a traffic in goods; under the new régime there is added, as the dominant and characteristic trait, trading in capital.
>
> *(Veblen, 1904: 75)*

> There is a multitude of real assets in the world which constitutes our capital wealth – buildings, stocks of commodities, goods in the course of manufacture and of transport, and so forth. The nominal owners of these assets, however, have not infrequently borrowed *money* in order to become possessed of them. To a corresponding extent the actual owners of wealth have claims, not on real assets, but on money.
>
> *(Keynes, 1972: 151; emphasis in the original)*

Veblen (1904) distinguishes between the old regime, where trading is a traffic in goods for final consumption, and a new regime where 'there is added, as the dominant and characteristic trait, trading in capital', where the ends sought from trading goods and trading capital are not the same. The buyer of durable and perishable goods buys for consumption, but the last 'negotiator of capital . . . in substance he buys in order to sell again at an advance'. This process of buying and selling on, according to Veblen, drives a process of capitalization and recapitalization where the connection between the earnings capacity of tangible asset investment and capitalization becomes increasingly hazy and disconnected. In relation to the earnings (liquidity) and debt accumulation, Minsky (1993) outlines three possible explanations validating debt leverage within a financial system: 'hedge, speculative and ponzi'. With hedge financing cash flows are sufficient to cover contractual repayment obligations (where the higher proportion of equity to debt is also taken into account). Speculative financing systems are able to service the cost of debt finance from their 'income account' even though cash flows are not sufficient to repay the principal sum borrowed. Speculative financing units thus need to ensure they have access to 'roll-over' credit which pays off previous borrowings. Ponzi financing units do not have sufficient cash to cover the cost of capital or to repay the principal sum, and so are engaged in borrowing or asset sales to raise cash to cover the cost of capital. Minsky (1993) employs these three categories of financing unit to suggest that, within financial systems, hedging and financial risk containment are possible, but that over prolonged periods of prosperity a financial system drifts towards a speculative or ponzi finance structure. In these circumstances the financial oscillations from this form of financing system increase and what matters, in these circumstances, is that the underlying liquidity/cash generative capacities of national business models have not been transformed to prevent leverage from unwinding and assets being liquidated. Rather than speculate on the fragility or instability of national economic business models, our purpose in this chapter is to reveal the extent to which capitalization (the market value of debt plus equity outstanding) in the advanced economies has moved ahead of GDP and earnings capacity (GOS). Our position is that advanced national economic business models are financialized because they are increasingly leveraged as capitalization accelerates ahead of GDP and surplus earnings capacity. In financialized business models, wealth accumulation and balance sheet recapitalization(s) are the Hollywood starry cast, and GDP trajectory, cost structure and cash extraction for wealth creation the stand-in extras.

Figure 5.12 plots the ratio of nominal global capitalization to GDP where the ratio increases from 2.5:1 to 3.5:1 over the period 1995–2007 and before the recent financial crisis. At a global level GDP increased over the period 1990–2010 by roughly \$40 trillion and a CAGR of 5 per cent, whereas global capitalization (domestic plus international securities and equity market value) increased over the same period by roughly \$155 trillion or a CAGR of 8.5 per cent. The growth rate of total capitalization was made up of an equity CAGR of 9.1 per cent and debt CAGR of 8.2 per cent whereby the overall ratio of debt to equity (gearing ratio) remained quite stable at roughly 2:1. The drivers of this disconnect between capi-

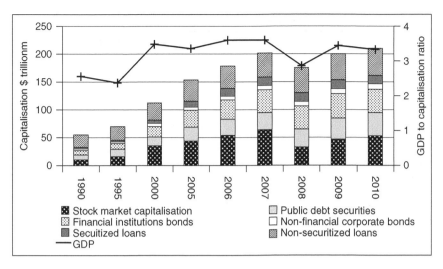

FIGURE 5.12 Global capitalization and capitalization to GDP ratio.

Source: McKinsey & Company.

talization and GDP are complex, but they include the low cost of servicing debt and the evolution of existing and new economic activities, within the advanced economies, that depend upon financial leverage.

Table 5.9 presents information extracted from the IMF 'Global Financial Stability Report' which includes additional items in the computation of national balance sheets that include stock market equity, outstanding bonds (private and public) and bank assets. Using this measure of capitalization to GDP gives a global ratio of 4:1 in 2009, increasing from 3.4:1 in 2003, and for the G7 group (accounting for two-thirds of global GDP in 2009) a ratio of 3.9 moving up to 5:1 in 2009. The picture is somewhat different for the emerging market countries where the increase in capitalization relative to GDP is more damped, apart from the Asian emerging markets which include China and India.

In 1990 we estimate that the US corporate, non-corporate and government sectors accounted for roughly one half of global market capitalization, and significantly longer-run national economic data reveal how the trajectories of GDP and capitalization evolve over the period 1950–2010. This time series can be split into two distinct thirty year sub-periods: 1950–1980 and 1980–2010. In the first period US GDP grew at a CAGR of 7.5 per cent and likewise capitalization (debt plus market value of equity) grew at a similar CAGR of 7.2 per cent. The second period, 1980–2010, marks a break with the past because the CAGR for US GDP growth was 5.8 per cent (below the previous period) and CAGR for total capitalization 9 per cent, significantly above the previous period (see Figure 5.13). Over an extended period of time there is a progressive divergence between capitalization (debt and equity) and GDP, especially during the period 1980–2010 as compound growths rates for GDP and capital accumulation diverge.

TABLE 5.9 Size of the capital markets, 2009

	GDP (trillion $)	Bonds, equities and bank assets to GDP (times)	
	2009	2009	2003
World	57.8	4.0	3.4
France	2.7	6.0	4.2
Germany	3.3	3.6	3.3
Italy	2.1	4.3	3.4
United Kingdom	2.2	8.4	4.9
Canada	1.3	4.7	3.4
United States	14.1	4.3	3.7
Japan	5.1	4.8	4.5
G7	30.8	5.1	3.9
Emerging market countries of which:	19.6	2.2	1.6
Asia	9.5	3.1	2.3
Western Hemisphere	3.9	1.8	1.3
Middle East and North Africa	2.0	1.2	1.0
Sub-Saharan Africa	0.9	1.3	1.1
Europe	3.3	1.1	0.7

Source: IMF, adapted by the authors.

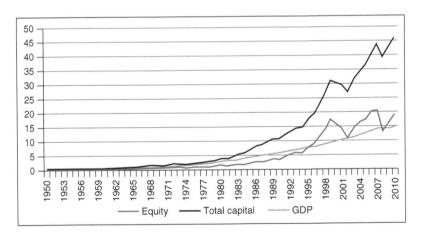

FIGURE 5.13 US GDP and capitalization, 1950–2010 ($ trillion).

Source: World Federation of Exchanges members (equity), and BIS Quarterly Review for outstanding domestic and foreign debt securities.

Within the US national business model the market value of balance sheet liabilities (debt and equity in the corporate, non-corporate and government sectors) has an equivalent value to assets. These assets are held predominantly in the form of real estate holdings and beneficial equity in pension funds growth accumulated by US households (see Figure 5.14).

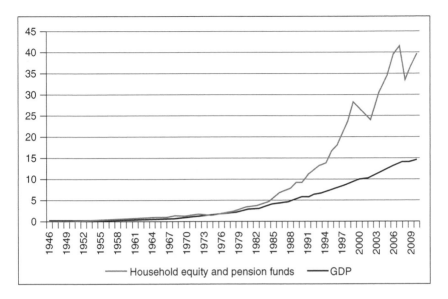

FIGURE 5.14 US household equity and pension funds ($ trillion).

Source: US Federal Reserve Board of Governors, Flow of Funds Z1. Table B.100 Balance Sheet of Households and Nonprofit Organizations.

This equivalence between assets and liabilities is not merely a neutral arithmetic identity and a product of national accounting and double entry book-keeping. Rather, it is the case that stakeholder motivation and financial condition for those holding assets and liabilities are variable and this is significant in terms of how financial disturbances emerge and transmit within national business models. We develop this position in more detail in the next chapter, but it is important to note at this point that the forces driving the accumulation and recapitalization of national business model balance sheets are complex and multi-faceted. On the one hand, we have corporate financial, non-financial and government accumulating debt and equity, and on the other, households accumulating and financing assets as entitlements to pension funds and claims on real estate.

Drivers of recapitalization

There are a number of drivers which account, in part, for the increased levels of global and national balance sheet capitalization. We have already pointed out that low global interest rates, especially in the advanced economies, reduce the cost of servicing debt, and thus for a given level of financial surplus it is possible to leverage the level of debt outstanding. We would also add the following factors: the emergence of a process of asset securitization, expansion of global mergers and acquisitions, development of financially leveraged business models, population demographics and the inflation of real estate trades.

Low interest rates

In the corporate, government and household sectors the progressive reduction in long-term interest rates increased borrowing capacity on a given level of surplus and contributed to the acceleration in the level of outstanding debt finance relative to GDP growth. Long-run interest rates in the USA and Europe fell steadily after 1980, progressively reducing from 14 per cent to 4 per cent by 2010. Although this has not always been the case, after reaching levels of 4 per cent in the 1960s, long-term interest rates increased steadily and, whilst prone to some cyclical movements, reached a peak of just over 14 per cent by 1980 (see Figure 5.7). The health warning is that interest rates can go up or down!

Asset securitization

The process of asset securitization involves packaging and selling on assets upon which repayments are being made, such as home, car and personal loans, to a purchaser who is financing the acquisition of these assets with funds they have generated from issuing securities (bonds/debt instruments).

> The process of securitisation creates *asset-backed bonds*. These are debt instruments that have been created from a package of loan assets on which interest is payable, usually on a floating basis. The asset-backed market was developed in the United States and is a large, diverse market containing a wide range of instruments. Techniques employed by investment banks today enable an entity to create a bond structure from any type of cash flow; assets that have been securitised include loans such as residential mortgages, car loans, and credit card loans. The loans form assets on a bank or finance house balance sheet, which are packaged together and used as backing for an issue of bonds. The interest payments on the original loans from the cash flows are used to service the new bond issue. Traditionally mortgage-backed bonds are grouped in their own right as mortgage-backed securities (MBS) while all other securitisation issues are known as asset-backed bonds or ABS.
>
> *(Teasdale, 2003: 1)*

Assets that are securitized are often sold on into a special purpose vehicle (SPV) or trust which is established as an independent company from the originator of the assets in order to establish a pool of cash-generating assets with an improved credit rating. The assets located in the SPV are subject to credit rating assessments by agencies such as Fitch or Standard and Poor's. Because the securitized assets are separated out from other assets of varying credit quality, the outcome is that the credit rating of securitized assets strengthens. On the liabilities side of the SPV there will be issued notes/securities which arise from investments made into the SPV by bondholders, the financing of which is managed (for a fee) by investment banks. The funds raised by the creation of the SPV allow the originator of these assets to raise additional funds at lower cost on the basis of a more favourable credit rating.

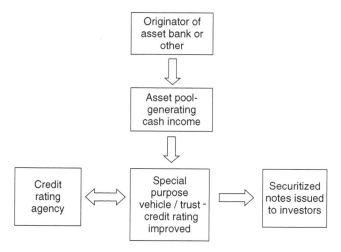

FIGURE 5.15   Securitization.

Source: The authors.

Table 5.10 reveals the significance of the securitization market, with accumulated issuances in Europe amounting to roughly €4 trillion and in the USA to $22 trillion. It is also clear from Table 5.10 that the annual market for securitized assets has dropped by about 40 per cent between 2008 and 2010 in the aftermath of the financial crisis. Moreover, as Table 5.11 indicates, the credit ratings on outstanding securitizations have also deteriorated significantly since the start of 2008 with the onset of the financial crisis in the USA and Europe. In the USA the largest global securitizations market operated with more than 80 per cent of outstanding balances receiving an AAA credit rating at the start of 2008, but at the beginning of 2011 AAA ratings covered just 30 per cent of outstanding balances. In Europe the credit rating for securitized asset balances held somewhat higher at 70 per cent AAA rated in 2011.

Changes in the regulatory environment granted banks the possibility to securitize their assets (loan books), further capitalizing these assets against additional bonds issued in the market and helping to inflate capitalization ahead of GDP in the advanced economies.

Global M&A deals

In 1985 the value of global mergers and acquisitions stood at just below $1 trillion and, before the financial crisis, in 2007, it was equivalent to $6 trillion or 12 per cent of global GDP (see Figure 5.16). The value of these deals tends to track global stock market indices, which had generally been inflating through the previous two decades and prior to 2007. The financing package associated with these deals contributed to inflating the value of debt outstanding on corporate balance sheets ahead of revenues. For example, in the S&P 500 group of companies, the level of

TABLE 5.10 Securitization in Europe and the USA, 2000–2011

	Europe (€ billion)	USA ($ billion)
2000	78.2	1,088.0
2001	152.6	2,308.4
2002	157.7	2,592.7
2003	217.3	2,914.5
2004	243.5	1,956.6
2005	327.0	2,650.6
2006	481.0	2,455.8
2007	453.7	2,147.1
2008	711.1	933.6
2009	414.1	1,358.9
2010	382.9	1,276.7
Q1 2011	114.4	265.3
Totals	3,733.6	21,948.3

Source: http://studio-5.financialcontent.com/sifma.

TABLE 5.11 Securitization balances and credit ratings, 2008 and 2011

	2011		2008	
	Europe	USA	Europe	USA
Outstanding balances	€2,076 bn	$6,792 bn	€2,135 bn	$7,056 bn
Aaa/AAA (%)	70.2	30.2	85.5	81.8
Aa/AA (%)	11.5	9.4	5.2	5.4
A/A (%)	7.5	5.7	4.4	3.9
Baa/BBB (%)	5.8	5.7	3.9	4.8
Ba/BB (%)	1.4	4.2	0.8	1.4
B/B (%)	1.0	7.3	0.1	1.1
Caa/CCC (%)	1.4	16.9	0.1	0.7
Ca/CC (%)	0.8	9.9	0.0	0.5
C/C (%)	0.4	10.7	0.1	0.5
Total	100.0	100.0	100.0	100.0

Source: http://studio-5.financialcontent.com/sifma.

debt outstanding in 1990 amounted to $1 trillion and by 2007 this debt outstanding had increased to $6 trillion, a six-fold increase when, over the same period, total sales revenues increased by a factor of less than three.

Population demographics: ageing and pensions

In the advanced economies, population demographics and increased longevity are adjusting the share of the population that will become dependent upon pensions in retirement (both state and private schemes), and this, coupled with a high average income per capita, requires a substantially higher level of equity and debt to finance retirement income.

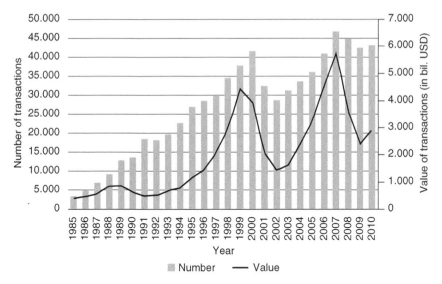

FIGURE 5.16 Announced merger and acquisitions worldwide, 1985–2010.

Source: IMAA.

By 2050, the median age of the world's people will be 38 years, 10 years older than in 2005. While the world's population will continue to grow to reach 9 billion by the middle of the century from 6.5 billion in 2005, it will also turn older. Much older. The worldwide old-age dependency ratio (the proportion of the population aged 60 years or older to the working-age population) is estimated to surge to 45% in 2050, from 19% in 2005.

(Standard and Poor's, 2006: 1)

Within the advanced economies the provision of state-funded and privately funded schemes requires additional capitalization to secure reasonable replacement incomes for those who become economically inactive. This will present a significant challenge to government-funded pay-as-you-go schemes when, as we have already observed, central government funding is already dependent upon high levels of debt financing to cover existing deficits. Moreover, privately funded schemes can only secure a decent replacement income in retirement in circumstances where equity values (stock markets) are also inflating and debt markets expanding to accommodate the financial demand for fixed-interest annuities. A Towers-Watson study of private pension funding, in thirteen major markets, has established the total market value of these funds to be capitalized at $26.5 trillion in 2010[3] with the USA accounting for roughly 50 per cent of overall funds. The value of these funds increased by 63 per cent over the period 2000–2010 and is equivalent to 76 per cent of annual GDP for this group of countries.

With regards to state-funded pension arrangements, a report by Standard and Poor's (S&P), *Global Greying: Aging Societies and Sovereign Ratings* (2006), establishes the connection between pensions and other age-related state-funded provisions and the amplification of government deficits and net debt financing arrangements going forward. The S&P report regards the growth in government funding for an ageing population, especially pensions, as being a major contributor to underlying increases in government deficits and the net debt burden going forward without substantial fiscal adjustments.

> Although the median general government net debt burden will remain relatively steady at about 32%–33% of GDP through to 2015, it will start to rise slowly thereafter, accelerating sharply from the late 2020s. By the mid-2030s the net debt burden will surpass a still manageable 80% of GDP, but will reach an overpowering 180% of GDP by 2050.
>
> *(http://www.savings-bond-advisor.com/Global-Graying.pdf)*

The S&P report goes on to consider what would happen to government sovereign debt ratings if government deficits and net borrowing to GDP ratios continue to run on their current trajectories. The S&P report observes that, using current credit rating benchmarks, most sovereign government debt would be rated 'speculative' by 2050, and that 'The scenario does reveal the dimension of the task that governments face in pruning benefits granted by unfunded state-run social security systems and/or achieving further fiscal belt-tightening' (Standard and Poor's, 2006: 2).

Within the advanced and developing economies, ageing populations on higher incomes are encouraged to finance their pension arrangements privately or they are covered by state pay-as-you-go schemes. The combination of population dynamics, higher average earnings and low interest rates is putting additional pressure on capital markets to inflate the debt coupon pool to provide income and annuities for both public and privately funded pension schemes.

Property and real estate

Apart from pensions, real estate, as a household beneficial asset, is also an important driver of global capitalization. Over the period 1995–2008 the ratio of real estate to GDP increased from 1.6 to 1.8; with global GDP in 2008 at $61 trillion, global real estate was valued at $90 trillion. In circumstances where property prices inflate above nominal GDP, this puts additional pressure on banks to expand mortgages ahead of GDP (see Figure 5.17). To decouple loans from deposits and savings, which are tied to GDP, banks have used securitization (see previous section) to buy and sell on assets as a means to secure additional loan-making capacity.

Leverage for holding gains

Leverage encapsulates the complex process by which global balance sheet capitalization (debt and equity outstanding) have moved ahead of GDP. The elements

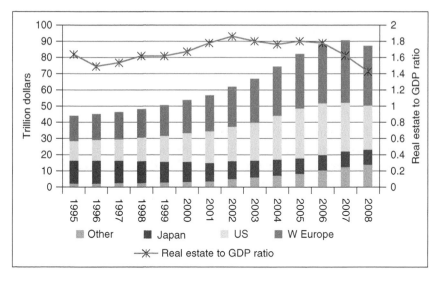

FIGURE 5.17   Global real estate value relative to world GDP.

Source: McKinsey & Company.

driving leverage are complex and include lower interest rates, the development of new financial products, corporate restructuring, population demographics and real estate inflation. In a credit-based economy, where assets can be actively traded, it is possible for corporate and non-corporate agencies and households to participate in the extraction of holding gains which can serve as additional collateral to extend borrowing capacity. Households, for example, can convert holding gains into additional financial leverage; governments extend their borrowing at times when interest rates are low; the corporate sector extracts holding gains from inflated assets to boost reported comprehensive income and inflate shareholder equity to leverage further borrowing capacity. In this volume we consider how the banking, private equity and real estate business models depend upon asset appreciation and holding gains upon which to generate additional financial leverage.

Ongoing recapitalizations in a credit-based economy are a precondition for leveraging additional finance. Initially the extension of a credit facility might be assured because interest rates are low and the earnings/surplus to interest cover ratio relatively high. However, in a brisk market, when asset values are inflating and where there is a strong possibility of selling assets on at a profit, the difference between the market and book value (goodwill) acts as a substitute for the interest cover ratio. The result is that:

> The economy's credit flows shift progressively away from the real economy and increasingly into financial asset market, with ever growing financial asset returns and individual net worth figures, and a growing debt service burden

on the real economy. Consumption – and the production that depends on it – may become financed more by fresh credit and debt flows from the FIRE [finance, insurance and real estate] sector based on capital gains, than by real-sector wages and profit.

(www.rug.nl/feb/Onderzoek/Onderzoekscentra/CIBIF/ Workshops/DirkBezemer1.pdf)

Bezemer makes a significant point that credit is decoupled from the real economy and becomes increasingly locked into financial asset trades where capital gains act as collateral for further ongoing capitalizations. Moreover, Bezemer notes that household consumption is not only financed by credit flows linked to income and wages, but is also leveraged out of capital gains on inflated assets.

Summary

In this chapter our objective has been to review the global context within which business models evolve and also adapt. This is one where the resource capacities for generating income growth and that for ongoing capitalization are unevenly distributed globally. In terms of share of the global population, numbers economically active and employment costs paid per hour, the developing and industrializing economies of India and China are capturing a greater share of global GDP, and their growth trajectories are far stronger than those of the advanced economies. They are also in receipt of an increased share of foreign direct investment (FDI) by overseas firms eager to capture cost reduction in the face of competitive price erosion. Furthermore the balance of trade is adjusting with advanced economies generally in deficit and developing countries in surplus and net exporters of capital. On the other hand, capitalization (debt and equity) for wealth accumulation is still the preserve of the advanced economies, and even though the drag on GDP growth has reduced the G7 group's share of global GDP to nearer 50 per cent, their command of global capitalization (bonds, bank assets, equities) remains at roughly 70 per cent and in recent years capitalization has moved further ahead of GDP. In this chapter we have shown that whilst capitalization has accelerated ahead in the advanced economies, there has been no significant transformation in cost structure and gross operating surplus (cash) in their national accounts. Capitalization has become increasingly disconnected from income and surplus generating capacity, and this is explained partly by historically low interest rates but also significant changes to the nature of national and sub-national business models that facilitate capitalization ahead of liquidity.

6

ACCOUNTING FOR NATIONAL BUSINESS MODELS

Introduction

We have previously established our position which is to argue that generating a surplus (for liquidity) and ongoing recapitalizations (for solvency) are a central financial feature of national business models. In this chapter we unlock national business models to explore the risks attached to maintaining ongoing capitalization where this runs ahead of GDP and operating surplus, and where financial adjustments are transmitted, amplified and made porous by accounting systems. Our starting point is to situate national business models within an institutional context: corporate (financial and non-financial), government and households. We consider the extent to which cost structures in these institutional sectors are transformed and argue that the arithmetic identity of assets ≡ liabilities conceals variable motivations and calculations embedded in corporate financial, non-financial and government-directed business models. We try to answer a series of questions. To what extent are the capitalizations of national business models grounded in a transformation of surplus (liquidity)? How are different institutional sectors able to inflate balance sheet capitalization ahead of surplus? And what role does accounting play in transmitting and amplifying adjustments within the financial system of national business models?

GDP: deconstructed by institution and cost structure

The primary statements provided in the national accounts for countries tend almost exclusively to focus on gross domestic product (GDP) by income, expenditure or by output. This emphasis on GDP growth is reinforced by the business press and political pronouncements on the state of an economy where again what matters is whether GDP is growing from one quarter to the next. Rarely do we find information which deconstructs GDP into its institutional components – corporate non-financial, financial and government – to reveal the extent to which GDP growth is also synonymous with changes in liquidity (operating surplus).

In this section we adopt the accounting framework outlined in Chapter 2 and also utilized in the previous chapter to consider the extent to which the main institutional sectors of national business models of the advanced economies for which we have data – Germany, the UK, the USA and Japan – have transformed their operating cost structures for additional liquidity. In the accompanying figures we compute institutional sector gross operating surplus (GOS) after deducting external and intermediate expenses and internal labour costs, and express this as a share of gross output (the GOS margin). If the GOS margin increases we assume that institutional sectors are reducing their total operating costs and are stretching their surplus (liquidity) out of total income (gross output)

In Figures 6.1–6.3 we identify the share of operating surplus (GOS) in gross output (GO) for Germany, the UK and USA for the financial, non-financial and general government institutional sectors which in aggregate account for approximately three-quarters of total national GDP. Starting with the non–financial corporate sector, which accounts for the larger share of national GDP, between 50 and 60 per cent,[1] we find that the share of operating surplus in gross output remains steady in the range 15–20 per cent for all three economies. For the broad financial corporate sectors, which account for 6 per cent of GDP in Germany and roughly 16 per cent in the UK and USA, the share of operating surplus in gross output is not only far more volatile than the corporate sector, it is generally (in the USA and Germany if not in the UK) on a clear downwards trajectory. General government share of GDP is at 10 per cent for Germany and roughly 14 per cent for the USA and UK; the operating surplus has gently deteriorated in the UK and USA from 10

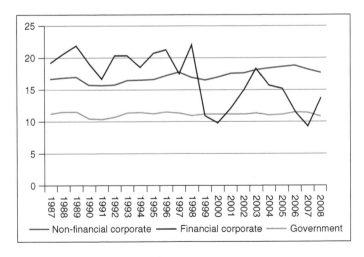

FIGURE 6.1 Germany: GOS in GO (%).

Source: www.destatis.de/jetspeed/portal/cms/Sites/destatis/Internet/DE/Navigation/TopNav/Kontakte.psml.

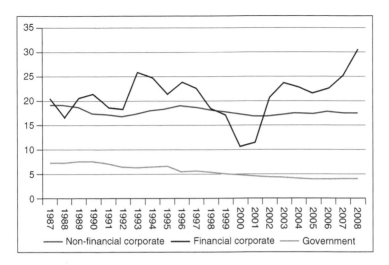

FIGURE 6.2 UK: GOS in GO (%).

Source: ONS Blue Book, various years, www.statistics.gov.uk/downloads/theme_economy/
bluebook2010.pdf.

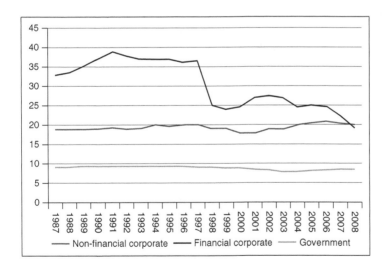

FIGURE 6.3 USA: GOS in GO (%).

Source: Federal Reserve Board: Flow of Funds Z1; US Bureau of Economic Statistics.

per cent to around 5 per cent and is holding steady in Germany at 10 per cent. By
disaggregating national business models into their constituent institutional sectors,
it is possible to identify the extent to which cost structures have been transformed.
The picture, especially for the non-financial corporate sector, is one of relative
stability in costs structure over a period of time. In the following section we review
the pattern of capitalization to operating surplus GOS.

Institutional sectors: earnings surplus and capitalization

In this section we blend operating surplus with total capitalization (debt and equity) to reveal the operating margins that underpin capitalization in a number of the main advanced economies. Our objective is to reveal general patterns in terms of the trajectory of capitalization relative to operating surpluses such that, if the percentage falls, capitalization is running ahead of operating surpluses.

In Figures 6.4–6.7 the patterns of GOS to total capitalization (debt and equity) are shown for the three main institutional sectors – non-financial, financial corporate and government. A similar pattern emerges with the rate of balance sheet capitalization generally running ahead of operating surplus. With regards to the non-financial corporate sector, the rate of increase in capitalization relative to operating surplus forces the ratio down by roughly one-third in Germany, the USA and UK, and it holds flat in Japan. With regards to the financial corporate and general government institutional sectors, there are similar patterns: both operate with very narrow margins/surplus relative to balance sheet capitalization of 2–5 per cent. The financial sector business model depends upon trading a large volume of assets to skim a margin between interest received and paid, the spread between bid/ask asset prices and commission fees on managing and trading assets. Within the main institutional sectors, financial corporate and government account for the greater share of capitalization (debt and equity). As at the end of 2009, roughly two-thirds of debt and equity outstanding were located in the financial corporate and general government institutional sectors.[2]

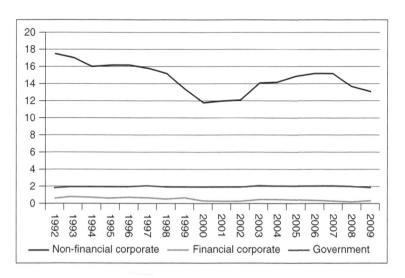

FIGURE 6.4 German institutional sectors: GOS as % of debt and equity.

Source: www.destatis.de/jetspeed/portal/cms/Sites/destatis/Internet/DE/Navigation/TopNav/Kontakte.psml.

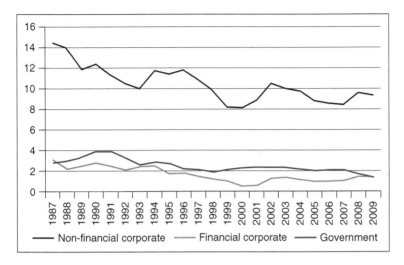

FIGURE 6.5 UK institutional sectors: GOS as % of debt and equity.

Source: www.statistics.gov.uk/statbase/tsdtables1.asp?vlnk=bb.

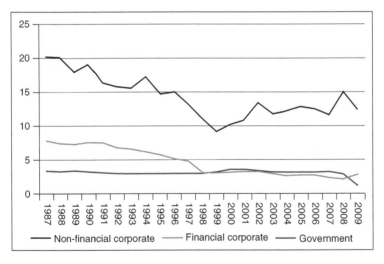

FIGURE 6.6 US institutional sectors: GOS as % of debt and equity.

Source: US Federal Reserve.

Within these institutional sectors, the sheer scale of capitalization outstanding relative to surpluses means that adjustments, when triggered, involve 'lumpy' disturbance in to assets and liability values in sector balance sheets that can easily threaten their solvency. Adverse adjustments to asset and liability values are not hedgeable or containable because double entry book-keeping transmits financial recalibrations within and across institutional boundaries. The role of accounting in transmitting and amplifying financial adjustments is also discussed in the following section.

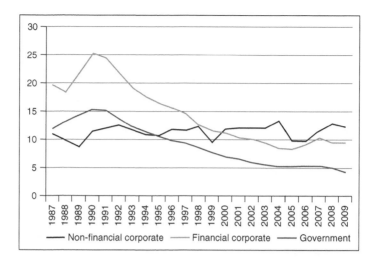

FIGURE 6.7 Japanese institutional sectors: GOS as % of debt and equity.

Source: www.esri.cao.go.jp/en/sna/kakuhou/kekka/h21_kaku/23annual_report_e.html#c1.

Capitalization at risk: activation, transmission and amplification

In this section we consider some of the factors that activate recapitalizations between assets and liabilities and how the accounting system transmits and amplifies adjustments. Our accounting framework of analysis takes as its starting point the national balance sheet accounting identity where assets and liabilities held by corporate and government on the left-hand side of the identity are balanced by the beneficial holdings of assets and liabilities by households on the right-hand side. This is a somewhat simplified account because some assets and liabilities net out on one side or the other and some do not move across one side to the other.

$$\text{Corporate} \quad + \quad \text{General Government} \equiv \text{Households}$$

Financial   Non-Financial

However, the significance of the analysis is that it captures a significant proportion of national balance sheet capitalization where the object is to consider how adjustments activated on one side of the arithmetic identity transmit across institutional boundaries where accounting systems amplify financial adjustments when they are marked to market. Furthermore, as capitalizations adjust, financial leverage moves into reverse, with the result that injections into GDP from holding gains become withdrawals as holding losses work their way through.

Household sector: capitalization at risk

We start with the balance sheet of households in the USA, Germany, UK and Japan where we have added together the value of tangible assets that are real estate (and in

Japan also land values), pensions, equity investments, bonds and loans outstanding, and track these values relative to household disposable income. In the case of the USA, Germany and the UK, the value of tangible assets, financial assets and loans outstanding increases relative to disposable income over the period 1987–2009. Within the aggregation for each country there are some obvious differences: real estate price inflation in Germany was not as fast as in the UK, whilst in Japan real estate land values deteriorate such that levels in 2009 are half those in 1987. What we reveal in Figure 6.8 is that household asset values and liabilities generally increase relative to household disposable income in the UK, Germany and the USA, whereas there is a progressive and steady reduction in the Japanese case. This figure also reveals that in terms of the level of household asset and liabilities, in the aftermath of the recent financial crisis, it is the UK and USA that have experienced significant downward adjustments. Whilst there were adverse adjustments to asset and liability values of US and UK households prior to 2008, these were much smaller.

Focusing on the US households specifically, we can break down the components of assets and loans outstanding to reveal the sheer scale of household wealth accumulation and changes over time. Table 6.1 describes the extent to which the value of US household assets changed during and after the recent financial crisis, and it shows that a significant component of the loss in household net wealth arises from the reduction in the market value of housing stock (26 per cent), followed by the loss in value of corporate equities held by US households (15 per cent) as at the

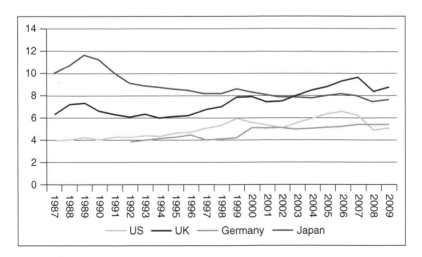

FIGURE 6.8 Household real estate, financial assets and loans outstanding to disposable income (ratio).

Source: UK: ONS Blue Book, www.statistics.gov.uk/statbase/tsdtables1.asp?vlnk=bb; USA: www.federalreserve.gov/releases/z1/; Germany: www.destatis.de/jetspeed/portal/cms/Sites/destatis/Internet/DE/Navigation/TopNav/Kontakte.psml; Japan: www.esri.cao.go.jp/en/sna/kakuhou/kekka/h21_kaku/23annual_report_e.html#c1.

end of 2010. The average US household's net equity held in real estate dropped by 50 per cent from roughly $16 trillion to $8 trillion as at the end of 2010. The housing market had already started to contract at the start of 2006, with a steep and steady reduction in new-build construction from 2.4 million homes at peak to 0.6 million per annum by mid-2009 and running into 2011. Price structures in the property market also deteriorated significantly, starting late 2006 and running through into 2011, with average prices down one-third according to the Case Shiller real estate price index (see Figure 6.9).

TABLE 6.1 US household key assets and liability balance sheet structure ($ billion)

	2006	2007	2008	2009	2010	Change (%)
Real estate at market value	25.0	23.3	19.6	18.8	18.5	−26.2
Corporate equities	9.6	9.6	5.8	7.3	8.2	−14.6
Pension fund reserves	12.8	13.4	10.4	11.9	13.4	5.2
Mutual fund shares	4.2	4.6	3.3	4.2	5.1	21.8
Credit market instruments	12.9	13.8	13.8	13.6	13.3	2.9
Of which mortgages	8.8	9.9	10.5	10.5	10.3	17.0
Net real estate equity	16.2	13.4	9.1	8.3	8.2	−49.7
Net wealth	38.7	37.1	25.3	28.6	31.9	−17.5

Source: US Federal Reserve Board Flow of Funds Z1, Household Balance Sheet Table B100, available at http://www.federalreserve.gov/releases/z1/current/z1r-5.pdf.

Notes: Credit market instruments include household mortgages and credit card borrowings. Net real estate equity is real estate assets minus mortgages on real estate outstanding. Net wealth is real estate, corporate equities, pension fund reserves and mutual funds minus credit market instruments outstanding.

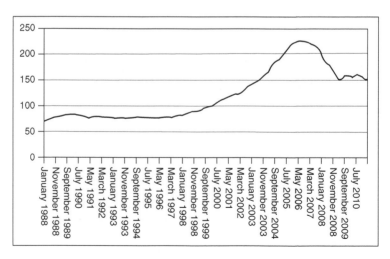

FIGURE 6.9 Case Shiller Composite-10 US house price index. January 2000=100. CSXR10 is a composite index of the house price index for ten major metropolitan statistical areas in the United States.

Source: S&P.

CoreLogic (NYSE: CLGX), a leading provider of information, analytics and business services, today released negative equity data showing that 10.9 million, or 22.7 per cent, of all residential properties with a mortgage were in negative equity at the end of the first quarter of 2011, down slightly from 11.1 million, or 23.1 per cent, in the fourth quarter.

While the average negative equity borrower was upside down by $65,000, there were wide disparities by state . . . New York borrowers were upside down by an average of $129,000, the highest average in the nation, followed by other high housing cost states: Massachusetts ($120,000), Connecticut ($111,000), Hawaii ($98,000) and California ($93,000). Ohio's negative equity borrowers were upside down by $31,000, the lowest average in the nation, followed by Indiana ($34,000) and Minnesota ($38,000).

(www.morningstar.co.uk/uk/markets/
newsfeeditem.aspx?id=145955873624330)

CoreLogic estimate that the collapse in house prices exposed one-fifth of homeowners to negative equity and that this group were 'upside down' by an average of $65,000 (when the equivalent median household income in 2008 was $50,000[3]). In addition the reduction in house prices reduced the potential for equity withdrawal, that is, raising additional mortgages on the back of inflated real estate values.

According to the Federal Reserve, US households' aggregate real estate assets rose by over a third between 2003 and 2006. Homeowners extracted part of this increased mortgage equity to fund consumption in other areas, such as automobiles and other consumer goods. It is estimated that income extraction from housing more than doubled between 2001 and 2005, with over $1.4 trillion extracted in 2005 alone. By one estimate, this housing-fuelled spending accounted for at least one-quarter of the growth in consumer expenditures.

(US Department of Labor, 2011: 4)

By tapping home equity, homeowners are able to lower their debt costs. For all these reasons, housing's contribution to household finances is unique and of great importance both to homeowners and the broader economy.

(Belsky and Prakken, 2004: 4)

In both the USA and the UK households have for some time remortgaged their properties to extract equity as the market value of household assets inflated. Figure 6.10 reveals the extent of mortgage equity withdrawals as a share of an individual's post-tax income in the UK using Bank of England data.[4] What this reveals is that a considerable share of annual incremental GDP growth is financed by leveraging income out of wealth accumulated in the inflated value of household assets in the UK. Likewise the average US homeowner was contributing significantly to annual incremental GDP growth rates by taking out housing equity loans. As at the end

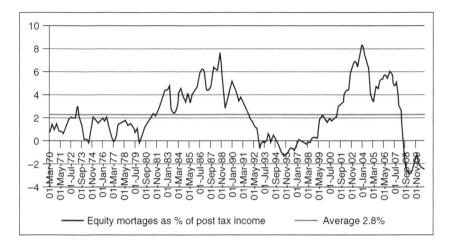

FIGURE 6.10 UK mortgage equity as % of individual post-tax income.

Source: Bank of England, data series LPQB3VH.

of 2007, and before the recent financial crisis, US household equity withdrawal mortgages outstanding amounted to $1.1 trillion and represented a significant boost to US household disposable income. In 2007 some $150 billion was released to US households as equity release loans; in 2010 this figure had gone into reverse at –$90 billion, an overall negative movement equivalent to 1.2 per cent of US GDP. The collapse in the housing market after 2007 reversed the trend in both the USA and UK whereby households could leverage real estate assets to boost current income and expenditure.

For the household pension and real estate capitalizations can inflate or undermine household wealth accumulation and generate injections and withdrawals into current income and expenditure circuits from realized holding gains and additional borrowing capacity. Adjustments in the capitalization of stock market values can also impact positively or negatively on the corporate sector and we illustrate this through pension provisions, goodwill and share buy-backs. We then turn to consider the financial corporate sector which operates with thin margins and high levels of capitalization where small adjustments in the balance sheet can trigger large swings in profits, adjustments to credit ratings, market valuations, and goodwill impairments and solvency. Finally we consider the nature of central government business models and how these are dependent upon debt roll-over refinancing to finance annual deficits. The challenge to this business model is that roll-over debt refinancing depends upon favourable credit ratings and low interest rates to keep it all going.

Corporate sector: capitalization at risk

The corporate sector has become increasingly reliant upon extracting financial leverage from its own market capitalizations and we illustrate this dependency with three examples: pension funding, goodwill accounting and share buy-backs in the US corporate sector. In 1999 stock markets in the USA, Europe and Japan peaked at roughly $30 trillion and at the end of 2006 these stock markets peaked again at $35 trillion before collapsing to $20 trillion, followed by a further halting recovery after the recent financial crisis (see Figure 6.11). As at the end of 2010 the value of stock market capitalization in these main markets was no higher than in 1999 and down on the peak of 2007. Faltering stock market values reduce the beneficial value of household pension funds, and for the corporate sector pension liabilities (employee claims) ran ahead of assets (corporate provision).

Capitalized pensions

The US corporate post-war social settlement included the provision of pensions and health care for retired employees, but as a larger number of the population live longer this is putting additional strain on the US corporate sector in terms of the financial provision for pensions and health care in retirement.

> For over fifty years, the relationship between employee and employer not only encompassed the exchange of services for compensation, but extended to obligations in the form of pensions and Other Post Employment Benefits (OPEB), specifically medical care. These benefits are staples of the American dream and marketplace with their related expenditures built into the cost of products and services.
>
> *(Standard and Poor's, 2011: 3)*

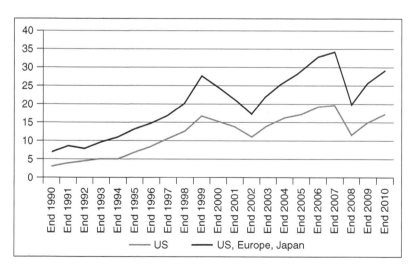

FIGURE 6.11   USA, Europe and Japan: stock market values ($ trillion).

Source: World Federation of Exchanges, www.world-exchanges.org/statistics/time-series/market-capitalisation.

After the US recession in 2000–2001, the economic recovery thereafter and over the following five years to 2007, the S&P 500 group of companies delivered twenty-two quarters of positive operating profit and experienced a recovery in stock market values. This enabled S&P 500 firms to make minimal contributions to their pension funds such that they were often 'taking a pension holiday'. In effect buoyant ongoing inflated stock market capitalizations helped to close the funding gap between the value of assets (pension funds invested) and liabilities (employee pension fund entitlements). Although pension assets exceeded liabilities by 2007, other post-employment benefits (OPEBs) covering health-care entitlements in retirement remained in deficit as US firms failed to make good the deficiency (see Table 6.2). In the USA, the corporate sector is under a regulatory obligation to make good pension deficiencies, but with regards to post-employment health-care benefits regulatory requirements are generally weaker: 'Unlike pensions, which have required funding and legal standing, most OPEBs are not regulatory in nature' (Standard and Poor's, 2011: 12).

As stock market values deteriorated after 2008, the deficit on pension funds opened up again: in 2010 the gap between assets and liabilities in the S&P 500 group of firms stood at $245 billion and the total funding gap that includes both pensions and other post-employment benefits stood at $455 billion, equivalent to one-third of S&P 500 cash earnings in 2010. When stock market values are inflating, the US corporate sector's obligation to finance pension funds from real cash was covered instead by holding gains from inflated stock market values. This, in turn, allowed US firms to make 'minimal' contributions, that is, until stock market values declined after October 2007.

> The gains of the 2002–2007 bull market improved pensions and allowed for minimal corporate contributions. The bear market of October 2007 through March 2009 quickly exposed the extent and size of the liability to current and future retirees. However, the accounting treatment has helped to hide these obligations via smoothing and a lack of full disclosures.
>
> *(Standard and Poor's, 2011: 12)*

TABLE 6.2 S&P 500 firms' pension and other post-employment benefit (OPEB) funding status

	Pension funding status	OPEB funding status	Total funding	EBITDA	Funding as a share of EBITDA
	($ billion)	($ billion)	($ billion)	($ billion)	(%)
2010	−245	−210.1	−455.1	1,500	30.3
2009	−260.7	−214.6	−475.3	1,319	36.0
2008	−308.4	−257.2	−565.6	1,505	37.6
2007	63.4	−269.1	−205.7	1,971	10.4
2006	−40.3	−293.7	−334	1,865	17.9
2005	−140.4	−320.9	−461.3	1,171	39.3
2004	−164.3	−286.9	−451.2	1,480	30.5

Source: www.spindices.com/assets/files/sp500/pdf/SP_500_OPEB-Pensions-May26-2011.pdf.

Note: EBITDA taken from Compustat data for S&P 500 ThomsonOneBanker.

In a competitive global market US corporations are increasingly retreating from their employee pension and post-retirement health-care provisions, and actively encouraging employees to take out private provision, thus shifting the financial risk from employers to employees and households. This process of financial risk transfer is accelerating as the average employee in the USA is living longer and thus placing additional financial demands on pension fund assets and health-care plans. In addition the US corporate sector cannot rely on the capital market to continuously inflate asset values and take holding gains to fund pension holidays rather than pay out *real* cash. 'Just as defined pensions shifted to defined contributions and 401K-type savings accounts, the responsibility of providing post-retirement medical care is now shifting from corporate programs to individuals and to US social policy' (Standard and Poor's, 2011: 9).

Reductions in stock market capitalization are transmitted and absorbed via pension fund accounting into the US corporate accounts where inflated pension and health-care liabilities are being smoothed because the corporate sector is struggling to maintain earnings, investor confidence and stock market values

Capitalized goodwill

Corporate sector restructuring involves undertaking business combinations where the acquiring firm absorbs the market value of the acquired firm, not its book value. In situations where stock market values are inflating, it is often the case that the market value of a company acquired will exceed its historic book value as recorded in its balance sheet. The difference between market and book value is accounted for in the acquiring firm's accounts as 'goodwill on acquisition'. During the period 1990–2010 the market to book value increased from a factor of 1.8:1 to 2.9:1 before dropping back to 1.8, but as Table 6.3 reveals the majority of merger and acquisition deals, by value, took place at times when the market to book value was generally above 2:1.

Recent adjustments to accounting standards (after year 2000) have changed the way in which goodwill is treated. Rather than being amortized and expensed over a number of years, it is accumulated in corporate balance sheets, and in the S&P 500 this amounted to $2.6 trillion or one-quarter of S&P 500 market value in 2011. Periodically auditors are required to assess the extent to which this accumulated goodwill is, or is not, impaired (www.iasplus.com/dttpubs/0807ifrs3guide.pdf).

TABLE 6.3 Global merger and acquisitions and market to book multiples, 1990–2010

Year	Market to book multiples	Global merger and acquisition deals ($ trillion)	
1990	1.8	1985–1990	1.9
1995	2.2	1990–1995	1.9
2000	2.9	1995–2000	8.8
2005	2.3	2000–2005	9.7
2010	1.8	2005–2010	16.6

Source: McKinsey & Co.

When one firm buys another, the target's goodwill – essentially the premium paid over its book value – is added to the combined entity's balance-sheet. Goodwill and other intangibles on the books of companies in the S&P 500 are valued at $2.6 trillion, or 10% of their total assets, according to analysts at Goldman Sachs.

(The Economist, 22 January 2009)

As accounting standards no longer require goodwill to be amortized, where the market value to book value of US firms acquired averaged three or more[5] during the period 2000–2009 this accelerated the accumulation of goodwill held as an asset on US corporate balance sheets. The accumulation of goodwill in the US banking sector was, in 2008, equivalent to 40 per cent of shareholder equity,[6] and in the S&P 500 in 2008 goodwill was also equivalent to an average 40 per cent of shareholder equity (see Figure 6.12). Roughly one-fifth of the S&P 500 stock market value is located in firms which have accumulated goodwill that has now reached between 75 and 100 per cent of shareholder equity. Our point is that there is substantial financial risk attached to goodwill capitalized and accumulated in both the US and European corporate sectors which, if charged off, could undermine the solvency of a large proportion of the advanced economy corporate sector.

In circumstances where the earnings generated from an acquisition are such that the cash earnings discounted or current market valuations do not align with the balance sheet carrying value of goodwill attached to these assets, it (goodwill) may be deemed to be impaired.[7] Goodwill impairments are charged off against income and, in turn, this transmits into the balance sheet, reducing shareholder funds/equity as the reduction in assets (goodwill) is accounted for as a reduction in liabilities (shareholder funds) to maintain assets ≡ liabilities.

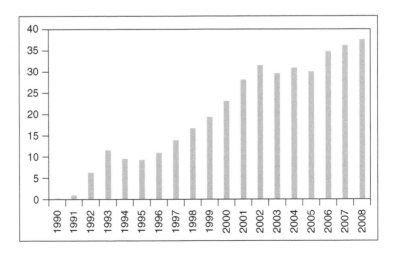

FIGURE 6.12 S&P 500 goodwill as % of equity, 1990–2008.

Source: ThomsonOne Banker, Compustat dataset S&P 500 index.

The previous version of IAS 36 required goodwill acquired in a business combination to be tested for impairment as part of impairment testing the cash-generating unit(s) to which it related. It employed a 'bottom-up/ top-down' approach under which the goodwill was, in effect, tested for impairment by allocating its carrying amount to each cash-generating unit or smallest group of cash-generating units to which a portion of that carrying amount could be allocated on a reasonable and consistent basis. The Standard similarly requires goodwill acquired in a business combination to be tested for impairment as part of impairment testing the cash-generating unit(s) to which it relates.

(IAS 36: IN11)

In circumstances where the corporate sector earnings capacity are damaged because of a traditional product market recession, this could then trigger a write-down of goodwill capitalized in corporate balance sheets. In the recent US and European banking crisis, the financial damage caused by writing off irrecoverable loans was very quickly magnified by even larger goodwill impairment charges.

Capitalizing upon share buy-backs

In the USA the S&P 500 group of companies have increased the deployment of profit and cash to finance an increase in share buy-backs relative to dividends over the past two decades. The total amount of profits appropriated for dividends totalled $2.2 trillion over the period 1998 to 2010 in the S&P 500, whilst share buy-backs (SBBs) amounted to $3.1 trillion, exceeding dividends by 50 per cent. In the earlier period, 1998–2004, dividends paid were roughly equivalent to SBB at 40 per cent of operating profits, but thereafter share buy-backs took up an increased share of earnings and cash. In 2007, at the end of a bull market, the value of US S&P 500 SBBs was equivalent to distributing all operating profits, with dividends taking a further 40 per cent share. The onset of the financial crisis in 2007, and the collapse of stock market values and uncertainty over the price at which to pitch share repurchases, had an obvious negative impact on the volume and value of SBBs. However, during the first quarters of 2011 SBBs recovered and are again surpassing the share of dividends paid out of operating profit (see Figure 6.13).

Approximately, $299 billion was spent by S&P 500 companies on share repurchases last year which represents a whopping 117% increase over the $138 billion spent in 2009, says Howard Silverblatt, Senior Index Analyst at S&P Indices. At this point the practice is not as deep as it was in the heydays of 2006–7, but companies are certainly back in the buyback business. While 2010 expenditures are still just half of what was seen in 2007, last year's activity resulted in a record year-over-year percentage and dollar increase for stock buybacks.

(Reuters, 2011)

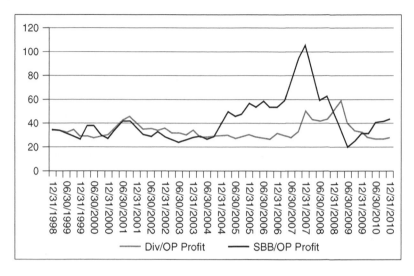

FIGURE 6.13 S&P 500 dividends and SBBs out of profits (%).

Source: www2.standardandpoors.com/spf/pdf/index/121307_SP500_THREE_YEARS_OF_
BUYBACKS.pdf; http://www.reuters.com/article/2011/03/23/idUS139424+23-Mar-2011+
PRN20110323.

To understand the motivations governing share buy-backs we can distinguish between corporate profits employed to pay dividends and corporate profit/cash utilized to buy back shares. Dividends are profit/cash distributed to shareholders whilst, in share buy-backs, shareholders receive cash but the company retains the repurchased shares as treasury stock on balance sheet; these can be used at a later date to finance executive stock option bonus schemes, cancelled to reduce shares outstanding or used in financing corporate acquisitions. One of the key motivations is to obtain financial leverage from SBB holding gains. In a bull market the implicit market value of treasury stock repurchased in an earlier period increases and this financial gain is realized when treasury stock is employed in exchange in a corporate acquisition.

In a report on share buy-backs in 2007, before the deterioration in stock markets, Standard and Poor's revealed that the balance outstanding on treasury stock amounted to $1.3 trillion at cost. However, at that point in time the market value

TABLE 6.4 S&P 500 treasury stock at cost and market value, April 2007

	$ million
Cost of treasury stock	1,282
Market value of treasury shares	1,962
Difference	680
Market value of companies	9,960

Source: www2.standardandpoors.com/spf/pdf/index/121307_SP500_THREE_YEARS_OF_BUY-
BACKS.pdf.

of this treasury stock stood at roughly $2 trillion and represented a holding gain of around $0.7 trillion, a 50 per cent gain on the funds originally employed to buy back shares. During the bull market, corporate acquisitions funded, in part, by an exchange of treasury stock would have realized significant holding gains for shareholders. We now turn to consider the impact of recapitalization upon the financial corporate sector in terms of how balance sheet adjustments amplify financial instability within this institutional sector, which is reliant upon leverage and high volume asset trades to generate a return on equity.

Financial corporate: capitalization and leverage

The business model governing the financial institutional sector of the main advanced economies has already been described in this chapter as one which generates thin operating margins whilst turning over a significant volume of financial assets. Banking and financial services are generally 'leveraged' business models because they operate with a relatively low equity to total assets ratio. A thin profit margin on assets is converted to a relatively high return on shareholder equity because the asset to equity leverage ratio is high. The return on equity (ROE) is defined as:

$$ROE = [\text{net income/assets}] / [\text{equity/assets}]$$

If a typical net income to assets ratio is 2 per cent and the equity to assets ratio 10 per cent, then the ROE would be 20 per cent. However, as different accounting standards and regulatory frameworks are in place across countries, the measure of assets included in the leverage calculation can vary.

> As a result of differences in accounting regimes, balance sheet presentation, and domestic regulatory adjustments, however, the measurement of leverage ratios varies across jurisdictions and banks. Accounting regimes lead to the largest variations. In particular, the use of International Financial Reporting Standards results in significantly higher total asset amounts, and therefore lower leverage ratios for similar exposures, than does the use of US generally accepted accounting principles. The reason is that under International Financial Reporting Standards netting conditions are much stricter and the gross replacement value of derivatives is therefore generally shown on the balance sheet, even when positions are held under master netting agreements with the same counterparty.
>
> *(World Bank, 2009: 2)*

In the USA, prior to 2008 and the onset of the financial crisis, commercial banks operated with a 15:1 asset to equity ratio, but investment banks such as Lehman Brothers were operating leverage ratios at 20–30:1. Significantly, 'the larger US investment bank holding companies and their subsidiaries were regulated by the Securities and

Exchange Commission and thus were not subject to a leverage limit' (ibid.), and in continental Europe the leverage ratio stood at approximately 30:1 and in the UK 25:1 (ibid.). In the aftermath of the banking crisis the focus has been on reducing the lever-age ratio by increasing the value of equity relative to total assets, which would dampen bank lending capacity and, it is suggested; help contain financial risk within a bank's balance sheet. In our case on banking (see Chapter 8) we argue that the focus has been on redefining capital adequacy rather than questioning the viability of the bank-ing business model and the capacity of firms to withstand what are relatively modest adjustments to balance sheet capitalization, for example, asset (loan) write-downs.

We first consider the relationship between the margin generated on assets in the US commercial banking system and its leverage ratio. Figure 6.14 reveals that the return on assets generated within the US banking business model is thin, averaging just 1 per cent over the period 1988–2010. During that period the asset to equity ratio fell from 16:1 to 10:1 which acted to put a brake on the return on equity, which held at roughly 14 per cent over the period up until 2003, before gently falling to 10 per cent before the recent financial crisis.

The onset of the crisis in the US banking business model was initially activated by a relatively small increase in household mortgage charge-offs, but became of signifi-cance when the return on banking assets averaged just 1 per cent. During the period 2007 into 2011 the percentage of assets that were charged off exceeded 1 per cent and reached at their peak more than 3 per cent, forcing many US banks into loss-making positions. In the G7 group of countries as a whole the unweighted share of non-per-forming loans in total loans moved up from 2.6 to 4.8 per cent by 2010.[8]

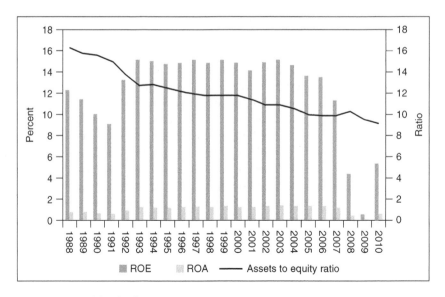

FIGURE 6.14 US banks: leveraging return on assets.

Source: http://research.stlouisfed.org/fred2/release?rid=55&soid=6.

As at the start of 2011, 10 per cent of US household real estate and 7 per cent of commercial real estate mortgages were delinquent,[9] that is, roughly $0.5 trillion, and of this total approximately 1.7 per cent were being charged off by US banks, that is, $60 billion for the year ended June 2011 when banking sector pre-tax operating profits were $77 billion (see Table 6.5). Over the period 2006–2009 OECD data on banking financials revealed a 70 per cent reduction in aggregate net income for the G7 group of countries. The triggers prompting US households and commercial real estate investors to default on their loan repayments related to higher levels of unemployment and a collapse in the housing market price structure. US banks were forced to write off loans which in turn undermined profits, triggering a reduction in market valuations, goodwill impairments and downgrades to the credit ratings of financial institutions.

In June 2007 the Royal Bank of Scotland (RBS) share price was being quoted at more than £6 per share, but by mid-2009 this had collapsed by 95 per cent to 30 pence per share. This loss of market value initiated goodwill impairments, amplifying the financial damage to reported profits and reducing shareholder equity below levels set by Basle II capital adequacy criteria. Over a period of two years, 2008–2009, the reduction in shareholder equity amounted to £60 billion from loan losses and goodwill write-downs. In circumstances where the share price was collapsing it was not possible to raise additional equity and so the equity 'cure' was provided by the UK taxpayer through a government bailout.

> Over the past decades financial innovation has fundamentally changed the structure of the financial system. This trend is exemplified by credit risk transfer instruments such as structured credit products, through which portfolios of credit exposures can be sliced and repackaged to meet the needs of investors. Banks funded a growing amount of long-term assets with short-term liabilities in wholesale markets through the use of off-balance-sheet vehicles, exposing themselves to credit and liquidity risk by providing facilities to these vehicles. Moreover, they also held structured credit instruments on their own balance sheet, exposing themselves to embedded leverage and increasing their asset-liability mismatch and their funding liquidity risk.
>
> *(World Bank, 2009: 4)*

TABLE 6.5 US real estate and consumer loans charged off in total loans outstanding (%)

	Real estate loans	
	Residential	Commercial
2011Q2	1.68	1.66
2010Q4	1.96	1.90
2009Q4	2.82	2.79
2008Q4	1.59	1.88
2007Q4	0.44	0.21
2006Q4	0.12	0.01
2005Q4	0.06	0.01

Source: US Federal Reserve.

The financial services sector business model depends upon financial leverage because this is the mechanism by which a reasonable return on equity can be generated when margins, commissions and fees on assets traded are so thin. Developments within the financial services business model have significantly involved the repackaging of assets, for example securitization (see previous chapter), that served to adjust the funding arrangements of banks where traditionally short-term liabilities (deposits) funded longer-term assets such as household thirty-year mortgages. This change served to inflate assets and balance sheet capitalization ahead of banks' earnings capacity, leaving the business model exposed to relatively small recapitalization adjustments. In a keynote address to the Bank for International Settlements, Már Gudmundsson observed in 2008:

> It is becoming more widely recognised that the financial system has a natural tendency to amplify business cycles through a reinforcing feedback loop with the real economy and that certain aspects of accounting frameworks and capital regulation can increase this tendency . . . Finally, the financial sector will become smaller and less leveraged. That is the only way the sector can be returned to soundness and profitability in the environment that is likely to prevail in the post-crisis period. However, such retrenchment has to be seen against the earlier growth of the sector.
>
> *(Bank for International Settlements, 2008)*

If the financial services sector does become smaller because it is forced to reduce leverage (and hence capitalization), this will have significant implications for the advanced economies because the financial sector accounts for a significant block of global capitalization. The capitalized value of investment funds, bank assets, insurance, mutual and pension funds in the financial institutional corporate sector is not only the asset base from which to extract a return on equity for shareholders, but also the accumulated asset base from which households extract holding gains, leverage their financial position and secure incomes when economically inactive.

Government: capitalization ahead of surplus

Our analysis in the previous chapter reveals that banks operate with very slim operating surpluses (and in a number of cases deficits) after covering the interest burden on debt financing. Governments are somewhat similar to banks in terms of their outstanding debt to surplus ratios, but unlike the banks they are not regulated and are not required to maintain capital reserves as a cushion against bad debts and capital at risk. Rather governments are, by their nature, assumed to be able to underwrite the cost of debt from income streams and capable of modifying fiscal policy to generate an additional surplus or reduce public expenditures. However, the recent financial crisis calls into question this business model in terms of the capacity of governments to finance their roll-over debt and act as 'triple A' rated counterparties. Greece's accumulated debt in 2010 was equivalent to 140 per cent of GDP and roll-over financing could amount to roughly 252 billion euros through to 2020. The difficulty facing Greece, at the time of writing, is that the cost of refinancing this debt, as it comes up for renewal, has risen significantly, with long-term interest rates on government bonds approaching 25 per cent towards the end of 2011 (see Figure 6.15).

Government borrowing, at such high interest rates, would put additional pressure on budget deficits in Greece which already stand at just over 13 per cent of GDP (see Table 6.6). To avoid recapitalizing the economy at this level of interest rate, funds from the IMF and European Community at 3.3 per cent had to be sought. However, undoing this level of capitalization will involve significant negative leverage and fiscal rectitude as the following comment from the IMF on Greece indicates.

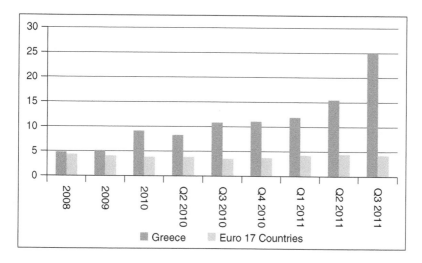

FIGURE 6.15 Long-term interest rates, Greece and euro area, 2008–2011 Q3.
Source: OECD.

TABLE 6.6 Eurozone government deficits and borrowing as a per cent of GDP

	Deficit to GDP (%)		Government debt to GDP (%)	
	2000	2010	2000	2010
European Union (27 countries)	0.6	−6.4	61.9	80.0
European Union (25 countries)	0.6	−6.4	62.0	80.7
Germany	1.3	−3.3	59.7	83.2
Ireland	4.7	−32.4	37.8	96.2
Greece	−3.7	−10.5	103.4	142.8
Spain	−1.0	−9.2	59.3	60.1
France	−1.5	−7.0	57.3	81.7
Italy	−0.8	−4.6	109.2	119.0
United Kingdom	3.6	−10.4	41.0	80.0

Source: http://epp.eurostat.ec.europa.eu.

On fiscal policy, the program has strong measures – many of them front-loaded – to reduce government spending and raise revenue as well as sweeping reforms to modernize the public sector. Fiscal measures of 11 per cent of GDP over three years will be added on top of the 5 per cent of GDP in measures already taken earlier this year by the authorities, for a total of 16 per cent of GDP. The adjustment is designed to get the general government deficit to well below 3 per cent of GDP by 2014 (from 13.6 per cent in 2009) and begin to lower the debt-to-GDP ratio from 2013 onwards.

(IMF, 2010)

The Italian government has roughly €1.6 trillion of bonds outstanding and here too there have been signs of a lack of confidence in Italian sovereign bonds, such that the ten-year bond yields on Italian securities rose to 6.5–7.0 per cent in November 2011, adding further pressure on the country's government to reduce spending and raise taxes.

Italian 10-year yields rose 10 basis points to 6.29 per cent, after climbing to 6.40 per cent. That difference in yield with German securities widened to as much as 462 basis points. The spread between French and German 10-year securities reached a euro-era record 141 basis points.

(Businessweek, 3 November 2011)

Over a relatively short period of time governments in Europe have moved considerably more into deficit as expenses exceed incoming revenues from taxes, and the scale of sovereign debt outstanding to GDP also increased from 60 to 80 per cent. In some countries the level of public sector capitalization is equivalent to or above the value of annual GDP (Greece, Italy and Ireland) and this is also coupled with high annual government funding deficits above 10 per cent of GDP (Ireland and Greece). The deterioration in sovereign debt credit ratings, most notably with Greece, has implications for institutions that have Greek bonds on their balance sheets. According to the *Financial Times*:

French banks are among Greece's biggest creditors, with $53bn in overall net exposure to Greek private and public debt, according to the latest figures from the Bank for International Settlements. German banks are also exposed with $34bn, including loans made through KfW.

(Financial Times, 15 June 2011)

A number of Greek and European banks have significant exposure to Greek sovereign debt[10] and the wealth at risk transmission mechanisms are further complicated because credit risk is also insured; for example, American International Group (AIG) issues credit default swaps (CDSs) to protect lenders, and at the height of the financial crisis in 2008–2009 AIG required $100 billion of federal government support to maintain solvency.

US government debt to GDP fell consistently over the period 1950–1980, reaching 30 per cent of GDP, but thereafter it increased consistently and has reached 90 per cent of GDP if we exclude agency debt.[11] With the inclusion of agency debt the ratio reached a low of 40 per cent and currently stands at 120 per cent of GDP (see Figure 16.6). The recent acceleration in total government debt funding requirements forced the treasury to seek permission to extend borrowing capacity, prompting the IMF to issue a warning. In the USA the federal government borrowing requirement is set by Congress and this currently stands at $14.3 trillion. The IMF is concerned to extend this borrowing requirement, whilst at the same time the US government should consider how the accumulated value of debt outstanding will be progressively reduced. However, as we write, internal political wrangling and indecision in Congress over the extent of cutbacks is leading to heightened uncertainty.

> The International Monetary Fund warned US lawmakers Wednesday that a failure to raise the nation's borrowing limit would pose serious risks to the global economy and financial markets.
>
> The US last month reached its $14.3 trillion borrowing limit. The US Treasury has said that it can keep the country operating for a couple months by employing various bookkeeping maneuvers. But if Congress doesn't raise the borrowing limit by Aug. 2, Treasury Secretary Timothy Geithner has said the country will default on its debt.
>
> *(The Times, 30 June 2011)*

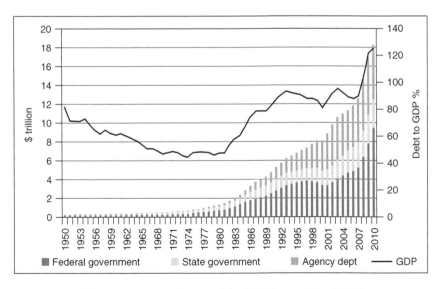

FIGURE 6.16   US government and agency debt ($ trillion and % of GDP).

Source: www.usgovernmentspending.com/debt_deficit_history.

Of the outstanding US debt for the year end 2010, some $9 trillion is held by the public and is marketable with a range of maturities. It is estimated that within the next four years $5 trillion of this debt will come up for renewal upon maturity.

> As of September 30, 2010, $8,476 billion, or 94 per cent, of the securities that constitute debt held by the public were marketable, meaning that once the Federal Government issues them, they can be resold by whoever owns them. Marketable debt is made up of Treasury bills, Treasury notes, Treasury bonds, and Treasury Inflation-Protected Securities (TIPS) with maturity dates ranging from less than 1 year out to 30 years. Of the marketable securities currently held by the public as of September 30, 2010, $5,180 billion, or 61 per cent, will mature within the next 4 years . . . As of September 30, 2010 and 2009, notes and TIPS held by the public maturing within the next 10 years totaled $5,673 billion and $4,169 billion, respectively, an increase of $1,504 billion.
>
> *(US Government Accountability Office, 2010: 13)*

The central structural issue is that the government business model of the advanced economies has itself also become increasingly capitalized relative to gross receipts minus expenditures, and this is also threatening the stability of the financial-corporate sector which is variably exposed to sovereign debt with uncertain credit ratings. Capitalization at risk is being transferred from one institutional sector (government) to another (financial corporate) in the double entry book-keeping roundabout.

> Statistics released in the BIS's Quarterly Review says European banks held $136 billion in foreign claims from Greece at the end of December 2010, led by France and Germany with $56 billion and $40 billion in foreign claims respectively.
>
> *(Central Banking.com, 6 June 2011)*

Financial and government institutional sectors in the advanced economies have leveraged their balance sheets, forcing capitalization ahead of surplus generating capacity. Relatively small realignments could force heavy deleveraging and initiate significant financial damage elsewhere as transmission adjustments work their way through. Moreover, as we now argue, the process of accounting, centred upon recording market values, serves to amplify financial realignments.

National business models: capitalization at risk

In this chapter we observe how a national business model can be deconstructed into its institutional components: corporate financial, non-financial, government and households. We find that ongoing capitalization in the advanced economies has moved ahead of GDP and cash earnings/surplus in the corporate and government sectors where leverage is possible. For households, this has underwritten inflated real estate values and accumulates pension funds for a growing proportion of the population that are economically inactive. Although earnings and surpluses have not been transformed in the corporate and government sectors, balance sheet capitalization has been transformed. A complex series of explanations account for this: historically low interest rates, population dynamics, mergers and restructuring, as well as new leveraged business models. In a credit-based economy the trade in assets generates ongoing recapitalizations where the collateral becomes disconnected from the original tangible assets because the collateral includes goodwill arising from inflated asset values. When balance sheet capitalizations are on an upwards trajectory, it is possible to also extract holding gains to boost consumption and generate further financial leverage. In the corporate sector holding gains reduce the need to provide real cash for pensions, and household equity is used to extract additional loans that leak into consumption expenditure and boost GDP. Within the corporate and government sectors leverage and holding gains are not secure when underlying liquidity is not transformed and where there is also the continued need for access to debt and equity funding to maintain balance sheet solvency. When capitalizations run ahead of earnings/surplus capacity, there is always a possibility of asset liquidations which are transmitted and amplified by accounting systems.

Capitalization at risk: transmission

Within a national business model, corporate plus government capitalizations are reflected in the beneficial value of household real estate assets and pension funds. A variety of triggers can initiate recapitalizations within and across institutional sectors and the process of double entry book-keeping transmits rather than contains financial disturbance. For example, deteriorating household employment and income levels can lead to a rise in mortgage loan defaults that in turn can significantly reduce bank profits which are a very thin margin on assets held. This may lead to a reduction in the market value of banks and, in turn, an increase in goodwill impairments that reduce shareholder equity as balance sheet asset values are 'marked to market'. Government's accumulated capitalizations (as debt outstanding) may not be sustainable if credit ratings are adjusted and interest rates increase. And there is also the possibility that, as in the Greek case, debt may have to be written down, forcing banks to take a 'hair cut' on their holdings of sovereign debt. In November 2011 the investment bank MF Global filed for Chapter 11 bankruptcy as the extent to which its exposure to high risk European government bonds became clear: 'MF's demise comes less than two years after it was intentionally transformed from a dull institutional broker to an ambitious investment bank by its new chief executive, Jon Corzine' (*The Economist*, 5 November 2011).

> MF Global's decline accelerated last week as the New York-based company revealed more details about its European exposure, posted a larger-than-expected quarterly loss, and was downgraded by major credit rating agencies to 'junk' status. Many investors were also spooked by MF Global's roughly 30-to-1 leverage ratio, based on more than $40 billion of assets and just $1.4 billion of equity. Corzine himself has said that much leverage is unacceptably high.
>
> *(Firstpost, 5 November 2011)*

Financial amplification

In the corporate sector the financial transmission mechanism governed by double-entry book-keeping operates to adjust asset values in line with liabilities, but the accounting system itself can amplify financial adjustments because capitalization and recapitalizations are computed on the basis of fair value accounting (FVA), that is, marking assets and liabilities to market value (FASB, 2001b). The standards-setting regulatory bodies such as the Financial Accounting Standards Board (FASB) in the USA and International Accounting Standards Board (IASB) are persuaded that FVA provides relevant information for investors concerned with reading valuations from the balance sheet rather than just cash flows. FVA therefore reflects the primacy of shareholder stakeholders within the setting of accounting standards and of structuring corporate financial disclosures. This not only has negative implications in terms of how broader stakeholder interests are affected by adjustments, but mechanically capital market recapitalizations are driving financial reporting. In an earlier period, under historic costing and conservative accounting, the market value of assets would only be recognized when sold at arm's length. FVA, by way of contrast, adjusts asset values up and down depending on capital market conditions, reporting realized and unrealized holding gains in the comprehensive income statement. Assets marked down can also be marked back up again where financial volatility is imported into the financial accounts and the reporting entity treated as if it were 'liquidating' rather than acting as a 'going concern'. Moreover, the role of accountants as reporting agents undertaking FVA must now be supplemented with a host of external support from actuaries (pension fund asset and liability computations) and market value expertise for specific assets (property) and credit agencies for ratings.

> Most prior research shows that the adoption of FVA translates into more volatile results (earnings). Hence financial markets' extreme volatility over the past few years has contributed to raise financial institutions' volatility, potentially amplifying the perception by investors, regulators, and governments as to the seriousness of the crisis. More practically, the drop in reported earnings is even more dramatic in light of the record earnings reported in prior years with FVA pushing down earnings in the current period but boosting earnings in prior years.
>
> *(Magnan, 2009: 7)*

We illustrate this point with the accountant's treatment of capitalized goodwill which represents the difference between the market and book value of business combinations. Goodwill is a significant component of the S&P 500 asset side of the balance sheet and equivalent to 40 per cent of total shareholder equity. There are circumstances (triggers) that can initiate an impairment of goodwill held in corporate balance sheets. For example, as previously noted, in the case of the Royal Bank of Scotland (RBS), an initial write-down of non-performing real estate loans triggered further and ever more substantial write-downs of goodwill arising from previously acquired businesses such as ABN Amro.[12] The process of FVA at RBS amplified adjustments to balance sheet capitalization which, when charged against profit and then into shareholder funds, compromised the activity as a 'going concern'. These recapitalizations are very large and lumpy, and inflated by the sheer scale of outstanding values. Moreover, our framework of analysis sets up the process of recapitalization within an accounting framework where assets ≡ liabilities but where the identity, motivations and financial condition of the institutional actors on one side do not correspond with those on the other.

Within this wealth accumulation and value at risk framework it is possible to explore how financial adjustments transmit and amplify within the realm and system of accounting. It is generally assumed that institutional sectors have the capacity to hedge financial risk, but when we open up the assets ≡ liabilities identity into its constituent stakeholder counterparties, where double-entry book-keeping operates, we find that financial adjustments and disturbance are permeable across institutional boundaries. For example, if households default on their mortgage loans outstanding, it is possible to observe how this impacts the viability of the financial corporate sector business model, or, should there be a threat of government default on sovereign bonds, one can see how the financial adjustments and risk transmit into the balance sheets of banks and insurance firms within the financial corporate sector. The advanced economy institutional business models have become financially leveraged as capitalizations have run ahead of liquidity. When the financial system is damaged, adjustments are transmitted, amplified and made porous by accounting systems and this fundamentally limits containment by financial hedging. Within the prism of double-entry book-keeping we are, as Minsky (1993) would observe, mostly in a speculative or ponzi *modus operandi*.

7

BUSINESS MODELS

Adaptation and restructuring

Introduction

In this chapter we explore two forms of 'generic' restructuring that are common to all types of business model. These two forms of corporate restructuring are business combinations (mergers/acquisitions), and off-shoring and out-sourcing. Both of these reside within the manager's corporate strategy tool-kit and can be deployed to modify corporate financial performance. The purpose of this chapter is to explore the extent to which these generic restructuring tools have the capacity to generate financial transformation and to what extent contradictory forces are in play within the stakeholder information pool that constitutes corporate sector business models.

Business models restructured: business combinations

In Figure 7.1 the number and value of global mergers and acquisitions is shown and it reveals a volatile cyclical pattern with the value of deals falling during the 2000–2001 recession before recovering to a new peak by 2007, before the recent financial crisis. At their peak in 2007 global M&A deals amounted to approximately $6 trillion, equivalent to 12 per cent of global GDP in that year, before collapsing by 50 per cent to $3 trillion and 5 per cent of global GDP, before yet again recovering. The pattern of M&A deals by value so significant that they reflect changes in the market value of global equities.[1]

In the USA a similar picture emerges where there is again a volatile cyclical movement (see Figure 7.2). The market value of deals peaked in 1999 at roughly $2.5 trillion, then collapsed to roughly $600 million before recovering to reach another peak in 2007 at $2.2 trillion, followed yet again by a collapse in the aftermath of the 2007–2009 financial crisis. In the case of the USA, which accounts for

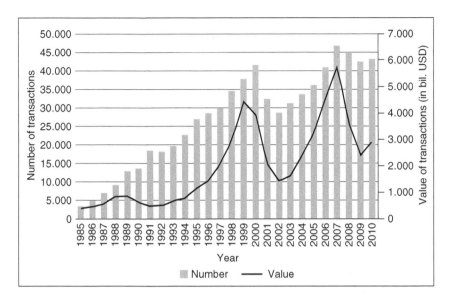

FIGURE 7.1   Announced mergers and acquisitions worldwide, 1985–2010.

Source: www.imaa-institute.org/images/figure_announced%20mergers%20&%20acquisitions%2
0(worldwide).jpg.

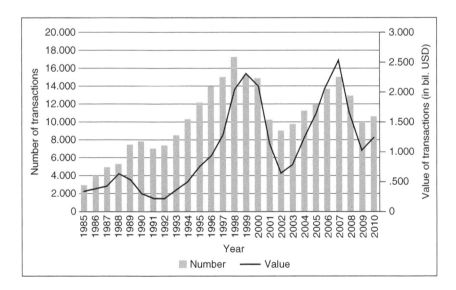

FIGURE 7.2   Announced mergers and acquisitions in the USA, 1985–2010.

Source: www.imaa-institute.org/images/figure_announced%20mergers%20&%20acquisitions%2
0(united%20states%20of%20america).jpg.

roughly 40 per cent of global M&A deals by value, the corporate sector is turning over the equivalent of total S&P 500 market value every five to six years.

The dominant rationale put forward to justify mergers and acquisitions (henceforth business combinations) is that these deals will lead to improved financial performance and value creation for wealth accumulation (Rappaport, 1979). The motivations and justifications for business combinations are many and varied, but significantly include reducing costs from scale, differentiation from economies of scope, consolidating market share, and appropriating synergies from vertical and horizontal integration. That is, business combinations can generate favourable cost structures by adjusting relations with customers, suppliers and competitors for financial gain. Within the context of a focal firm within its business model, corporate acquisitions provide opportunities to arbitrage existing stakeholder arrangements and modify operating financials. Our use of the term 'information' differs from that employed by economists, where the quality of 'asymmetric' information is of interest, for example, where one party has access to more or less information than the other party or where information is imperfectly distributed between a principal and agent in contractual relations. In this chapter our argument is that the focal firm, subtended within its business model, is pooling information so as to dynamically arbitrage and modify stakeholder relations to generate additional cash resources and inflate capitalization. The information pool within which these calculations take place includes physical, financial, institutional and regulatory numbers and narratives which are further refracted, classified and manipulated through a process of financial reporting and accounting. Thus a focal firm's reported financials congeal the outcome of complex stakeholder interactions and accounting manipulations, where the connection between action(s) and outcome(s) is less than clear-cut. That is, we should expect discrepancies to arise between 'policy narratives' that promise transformation and the financial 'numbers' that record outcomes. The following quote from a KPMG report on 'World Class Transactions' in 2001 is a good example of what we mean.

> The survey found that 82% of respondents believed the major deal they had been involved in had been a success . . . We found that only 17% of deals had added value to the combined company, 30% produced no discernible difference, and as many as 53% actually destroyed value. In other words, 83% of mergers were unsuccessful in producing any business benefit as regards shareholder value.
>
> *(KPMG, 1999: 2)*

In this chapter the intention is to explore this type of 'narrative-numbers' contradiction, for example in accounting for business combinations in the S&P 500 group of companies which account for roughly one-quarter of global market value and 40 per cent of business combination transactions by market value. Here our attention is on how corporate acquisitions are financed and accounted for and the impact that this has on capitalization relative to liquidity in the S&P 500 group of companies.

In the S&P 500 the average business combination will be financed with cash (own and borrowed funds) which accounts for roughly 65 per cent of total consideration, whilst the exchange of shares represents roughly 14 per cent and the residual 21 per cent comprises a mix of financing options.[2] Thus, having access to healthy cash reserves and a favourable credit rating to facilitate debt financing at relatively low interest rates matter in relation to putting together the 'cash' component of a deal. The S&P 500 constituent group have increased their cash reserves relatively steadily in recent years from roughly $400 billion in 2000 to $1 trillion in 2010 and up from 6 to 10 per cent of total sales.[3] Lower interest rates have helped to keep the cost of debt financing out of free cash flow[4] reasonably steady at approximately 30 per cent.[5] In addition the ebb and flow of the market value of the S&P 500 (see Figure 7.3) extend or, at times, restrict the scope for deploying treasury stock as part of a deals financing structure. In a situation where stock market values are inflating, the acquired company investors will be more confident that treasury shares used in exchange, and to part-finance a deal, will also inflate in value and will be more attractive as a financing component.

Throughout the period 1990–1999 the market value paid for business acquisitions moved ahead of their balance sheet book value and this peaked at the end of this period at 5:1 in 1999 as the tech bubble was about to burst (see Figure 7.4). That is, the market value of the average S&P 500 corporate acquisition would be priced at a value which was five times greater than the book value of equity. After reaching this peak, S&P 500 market to book values retreated, but they still hovered around 3:1 during the past decade until the recent financial crisis when it fell back to 2:1. In addition to paying the market value of equity, it is often the case that the

FIGURE 7.3   S&P 500 market value index, 1990–2011.

Source: Yahoo finance UK.

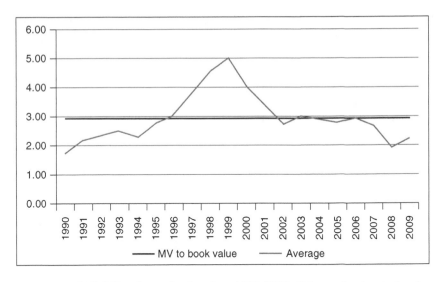

FIGURE 7.4 S&P 500 price to book value, 1990–2009. Price to book calculated as market value to equity.

Source: ThomsonOneBanker.

acquiring company will pay what is termed a 'control' premium, over and above market value. In recent years this control premium has averaged approximately 15–20 per cent[6] and would increase the average market to book value of an average deal from roughly 3:1 to 3.6:1 during the period 2000–2010.

Prior to 2001, in the USA, the income statements and balance sheets of the acquiring and acquired company would have been pooled together, that is, simply blended. Under this accounting regulation it would be the historic balance sheet values of both companies that would have been combined and the market value would be 'dust in the wind' for the purpose of consolidating the two firms (Andersson *et al.*, 2008a). In the USA after 2000, the accounting standard SFAS 141 'Business Combinations'[7] recommended that, for all transactions, the market value of the acquisition be taken into account and the difference between market and book value accounted for as goodwill arising from the acquisition, and shown in the acquiring firm's accounts.

> This Statement, together with the IASB's IFRS 3, *Business Combinations* (as revised in 2007), completes a joint effort by the FASB and the IASB to improve financial reporting about business combinations and to promote the international convergence of accounting standards. Statement 141 and IFRS 3 (as issued in 2004) both required use of the acquisition method rather than the pooling-of-interests method to account for business combinations.
>
> *(FASB, 2007)*

This change in the accounting standard governing how firms account for business combinations significantly modified the information pool within which corporate and business model restructuring was to take place. Practically it had a significant impact on the acquiring firm's balance sheet because it must now absorb the market value of a business combination, where the difference between the book value and market value of the business acquired is accounted for as an intangible asset, 'goodwill'. The financial measure of goodwill is also itself subject to a modified accounting treatment where it is accumulated (not depreciated on an annual basis) and subject to periodic impairment testing.[8]

> The Board concluded that amortization of goodwill was not consistent with the concept of representational faithfulness, as discussed in FASB Concepts Statement No. 2, *Qualitative Characteristics of Accounting Information*. The Board concluded that non-amortization of goodwill coupled with impairment testing *is* consistent with that concept. The appropriate balance of both relevance and reliability and costs and benefits also was central to the Board's conclusion that this Statement will improve financial reporting.
>
> *(FASB, 2001c)*

These accounting adjustments favoured certain groups of firms, that is, those paying inflated prices for a business combination which would add a significant lump of goodwill into the acquiring firm's balance sheet. Depreciating this goodwill would lead to a lowering of reported earnings and reduction in the value of shareholder equity as asset values and liabilities adjust. The adjustment to fair value reporting was a socially constructed move which involved recalibrating balance sheets to reflect the market value of assets and liabilities for shareholders, where a compromise was struck such that goodwill would be allowed to accumulate in the acquirer's balance sheet (rather than amortized and depressing earnings) unless, however, the goodwill was deemed to be impaired.

Andersson *et al.* (2008a) argue that the change from historic cost pooling of assets and liabilities to fair values in business combinations modified the orthodox value-creating models which had previously (if often erroneously) assumed a left to right causality between improved operating financials and generating market value for shareholders.

> There has always been an active market for corporate control in the US but the difference in recent years is that business combinations should be accounted for at 'fair value' with the result that wealth accumulation, arising in the capital market, is being absorbed onto corporate sector balance sheets. Accounting for the fair value of capital market transactions modifies reported corporate financials and this process of value absorption adds additional right-to-left polarity to orthodox left-to-right *value creating* models.
>
> *Andersson* et al. *(2008a: 262)*

In a traditional value creating model, Stern Stewart Consulting suggest that firms that report higher EVA™ (profit after deducting a cost of capital) one year to the next will normally be rewarded with higher market valuations. This conventional value creating model depends upon constructing left to right causal relations where higher EVA would lead to higher market value. Andersson *et al.* (2008a) argue that left to right causal relations are difficult to establish under mark to market accounting, because the financial values on the left-hand side also embody market values from the right-hand side of the value creating relation. For example, the cash return on capital employed generated by the S&P 500 group of companies is not only a driver of market value, it is also a ratio that captures market value absorbed (by business combinations) in the balance sheet. Over the period 1990–2000 the S&P 500 group increased their average reported cash surplus margin from 16 to 20 per cent and sustained this higher level over the period 2000–2007. After the year 2000 and the change to fair value accounting for business combinations, the S&P 500 average cash return on capital has fallen steadily to just over 17 per cent in 2010, as balance sheet capitalization accelerated ahead of cash earnings (see Figure 7.5)

In Table 7.1 we illustrate the impact of mark to market accounting using a hypothetical business combination. Initially both companies share a cash ROCE of 25 per cent, but when company B is acquired we employ a 3.5:1 market to book value to estimate the its market value. When A and B are combined the capital employed is the debt and equity of company A (10,000) plus the market value of company B and its debt outstanding (9,000). After the business combination is accounted for the cash ROCE has fallen from 25 to 18 per cent.

We now consider the specific case of Pfizer to explore the difference between 'pooling' and accounting for 'business combinations at fair value', and its impact on

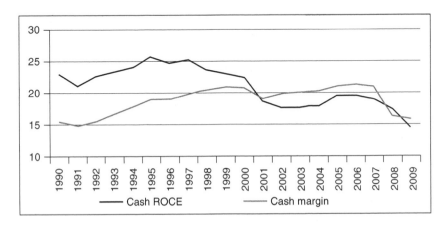

FIGURE 7.5 S&P 500 cash margin and cash ROCE (%). Cash surplus margin is earnings before interest, taxes, depreciation and amortization (EBITDA) as a per cent of total income. Cash ROCE is EBITDA as a per cent of long-term debt plus shareholder equity.

Source: ThomsonOneBanker.

TABLE 7.1 Business combination schematic

	Company A	Company B	A&B
Cash	2,500	1,000	3,500
Capital employed	10,000	4,000	19,000
Of which debt	5,000	2,000	
Of which equity	5,000	2,000	
Market value		7,000	
Cash ROCE (%)	25	25	18

Source: The authors.

Note: We assume a market to book value of equity 3.5:1.

key performance ratios. Since the year 2000 Pfizer has made a number of corporate acquisitions, the most significant of which being Warner-Lambert (2000, $90 billion), Pharmacia (2003, $55 billion) and Wyeth (2009, $60 billion). The acquisition in 2000 of Warner-Lambert was accounted for using the 'pooling method'.

> On June 19, 2000, we completed our merger with Warner-Lambert. We issued approximately 2,440 million shares of our common stock for all the outstanding common stock of Warner-Lambert. The merger qualified as a tax-free reorganization and was accounted for as a pooling of interests under APB No. 16, Business Combinations.
>
> *(Pfizer Annual Report 10K 2001: 44)*

The acquisitions made after the Warner-Lambert deal were all accounted for under the new accounting standard SFAS 141 'Accounting for Business Combinations' at their fair value. The impact of absorbing the market value of Pharmacia and Wyeth on to Pfizer's balance sheet forced balance sheet capitalization ahead of cash earnings and resulted in a significant increase in goodwill recorded in the balance sheet. In Figure 7.6 we calibrate goodwill as a percentage of shareholder equity to show that this increases from 10 to 40 per cent before a further adjustment pushed it up to 50 per cent after the Wyeth deal. Pfizer's cash ROCE drops from 50 per cent in 2001 to 10 per cent after the purchase of Pharmacia, before recovering back to 20 per cent over the period 2005–2009. Then again after the acquisition of Wyeth a similar pattern emerges, with the cash ROCE again depressed back down to 10 per cent and an additional jump in reported goodwill in the balance sheet.

The narratives of corporate restructuring often promise financial transformation from economies of scale and synergies that might reduce costs and transform operating financials. Our argument, from a business model perspective, is that the information content arriving from stakeholders filtered by accounting is complex and not straightforward. In the case of restructuring through business combinations, changes in accounting regulation and standards matter because this also modifies information content from which financial numbers are constructed. In the specific case of corporate acquisitions, SFAS 141 fair value reporting forces balance sheet

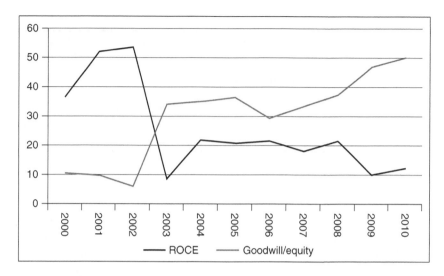

FIGURE 7.6 Pfizer cash ROCE and goodwill to equity (%). Goodwill is on corporate acquisitions.

Source: Edgar SEC dataset 10Ks for Pfizer, various years.

capitalization ahead of cash earnings, reducing reported ROCE when a business combination is substantial and the market to book values are high.

Although corporate restructuring promises to boost shareholder value and return on capital, the way in which we account for business combinations complicates matters. Where the acquired firm has a market to book value of 3 or more and represents a significant deal, the cash ROCE of the acquiring firm will almost certainly deteriorate. Moreover, the difference between book and market values leads to the accumulation of goodwill in the acquiring firm's accounts which is an additional risk if, at some future date, it is deemed to be impaired. All of this arises out of changes in accounting standards which impact upon the information pool within which focal firms operate within their business model. Accounting systems modify the information pool and this generates adjustments to reported financial numbers and sets up the possibility for amplified financial adjustments when market capitalizations can no longer be sustained.

We now turn to another broad restructuring strategy that can be deployed by firms, that of off-shoring and out-sourcing, which promise the possibility of reconfiguring the global financial value chain and higher returns for investors.

Business models restructured: off-shoring and out-sourcing

Off-shoring and out-sourcing are a significant element in the corporate management and consultancy restructuring portfolio where narratives often promise financial transformation. In a corporate context it helps if narratives about strategic initiatives align with financial performance. In their text *Financialisation and Strategy:*

Narrative and Numbers, Froud *et al.* (2006) reveal how financial numbers can be used by outsiders to critically assess transformative narratives issued by senior management and consultants.

Out-sourcing and off-shoring, it is argued, offer the potential to lower costs and increase efficiency (OECD, 2007), which in turn should transmit into increased earnings capacity (profit or cash surplus on capital employed) where organizational unbundling (Jacobides, 2003) reconfigures the mix of business activities undertaken by the firm along a value chain and where, ideally, internal cost reduction is not offset by increased external expenses and balance sheet capitalization. Gereffi (1994) reveals how leading brand companies seek to restructure their global value chains and the implications for corporate governance, technical transfer, the division of competences and the utilization of power within global markets to extract higher returns (Kaplan and Kaplinsky, 1998; Sturgeon, 1997). A recent OCED report (2007) observes that:

> This globalisation of the value chain is driven by companies' desire to increase efficiency, as growing competition in domestic and international markets forces firms to become more efficient and lower costs, as well as the desire to enter new emerging markets and gain access to strategic assets that can help tap into foreign knowledge.
>
> *(OECD, 2007: 1)*

The same policy brief observes that 'what is new is the speed and scale of the current wave of globalisation, and the associated phenomena of outsourcing and off-shoring' (OECD, 2007: 2). During the 1990s it was not only manufacturing capacity that was amenable to out-sourcing and off-shoring but also services. As Gordon *et al.* (2009: 373) observe, 'Since the end of the 1990s, however, service activities in advanced economies have taken initiatives to shift a much wider range of information-related functions to offshore locations in pursuit of labour cost savings, as they in their turn come to face more intense price competition.' A survey by the United Nations Conference on Trade and Development (UNCTAD) and Roland Berger Strategy Consultants also notes that 'So far, the focus is on back office services, but most service processes are potential future candidates for off-shoring. While they lag behind their US rivals, European companies – especially from the United Kingdom – see off-shoring as a way to reduce costs and improve their competitiveness' (UNCTAD, 2004: 1).

In research carried out by CAPCO consultants and the London Business School entitled 'Financial Services Factory', Gupta (2008) compares the current off-shoring project of financial services with that of car manufacturing in an earlier period (Williams *et al.*, 1994). CAPCO employ the term 'componentization' to describe how processes and functions can be decoupled from their existing geographic location to arbitrage labour cost (and exploit other non-price and knowledge-based assets) in order to reduce operating costs and improve earnings. In a global investment bank:

The offshore centre in India took over the responsibility of initiating (phone calls, faxes, e-mails, etc., to the counterparties) while the more experienced resources based in London processed exceptions. Using this model the investment bank was able to minimize their investment in knowledge transfer and training of the India-based staff while reaping as much as 40 per cent savings in operating costs.

(Gupta, 2006: 46)

According to a report by Duke University's Centre for International Business Education and Research (CIEBR), the financial crisis adds to the urgency to off-shore to save labour costs: 'The most prominent change is labor cost savings. The findings from the ORN survey conducted in November 2008 show that labor cost savings have become even more important (relative to ORN 2007/2008 findings) in the current economic situation' (PricewaterhouseCoopers 2009:1).

This acceleration and deepening of the global out-sourcing and off-shoring project by US and European firms also coincides with changes in corporate governance, where in an era of shareholder value, financial incentives based on performance become coupled to managerial remuneration. Mahony *et al.* (2006), Milberg (2008) and Milberg *et al.* (2010) integrate the motivation to out-source and off-shore with the pressure to generate higher returns to shareholders in the USA. Their argument is that the out-sourcing and off-shoring of services from the USA increased profits but that these additional earnings were not deployed into reinvestment and productive renewal, instead being distributed to shareholders: 'At the same time the cost savings from off-shoring are considerable, and the recent rise in off-shoring has corresponded with historic highs in the profits share of national income. Despite the profit increases, rates of investment have not grown accordingly' (Mahony *et al.*, 2006: 10).

Management consultants are especially prone to deploying narratives supporting the financial benefits that can arise from off-shoring and out-sourcing.

Companies that have allocated over 60% of their R&D expenditure offshore have displayed greater shareholder return, operating margins, market capital growth and return on assets.

(Business Insight, 2009)

Financial institutions that only move a single function off-shore typically report average cost savings of twenty per cent. In contrast companies that offshore multiple functions enjoy an average cost saving of 40 to 50 per cent or more, suggesting that there are significant benefits to expanding the scope for off-shoring activities.

(Deliotte, 2005:12)

Always under intense financial pressure, in recent years executives have turned to off-shoring their IT work in search of immediate relief. Labor arbitrage advantages delivered rapid cost cuts, to the accolades of shareholders and chief financial officers alike.

(Accenture, 2010:1)

Erturk *et al.* (2012) observe that we should be careful about conflating corporate strategy around a single purpose when it comes to extracting a return on capital for shareholders. Their analysis of Apple Inc. reminds us that strategy can combine low cost capture with considerable marketing and branding expense deployed to sustain price structures.

> In the case of Apple Inc., cost control and risk transfer works through low cost Asian assembly and crowd sourcing of the software apps, while heavy investment in branding and marketing of iPod, iPhone and iPad backs up a 'seduce and capture' retailing of affordable novelties which locks customers into utilities like iTunes software that impose high switching costs.
>
> *(Erturk et al., 2012)*

The business model framework of analysis outlined in this text argues that reported financial numbers congeal the outcome of a complex range of stakeholder interventions that invariably produce contradictory information content and financial outcomes. The usual narratives on off-shoring and out-sourcing suggest that cost reduction from arbitraging global labour is also commensurate with generating higher returns on assets/capital for shareholder value. Using financial numbers reported by the US Bureau of Economic Analysis (BEA) we can assess the extent to which US foreign affiliates are generating a higher return on invested capital relative to their US parents.

Revealing contradictory financial transformation from off-shoring and out-sourcing

In Table 7.2 we present a hypothetical example to consider how earnings capacity (cash ROCE or cash earned on assets employed) might be improved from out-sourcing and off-shoring. We assume that it is possible to arbitrage global labour markets and, by displacing domestic for foreign labour, to reduce internal employment costs by one-third from 42 per cent to 28 per cent of total income. Outsourcing and off-shoring labour-intensive functions, we assume, would only increase external procurement costs by 7 per cent of total income because, in this case, overseas external suppliers offer a 50 per cent labour cost saving. Out-sourcing thus increases external costs by 7 per cent and thereby also reduces value retained (after paying suppliers) from 60 to 53 per cent of total income, whereas the reduction in internal labour costs is 14 per cent, that is 42–28 per cent of total income. Therefore, in combination off-shoring and out-sourcing reduce total costs by 7 per cent (14 minus 7) and this increases the cash margin from 18 to 25 per cent of total income. Assuming also that the firm's capital/asset intensity remains constant (capital/assets employed to generate a financial unit of total income), the return on capital/assets would also increase from 18 to 25 per cent (see Table 7.2). Using

TABLE 7.2 Key financial operating ratios and earnings capacity

Firm	At_0	At_1
Total revenue/income	100	100
External procurement costs	−40	−47
Value retained	60	53
Employee expenses	42	28
Cash retained	18	25
Capital/assets employed (% sales)	100	100
Cash ROCE/cash to assets	18	25

Source: The authors.

Notes: Capital employed would be computed as long-term debt plus equity. Assets are tangible assets minus working capital (short-term assets minus short-run liabilities) and capital/asset intensity is found by dividing capital/assets employed into total revenue/ income.

the nature of expense accounting format described in Table 7.2, it is possible to compare US parent company financials with their majority owned foreign affiliate operations (but excluding finance and depository institutions). The US industrial sector has a long history of investment overseas and it is possible to identify the financial operating characteristics of US parent companies and their foreign overseas affiliates from the US Bureau of Economic Analysis (BEA) datasets.[9]

In 2008 majority owned US foreign affiliates accounted for assets, sales revenue and value added that was equivalent to roughly one-quarter of the assets, sales revenue and value added of their US parents. Over the period 1999–2008 US parent company employment fell by 2 million from 23 million to 21 million and employment in foreign affiliates increased by 2.3 million. The majority of the increase in overseas employment was located in developing regions – Asia-Pacific, China and Latin America – where labour costs are one-half to one-sixth of those in the USA (see Table 7.3). A significant motivation for US parent companies was to reduce total labour costs and pass this saving on in lower prices to maintain competitiveness. However, cost reduction is not the same as transforming cost structure, cash margins and the return on invested assets for shareholder value.

The Bureau of Economic Analysis has previously investigated this puzzle – why has the return on asset (ROA) performance of US foreign affiliates been below that of US parent companies in the 1990s?

> A longstanding question about foreign owned US companies is why their rates of return have been consistently below those of other US companies . . . The average ROA for foreign owned nonfinancial companies was 2.2 percentage points below that for US owned nonfinancial companies in 1988–97.
>
> (*US Bureau of Economic Analysis, 2000:1*)

The BEA research undertaken at this time tried to explain the difference as a 'measurement' problem where it was difficult to compare 'like with like' because the asset values of foreign affiliates are more current than parent company historic values.

Table 7.3 Labour costs: USA, Europe, Asia–Pacific, Latin America and the rest of the world

	1999			2008			Employment change 1999–2008 (%)
	Labour costs ($ million)	Employment (million)	Average employee costs ($ thousand)	Labour costs ($ million)	Employment (million)	Average employee costs ($ thousand)	
US parent	1,104	23.0	48	1,373	21.0	65	–8.7
Foreign							
Europe	153	3.5	43	257	4.2	61	19
Asia–Pacific	41	1.5	27	78	2.6	29	74
Of which China	2	0.3	7	9	0.8	11	207
Latin America	24	1.5	16	40	1.9	21	26
Rest of world	37	1.2	31	64	1.3	48	12
Total	255	7.8	33	438	10.1	43	30

Source: Bureau of Economic Analysis.

Thus adjustments to profits and asset values were made to narrow the difference. An alternative approach is to employ the cost structure and return on assets approach described in Table 7.2 to reveal whether there are differences between US parents and their foreign affiliates in terms of surplus and return on assets employed.

We start by deducting all external costs from total income to estimate the value retention rate in sales for both US parent companies and foreign affiliates and this is shown in Figure 7.7. This figure reveals that US foreign affiliates retain 4–5 per cent less value from their total income relative to US parent companies, and this suggests that the off-shore operations of US parent firms tend to out-source a greater share of their total financial value chain. However, as Figure 7.8 reveals, US overseas affiliates operate with a lower share of labour cost in sales revenue and, although US parent firms are reducing employment cost in sales from 19 to 15 per cent, foreign affiliates have reduced labour costs from 11 to 9 per cent of total income. The net result is that US foreign affiliates out-source a larger share of their financial value chains but operate with lower labour costs in total revenue, and this compensates to restore the cash surplus margin, where:

Cash surplus margin = total sales − (external costs + internal labour costs).

This analysis of the financial operating ratios of US parent companies and their majority owned foreign affiliates reveals more similarity than difference when it comes to the bottom line cash surplus margin (cash in sales) (see Figure 7.9). However, deconstructing the bottom line cash surplus margin into external and internal employment costs reveals differences between the parent and foreign affiliate (see Figure 7.10). US industry foreign affiliates operate with higher shares of external costs but lower shares of internal labour cost in total income compared with their US parents. In the final section we reveal the extent to which US

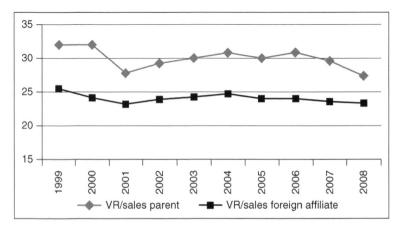

FIGURE 7.7 US goods-producing firms: value retention rate in sales (%).

Source: Bureau of Economic Analysis.

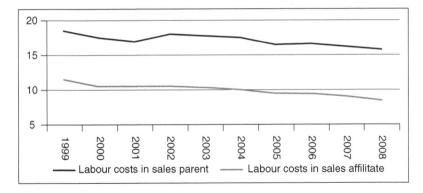

FIGURE 7.8 US parent and foreign affiliate labour costs in sales (%).

Source: Bureau of Economic Analysis.

majority owned foreign affiliates have actually delivered a higher return on assets, a key shareholder value performance metric.

The financial ratio of cash to assets employed shown in Figure 7.10 again reveals more similarity than difference between the US parent and foreign affiliates.[10] This, we argue, reveals the difficulty in translating strategic interventions into both cost reduction (for price competitiveness) and a higher return on assets for shareholder value simultaneously. To explore how these contradictions play out, we employ another company case, that of Molex Inc. A NASDAQ quoted company established in 1938, Molex conducts business for the manufacture and sale of electrical components, designing, manufacturing and distributing electrical and electronic devices such as terminals, connectors, planer cables, cable assemblies, interconnection systems, fibre optic interconnection systems, backplanes and mechanical and electronic switches. In recent years Molex has off-shored and out-sourced an increasing share of its factory space in overseas operations and especially low labour cost economies.

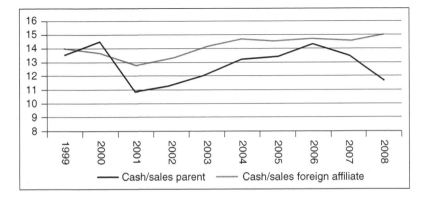

FIGURE 7.9 US industry parent and foreign affiliate cash margin in sales (%).

Source: Bureau of Economic Analysis.

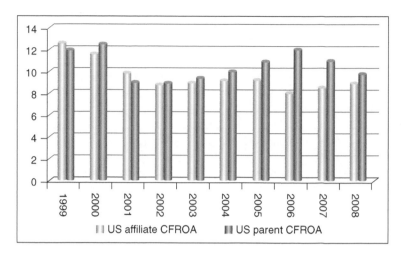

FIGURE 7.10 US parent and affiliate cash flow return on assets (CFROA) (%). CFROA is cash (value retained minus labour costs) as a share of total assets employed.

Source: Bureau of Economic Analysis.

In 2002 only 30 per cent of its factory space and 45 per cent of employment were located outside the USA, but by 2009 the share of factory space abroad had increased to 60 per cent and employment to 70 per cent (25,738 employees based in low cost regions out of a total worldwide workforce of 35,519).

The market for connector devices is competitive and fragmented, with the top ten firms supplying 54 per cent of the global market and Molex itself taking just a 7.5 per cent share. In this competitive market the struggle is to preserve margins when prices are eroding at the rate of 3–5 per cent per annum.[11] In these circumstances off-shoring and out-sourcing make sense because Molex, like many other US firms, is exposed to global competition, and is seeking cost reduction to restore price competitiveness. Yet the previous analysis of US parent and overseas affiliates suggests that cost reduction for price competitiveness may not modify cost structure for a higher return on capital for shareholders. Since the start of this decade, Molex has made a significant commitment to adjusting its geographic configuration by relocating operations out of the USA into China, Malaysia and Vietnam. Here we assess the extent to which this restructuring process has actually delivered stronger operating ratios for shareholder value.

For Molex, the period after 1990–2000 was one of relative stability in the key operating ratios. Value retained after deducting external costs was steady at 50 per cent and employment costs were also relatively stable, at 25 per cent of sales revenue (see Figure 7.11). After deducting both external costs and internal labour costs, the remainder, cash from operations, was also relatively steady, at 25 per cent of sales. The period after 2000 marks a break with the past as Molex more aggressively pursued its off-shoring and out-sourcing policy. First, the value retained by Molex out of sales revenue dropped from approximately 50 per cent to 40 per cent (prior

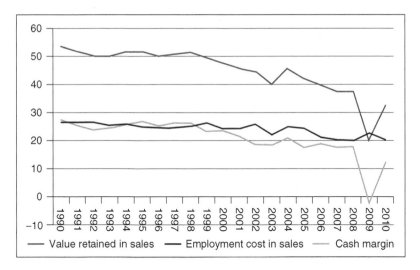

FIGURE 7.11 Molex Inc.: key financial ratios, 1990–2010.

Source: Annual Report and Accounts 10Ks, http://phx.corporate-ir.net/phoenix.zhtml?c=116886&p=irol-sec.

to the 2008 financial crisis and US recession). Second, labour costs drifted from 25 per cent to 20 per cent of total sales. However, this decline was not sufficient to compensate for the reduction in value retained, at 10 percentage points. The net effect of these changes is shown in Table 7.4, which indicates how the cash margin dropped from 25 to 20 per cent of sales.

It appears that shifting production capacity overseas and especially into China whilst accessing lower labour costs has not translated into a stronger cash surplus margin for Molex. Table 7.5 reveals that this is not exceptional. US foreign affiliates manufacturing computer and electronic equipment have increased their share of total sales relative to their US parents, but they do help to transform the cash surplus in the consolidated financials of both the parent and affiliate. Cash surplus margins are no different in the overseas affiliates than they are at home.

The challenge facing Molex and other US manufacturers is that off-shoring and out-sourcing are not translating into stronger operating margins and at the same

TABLE 7.4 Molex cost structure as per cent of total sales for 2000 and 2008

	2000	*2008*
Sales	100	100
External costs	(50)	(60)
Labour costs	(25)	(20)
Cash margin	25	20

Source: Annual Report and Accounts 10Ks, http://phx.corporate-ir.net/phoenix.zhtml?c=116886&p=irol-sec.

TABLE 7.5 US computer and electronic industry cash surplus margin (parent and foreign affiliates) ($ billion)

	Foreign affiliates		US parents	
	2008	1999	2008	1999
Sales	296.8	194.4	375.4	340
Value added	49.7	37.6	113.6	106.1
Labour costs	21.6	18.3	77.6	65.5
EBITDA (cash)	28.1	19.3	36	40.6
Cash surplus margin	9.5	9.9	9.6	11.9

Source: Bureau of Economic Analysis.

Note: Financial data for computers and electronic products taken from aggregation of ISI codes 3341–3346.

time balance sheet capitalizations are inflating ahead of cash surplus margins. The net result for Molex, after 1999, has been a steady fall in its reported cash ROCE.

In an earlier period, 1990–1999, the Molex cash ROCE remained steady at 30 per cent, but the period after 2000 marks a break with that past, with the cash ROCE drifting down and hitting 20 per cent before the global recession in 2008–2009. Molex's average market value (using the average of high, low share price during year) climbs from $2 billion in the early 1990s to $8 billion at peak in the year 2000, before tracking down with the cash ROCE to a market value of approximately $4 billion in 2010 (see Figure 7.12). Molex's off-shoring and out-sourcing policy reconfigured its financial value chain and network relations with its stakeholders to capture cost reduction and sustain competitiveness as price structures eroded. Analysis of the key financial ratios suggests that cost reduction cannot be equated with modifying cost structures and generating higher returns on capital employed for value creation and ongoing capitalization and wealth accumulation for shareholders. The weaker return on capital impacts negatively on market value and this, in turn, impacts on goodwill reported in the balance sheet accumulated from previous acquisitions. In 2009, $264 million of goodwill was written off by Molex, a sum equivalent to 10 per cent of shareholder equity. Untransformed operating financials have frustrated the share price and possible holding gains from treasury stock. Molex has repurchased treasury stock to the value of $1.1 billion ($22 per share), a sum equivalent to spending 15 per cent of cash generated from operations over the period 1990–2010. As at the year end 2011 its share price was $23 per share, limiting the extraction of holding gains that might have been realized if Molex's stock were, say, $30 and used to finance acquisitions.

Summary

In this chapter we have considered how focal firms in their business model might seek to restructure from off-shoring and out-sourcing and business combinations. The purpose of corporate restructuring, regardless of business model, is to modify stakeholder

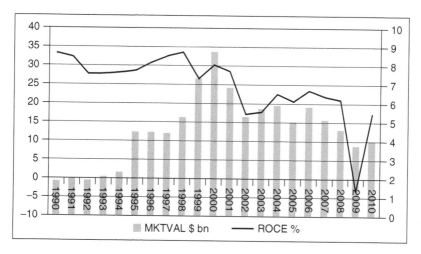

FIGURE 7.12   Molex cash ROCE (%) and market value ($ billion).

Source: Annual Report and Accounts 10Ks, http://phx.corporate-ir.net/phoenix.zhtml?c= 116886&p=irol-sec.

relations and adjust the information genotype to modify a reporting entities' operating financials. The problem is that the information genotype within which a focal firm and business model are subtended is complex, and thus financial transformation will not be straightforward. This is because the financial numbers embody complex and often contradictory forces where simple cause and effect relations are not operating (Andersson *et al.*, 2010).

In the case of business combinations there is the promise of cost reduction arising from synergies and rationalization, but the way in which financial transactions are accounted for is a significant element in the information pool. We note the impact of fair value reporting and how this accelerates balance sheet capitalization ahead of earnings capacity when the average US acquiring firm is required to absorb market to book values that averaged 3:1 over the past couple of decades. Changes in accounting standards also helped to modify the structure of the asset side of corporate balance sheets, introducing accumulated goodwill arising from acquisition. Accumulated goodwill is a new risk element if it is deemed to be impaired and injects additional volatility, which was not the case when a business combination was financially 'pooled'. Mark to market financial reporting encourages market value absorption on to corporate balance sheets, and so it also becomes difficult to identify a straightforward 'productive' tangible asset value creating process, because the financial numbers employed embody market value and the product of ongoing recapitalizations.

The struggle to maintain price competitiveness has encouraged adjustments to the global configuration of business models through another channel, namely outsourcing and off-shoring. In this chapter we have also assessed how this intervention adjusts stakeholder relations and the information network around financial settlements. Within this chapter our concern has been to distinguish between cost reduction and cost structure for return on capital, where accounting numbers can be used to reveal contradiction and ambiguity. In the case of US multinationals we are able to separate the parent company financials from those of their majority owned foreign affiliates. We find that, in general, US foreign affiliates are financially more disintegrated (relative to their parent) and this reduces value retained from sales revenue. On the other hand, US foreign affiliates tend to have a lower employment cost in total income relative to their parents and this helps to offset for the lower value retention rate. The bottom line is, however, that the average US parent and average US foreign affiliate deliver similar cash surplus margins and cash return on assets employed. This leads us to conclude that off-shoring and out-sourcing, whilst necessary to sustain competitiveness, may not be sufficient to transform financial value creating capacity for wealth accumulation and ongoing capitalization where cash surplus margins and return on assets/capital remain untransformed.

Finally, this chapter is all about the information pool within which business models subtend and how restructuring narratives promise to improve reported financials for shareholder value and wealth accumulation. Once we enter the prism of accounting, we are in a 'hall of mirrors' where it is often a case of 'now you see it, now you don't'.

8

US BANKING

A viable business model?

Introduction

The traditional 'productionist' view of the role of banking is that of mobilizing and directing savings into loans for financing investments into productive assets. In the process banks are managing the risk associated with a timing difference between loans made (relatively long-lived assets) and liabilities incurred in the form of deposits held on behalf of households (relatively volatile).

> Understanding the many roles that banks play in the financial system is one of the fundamental issues in theoretical economics and finance. The efficiency of the process through which savings are channeled into productive activities is crucial for growth and general welfare. Banks are one part of this process.
>
> *(Allen and Carletti, 2008: 1)*

The focus of the economics literature has been on two key aspects of banking. One aspect is the duration risk associated with the discrepancy between asset and liability risk and how timing mismatches can lead to a possible financial contagion. The other aspect concerns the classification of banking systems as either 'bank based' (e.g. in continental Europe and Asia) or 'market based' (e.g. in the UK and USA), and how differences in system characteristics help to explain variations in growth and economic development. Our argument is that banks are best viewed as operating within a particular banking business model (BBM) where market and non-market stakeholder relations have an impact on bank reported financials. From the mid-1970s on, US (and later European) banks have managed to disconnect their financing (from savings) through securitization, which facilitates the selling on of loans to other investors that raise their funds in the bond market. This process of securitization helped to disconnect the growth in banks' assets (loans) from GDP and household savings, thereby inflating banks' assets ahead of GDP and liquidity. Liquidity and possible loan charge-off risk are ameliorated by the need to maintain 8–10 per cent of equity funds in a bank's balance sheet to satisfy capital adequacy tests set out by the so-called Basle I–III regulatory agreements. The purpose of capital adequacy is to act as a financial buffer in circumstances where high risk assets (loans) become irrecoverable and have to be written off against earnings and thus also shareholder equity.

The banking crisis emerging in the USA in late 2007 running into 2011 had its origins in the expansion of securitization, which encouraged banks to move away from a 'retain and hold' balance sheet to 'originate and sell on'. That is, securitization provided a mechanism by which banks could sell on assets (loans) to special purpose trusts set up to modify the credit rating and risk-return model of bundled up mortgages. Investment banks and other investors drew upon fixed interest securities to help finance the purchase of these bundled up mortgages and thereby also provided additional funds upon which banks could re-lend. This process allowed banks to generate substantial growth in their capitalized balance sheets, fee income and interest income from asset leverage. The sheer scale of the increase in loans outstanding is clear when, later in this chapter, we compare the growth in bank loans outstanding to GDP in the USA.

What is more significant is that the process of 'originate to sell on' coupled with risk-return modelling and favourable credit ratings established a progressive disconnect between the balance sheet and operating fundamentals of the banking business model. These operating fundamentals are that liquidity is generally 'thin' and the margin between maintaining and losing solvency approval from auditors 'narrow'. This fragility was illustrated when, in 2007, a small fraction of US households initially defaulted on their mortgages. By 2009 this charge-off rate had reached only 2.8 per cent of outstanding mortgages, but it was sufficient to undermine banking profits and their stock market valuations and to trigger substantial goodwill impairments that in combination threatened the viability of the US banking business model.

The development of US banking and financial intermediation

The US finance sector's share of GDP gently increased from roughly 3 per cent in 1980 to a peak of 5.5 per cent in 2002 before gently falling off to below 5 per cent by 2009, and its share of employment in 'all industries' was steady at 3–4 per cent from 1980 to 2009 (see Figure 8.1).

Even though the share of US banking and financial intermediation (Federal Reserve banks, credit intermediation, securities, commodity contracts and investments) in GDP has increased the cost structure associated with financial intermediation, activity has changed significantly, and for the worse, over the past three decades. In the early 1980s, of income received, this sector would retain roughly 65–70 per cent after covering external costs. By 2009 the value retained within the sector had fallen to 50 per cent, reflecting increased out-sourcing and disintermediation of the banking financial value chain. This was not offset by a reduction

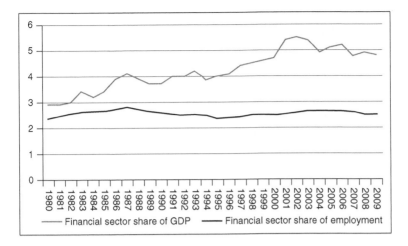

FIGURE 8.1   US financial sector share of GDP and employment (%).Value added is accounted for as Federal Reserve banks, credit intermediation and related activities, securities, commodity contracts and investments. Total employment is that for all industries.

Source: Bureau of Economic Analysis.

in the share of employment costs which accounted for a reasonably steady 30 per cent of total income. The combination of higher external costs and relatively stable employment compensation (employment levels remaining steady at around 3.2 million) in total income reduced the reported cash surplus margin (GOS in income) from 30 per cent to 20 per cent, a one-third reduction (see Figure 8.2).

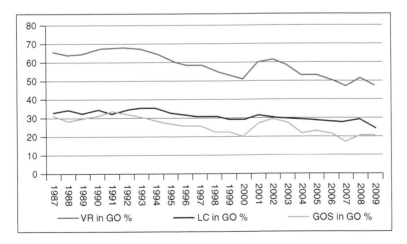

FIGURE 8.2   US finance sector cost structure. Gross output in financial services is net interest and dividends plus commission fees.

Source: Bureau of Economic Analysis.

It is well known that the banking business model is a low margin asset intensive activity and the US banking sector is no exception to this rule, generating a net income on total assets in the range 0.6–0.8 per cent for the period 1935–1980, with a step change to roughly 1.2 per cent thereafter and before the recent financial crisis. It is a business model that depends on extracting a surplus between interest paid and interest received and generating financial commissions on services provided and trading margins on own funds (see Figure 8.3).

From the post-war period up until the late 1970s, investor deposits into the banking system and thrift savings had been the main source of funding for extending credit to US households in the form of mortgage loans or consumer credit. The funding available for mortgages drifted upwards in line with the growth in national income (GDP) and savings. However, financing mortgages from such deposits was problematic because of the short-term duration (and thus volatility) connected with this type of funding. Using short-term deposits to finance long-term debt involved not only reconciling timing differences but also the added uncertainty relating to the inflow of deposits against which new additional mortgages could be raised. The Savings and Loan crisis in the 1980s changed the system for US housing finance from local and regional balance sheet lending by depositories to a national market based system of securities mortgage finance (Schnure, 2005).

Securitization, as we have already observed, involves repackaging and selling on balance sheet assets such as mortgages into a secondary market. Mortgage-backed securitization allowed banks to modify their balance sheet asset-liability risk exposure (and cost of capital) and significantly raised additional cash resources for lending to households. Securitization provided banks with the financial capability to increase the supply of mortgage funds to an increasing number of home-owning households

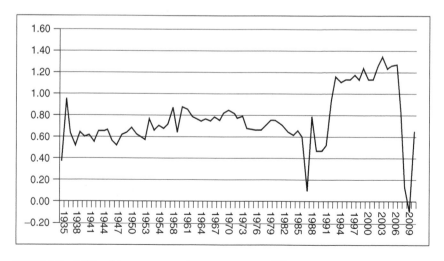

FIGURE 8.3 US banking sector net income on assets (%).

Source: Net income: www2.fdic.gov/hsob/hsobRpt.asp; assets: www2.fdic.gov/hsob/hsobRpt.asp.

paying more for their properties (Shiller, 2006a, 2006b). This break also coincided, as we have noted, with a change in US banking regulations and household demand for mortgage credit as the population of households, stock of housing and price levels increased. The US banking sector had operated under a 'retain and hold' policy up to the 1980s whereby customer deposits and matching assets were held on balance sheet. During this earlier period, growth in mortgage lending generally tracked the increase in investor deposits and thrift funds. The mid-1970s marked a break with the past because regulations now permitted banks to 'repackage and sell on' assets (loans) held on balance sheet into a secondary market. This change in regulatory framework established the foundation for a substantial growth in mortgage-backed securities, that is, bonds whose cash flows are backed up by household mortgage repayments. A secondary market would permit banks to sell mortgages they had originated to other investors to raise additional cash funding upon which they could increase the volume of mortgage lending. According to the American Securitization Forum:

> The first mortgage-backed securities arose from the secondary mortgage market in 1970. Investors had traded whole loans, or unsecuritized mortgages, for some time before the Government National Mortgage Association (GNMA), also called Ginnie Mae, guaranteed the first mortgage pass-through securities that pass the principal and interest payments on mortgages through to investors. (Ginnie Mae is a government agency that guarantees securities backed by HUD- and Veterans Administration-guaranteed mortgages.) Ginnie Mae was soon followed by Fannie Mae, a private corporation chartered by the federal government – along with Freddie Mac – to promote homeownership by fostering a secondary market in home mortgages.
>
> *(American Securitization Forum, 2003: 2)*

Altunbas *et al.* (2007) reveal that asset securitization increased bank liquidity and served to transfer credit risk off balance sheet into the wider financial market.

> First, asset securitization increases banks' liquidity while reducing banks' funding needs in the event of monetary tightening. Second, securitization allows banks to swiftly transfer part of their credit risk to the markets (including institutional investors such as hedge funds, insurance companies and pension funds) thereby reducing their regulatory requirements on capital.
>
> *(Altunbas* et al.*, 2007: 6)*

In their paper for the European Central Bank Altunbas *et al.* explore how securitization modifies the monetary transmission mechanism, increasing liquidity (even if there is monetary tightening). In addition, they observe that 'securitisation activity has also strengthened the capacity of banks to supply new loans to households and firms for a given amount of funding' (Altunbas *et al.*, 2007: 10).

Securitization thus allows a bank to remove and repackage assets that have built up on its balance sheet and sell these on in a secondary market, where credit risk is removed from the bank's balance sheet and cash reserves increased as loans are sold on. In turn, the reduction in both credit risk and increased cash in hand on balance sheet provides banks with the regulatory ability to raise additional loans for new or existing customers (Duffie, 2008). The availability of finance was no longer subject to monetary policy restrictions; rather prices and liquidity in national and international bond markets mattered. Mortgage-backed securities were sold on to investors that had varying appetites for risk, where sub-prime mortgage debt was blended with AAA rated mortgages and 'wrapped up' for investors. Bundling and blending products with varying types of credit risk met with general 'technical' approval because the process of diversification between high and low rates credit risk and wrapping it up into portfolios would both spread and limit risk (Frankel, 2006; Krinsman, 2007).

> With sufficient controls and the necessary infrastructure in place, securitization offers several advantages over the traditional bank-lending model. These benefits, which may increase the soundness and efficiency of the credit extension process, can include a more efficient origination process, better risk diversification, and improved liquidity.
>
> *(US Treasury Department, 1997: 7)*

The process of asset securitization accelerated from the early to mid-1990s such that by 2007 and before the onset of the banking crisis annual securitizations reached roughly $3 trillion per annum (see Table 8.1). For US banks the practice of securitizing and expanding lending capacity and taking advantage of the generally strong credit ratings associated with asset securitizations are, as we will argue later in this chapter, central to assessing capital adequacy and risk. As at the end of 2010 the accumulated balance of assets securitized in the USA had reached $11 trillion (see Table 8.2), up from $8.7 trillion as at the first quarter of 2008. Although the value of assets securitized outstanding increased over the period 2008 to 2010, the underlying credit rating of these assets has significantly deteriorated in the aftermath of the US banking crisis (International Monetary Fund, 2009).

At the start of 2008, some 87 per cent of securitized assets received a credit rating of Aaa/AAA or Aa/AA (essentially risk free and of high quality) but, by the end of 2010, this had fallen to 45 per cent and roughly one-third of securitized assets were rated as junk status (Caa/CCC and below). The extent to which the credit rating of securitized assets deteriorated in the US banking system impacts on the computation of asset values at risk. Banks asset structure is assessed on the basis of risk with scores of between 0 and 1, where safe assets such as government securities would have a zero weighting and riskier assets would be rated up to 1. Risk weighting and modelling approaches are set out in the various Basle regulatory agreements which have progressively tightened the assessment of asset risk in the banking system. However, US banks had a great deal of discretion in how they ran their risk modelling, and in the run up to the financial crisis US banks would have been, more or less, rating the risk of their securitized loans/mortgage stock at close

TABLE 8.1 US annual securitization issuances, 1996–2010 ($ billion)

	Securitization issuance ($ billion)
1996	661
1997	828
1998	1,431
1999	1,313
2000	1,021
2001	2,055
2002	2,718
2003	3,671
2004	2,649
2005	3,139
2006	3,241
2007	2,892
2008	1,298
2009	1,943
2010	1,711

Source: www.afme.eu/dynamic.aspx?id=194.

Note: Figures for 2008–2010 are converted from euros into dollars at year end exchange rates.

TABLE 8.2 US securitizations: balances outstanding and credit rating

	2008 Q1 (%)	2010 Q4 (%)
Aaa/AAA	81.7	33.7
Aa/AA	5.4	9.8
A/A	4	6.1
Baa/BBB	4.8	5.4
Ba/BB	1.4	3.9
B/B	1.1	6.1
Caa/CCC	0.7	15.4
Ca/CC	0.5	9.5
C/C	0.4	10.1
Total	100	100
Total value ($ billion)	8,695	11,074

Sources: www.afme.eu/dynamic.aspx?id=194; credit ratings: Moody's Investors Service.

to zero in their risk management models. In 2007 Lehman Brothers' gross leverage ratio stood at 30.7 (shareholder equity to all assets), but after adjusting for risk the net leverage ratio stood at 16.1, suggesting that the equity share of risk adjusted assets was just 6 per cent.[1]

Capital adequacy is the safety net of equity funding which is maintained on the liabilities side of a bank's balance sheet to cushion the impact of asset write-downs and damage to earnings capacity, and thus solvency. Capital adequacy is defined as 'tier 1' or 'tier 2' capital, that is, shareholder equity or shareholder equity plus preference share capital, and so tier 1 or tier 2 capital divided by a bank's total assets (that is, risk adjusted assets) reveals the extent to which it can cover its 'riskier' loans if these were to be charged off. In Figure 8.4 the ratio of US banking shareholder equity to total assets on balance sheet is shown for the period 1934–2010. This shows that very early on, the share of common stock relative to total banking assets becomes progressively diluted as retained and undistributed profits become a more significant component in the underlying accumulated value of US bank equity. Overall the value of equity relative to total assets is in the range 6–8 per cent for the post-war period up to 1990, and then it gently increases to around 10 per cent on average.

During the 1980s and following decades, US banks were thus able to expand their assets through a process of securitizing assets which also had the added advantage of not inflating assets at risk when credit ratings were also favourable. At the same time capital adequacy rates of 10 per cent on risk adjusted assets were deemed sufficient as a cushion against asset risk. The capital adequacy computation based on shareholder equity was reliant upon a continued expansion of retained profit rather than incremental injections of common stock. The combination of a low capital adequacy requirement coupled with 'low risk' attached to asset securitization meant that US banks could leverage their balance sheets to generate return on equity for shareholders whilst continuing to expand mortgage lending to US households.

From the early 1980s onwards, as asset securitization was implemented by US banks, they were effectively able to decouple mortgage lending from GDP (savings and investment flows), and this disconnection between that value of mortgages outstanding and rate of growth of US GDP is shown in Figure 8.5. For the period 1950–1980 the value of US mortgages outstanding grew in line with GDP,

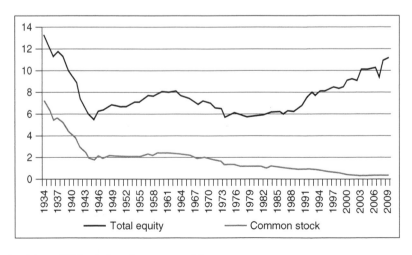

FIGURE 8.4   US banks' equity to assets (%).

Source: US Federal Deposit Insurance Corporation, historic banking financials.

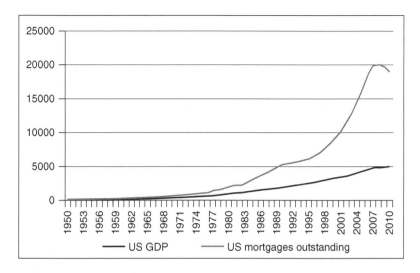

FIGURE 8.5   US mortgages outstanding and GDP nominal growth, 1950–2010. Index 1950=100.

Source: www.federalreserve.gov/releases/z1/current/annuals/a2005-2010.pdf, Table F6 Distribution of GDP and Table L217 Total Mortgages.

but thereafter changes in the regulatory framework opened up the possibility of securitization and mortgages outstanding decoupled from GDP. For the period 1980–2010 GDP grew at a compound annual growth rate (CAGR) of 5.5 per cent, but mortgage loans outstanding grew at a CAGR of 8 per cent. By 2010 the total value of mortgage assets held on the US bank balance sheets was roughly equivalent to annual GDP (Figure 8.5).

US banks, now able to move loans off balance sheet to investors, transformed the role of financial intermediaries in the mortgage market from 'buying and holding' to 'buying and selling' (Keys *et al.*, 2008) and thus, it is argued, transfer financial risk off balance sheet. And yet, US banks were among the most active buyers of their own structured products and, as such, credit risk remained in the banking system (Duffie, 2008). The increased distance between loan originators and the ultimate bearers of return and risk may also have contributed to diluting a lender's incentive to carefully screen and monitor borrowers (Petersen *et al.*, 2002). Borrowers were encouraged to fill in 'quick qualifier' loan applications and offered new products to extend the market, including adjustable rate mortgages (ARMs) and 'pick a payment' home loan deals which offered borrowing households the opportunity to switch from full repayment to a minimum-only charge similar to that for a credit card product. The nature of the US banking business model was such that, although the total value of mortgages outstanding increased four-fold over the period 1980–2008, the net income earned on assets was, as we have noted, structurally thin. Return on assets is thin because financial intermediation is about extracting net income from spreads and yields obtained on interest bearing assets (interest received minus interest paid) plus any fee income charged for services provided minus total employment costs and other expenses that are deducted from fee income. During the period 1980–2007 the net income margin expressed as a percentage of total assets held on balance sheet was very thin at approximately 1 per cent.[2] This margin earned on total assets could easily melt away in circumstances where a relatively small number of households default on repayments resulting in loan charge-offs at market value.[3] The factors driving up US household mortgage default rates during 2007 and into 2008 are complex and multi-faceted, but they include household leverage (high debt repayments out of disposable income), loss of employment, lower real income, negative equity and limited access to refinancing.

> Some borrowers may have taken on mortgages with high payments relative to income – either borrowing at high rates or borrowing too much relative to their ability to pay – because they planned to cash out equity, refinance, or sell the house in short order. Any such plans were likely thwarted as declines in house prices sapped equity, lending standards tightened and home sales fell sharply. Another group of borrowers with interest-only or pay-option ARMs have faced increases in their monthly mortgage payments as the loans have recast to fully amortizing. Other borrowers have faced job loss or cutbacks in their hours worked, and the resulting reduction in their financial resources has forced them into delinquency status. Another factor contributing to the rise in defaults and foreclosures has been a dramatic increase in the number of households with negative housing equity; that is, the combined balance of all of their mortgages exceeds the value of the underlying property. As of summer 2009, some estimates put the number of US households that are 'underwater' with their mortgages as high as 14 million or 27 per cent of US homeowners with mortgages in 2009:Q1.
>
> *(Federal Reserve Board, 2009: 9)*

After 2006–2007 the level of foreclosures on mortgage repayments increased significantly in the USA, reaching 2.3 million in 2008 and 2.8 million at the end of 2009, that is, roughly one in every forty US households (Krinsman, 2007).[4] Significantly a large proportion of defaulting mortgages were prime designated, rising from one-third to more than one-half of total foreclosures in 2009 (see Table 8.3).

> Estimates of loss severities, that is, the per cent of a loan's balance that is lost in a foreclosure, have increased significantly in the past 18 months and now are close to 50 per cent for prime, 60 per cent for near prime, and more than 70 per cent for subprime mortgages.
>
> *(Cordell et al., 2009: 7)*

As US households increasingly defaulted on their repayments these had to be charged off against profits, and data from the US Federal Deposit Insurance Corporation (FDIC) reveal that that during 2006–2008 the charge-off rate increased

TABLE 8.3 US household mortgage foreclosures (thousands)

| | Foreclosures loans (thousands) | | | |
	Sub-prime	Prime	Other	Total
2004	362	307	259	928
2005	406	295	190	891
2006	549	322	162	1,033
2007	871	564	157	1,592
2008	1,109	1,056	194	2,359
2009Q1	291	397	67	755
2009Q2	251	425	74	750

Source: Extracted from Cordell *et al.* (2009).

to 2.5 per cent for all real estate mortgage loans outstanding and still remains at 1.6 per cent in Q2 2011 (see Figure 8.6)

The previous US recession in the early 1990s increased the charge-off rate to roughly 1 per cent of real estate mortgages outstanding (value in 1990 = $0.8 trillion[5]). During the boom years and during the 1990s into the late 2000s, the charge-off rate remained a very small fraction of a per cent of total mortgages outstanding. Starting at the end of 2007 and running into 2008 the charge-off rate again increased, reaching a record level of 2.8 per cent of mortgages outstanding, which by this point in time had accumulated to $4 trillion. The impact of households defaulting on repayments resulted in a substantial financial risk transfer from households back

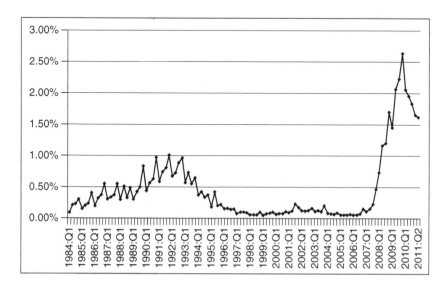

FIGURE 8.6   FDIC-insured institutions' net loans charge-off rates (%).

Source: Federal Deposit Insurance Corporation. See also www.federalreserve.gov/releases/chargeoff/chgallsa.htm.

into the US banking business model, compromising its viability and sustainability. Risk is amplified because relatively small percentages, in terms of total asset write-down, have the potential to completely undermine bank profitability, with further ramifications for goodwill impairments and market valuation adjustments. These in turn transmit risk back into the household in the form of a reduction in the market value of banks included in pension and mutual fund investments.

FDIC published in 2010 aggregate financial information for all insured US commercial banks (6,839 banks in total). For the year 2009 this group of banks reported a total net interest income and other income of $602 billion before employment compensation. Figure 8.7 shows the impact of loan charge-offs for this group of banks in the run up to and during the recent banking crisis. This reveals that in the late 1980s, when the increase in mortgage charge-offs hit just 1 per cent of outstanding mortgages (see Figure 8.7), there was significant damage to banking profits. Even in a good year US bank net income looked vulnerable; for example, Bank of America managed $1.7 trillion of assets in 2007, but provisions for loan losses in 2006–2007 reduced reported net income by one-third.[6] However, the significant jump in charge-offs running through 2008 into 2009, to 2.8 per cent on a platform of mortgages outstanding of $4 trillion, had the potential to completely undermine bank profits. From a peak of $186 billion in 2007, pre-tax profits of FDIC-insured banks collapsed to just $20 billion in 2009, with many banks now in loss-making territory after 'marking to market' the fair value of loans outstanding (Bernard *et al.*, 1995; see also FASB 157, 144 and 133).

The collapse in US banking profits triggered a substantial reduction in the collective market value of US banks, from an index peak of roughly 400[7] to a level of 150, a two-thirds reduction in market value (see Figure 8.8). As at October 2007 this group of financial institutions in the USA had a market value of roughly $2.5

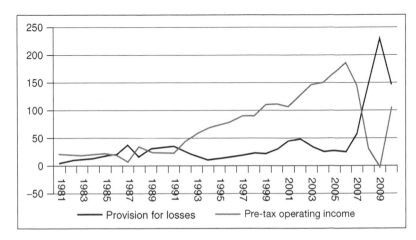

FIGURE 8.7 FDIC-insured banks: pre-tax income and provision for losses ($ billion).

Source: http://www.fdic.aov/bank/.

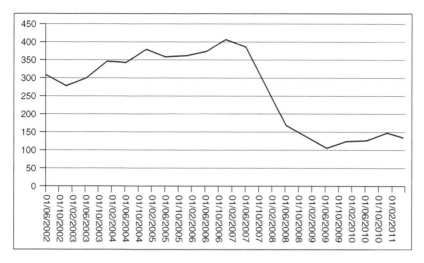

FIGURE 8.8 US banks' S&P 500 market value index, 2002–2011.

Source: Yahoo finance UK S&P 500 banking index.

trillion or around 22 per cent of S&P 500 market value. Yet by the end of 2010, the market value of these US banks stood at $1 trillion. As the market value of banks collapsed, this contributed to the reduction in the value of equities held by US household pension funds, which had, by end of 2009, depreciated by 18 per cent on 2007 levels, helped along by the banking crisis. In circumstances where the market value of a bank is downgraded, this calls into question the value of goodwill accumulated in the balance sheet of those banks that have been acquiring other banks and paying large market to book value premiums. There was an increased probability that goodwill would be judged to be 'impaired' because the carrying value in the balance sheet was below its market value.[8] In 2007, and just prior to the financial crisis, the FDIC reported that US banks held on balance sheet $450 billion of goodwill, equivalent to 40 per cent of total banking equity (capital adequacy) which is the buffer required to absorb loan write-downs and goodwill impairments. As US banks were writing down irrecoverable loans at market value, this triggered a collapse in the profits and market value of US banks and, in turn, required banks to make goodwill impairments.

Losses from loan charge-offs and goodwill impairments feed into the liabilities side of a bank's balance sheet to equalize assets and liabilities, but this will significantly reduce the value of reported shareholder equity. For many US banks this compromised their capital adequacy ratios: they were no longer solvent and 'going concerns'. FDIC records from January 2008 to November 2011 list 417 banks in the USA that had failed. The nature of the banking business model is such that it is fragile rather than robust, and at the height of the financial crisis US national and federal government agencies had pledged up to $3 trillion to underwrite assets and insurance-related products within the financial system to keep it all going.[9]

Everything is different for banks. Banks **love** high leverage. Whenever they make money, which is most of the time, they pay much of it out (to managers and shareholders), and they keep rolling over their huge debt, continuing to borrow more as they pay off what they owe. Equity is always a relatively small fraction of the total balance sheet. High leverage creates fragility because even a small change in the asset value can wipe out the equity and cause insolvency and financial 'failure'.

(Huffington *Post, 12 April 2010)*

The US banking business model is fragile, highly leveraged and employs financial instruments such as derivatives and hedge products to contain financial risk. In November 2011 MF Global, the seventh largest US bank, was exposed to a downgrading of sovereign bonds held in its portfolio. These speculative 'house' bets seem not to have been hedged and possibly also involved deploying segregated customer accounts to maintain liquidity.

MFGI held a long position of $6.3 billion in a short-duration European sovereign portfolio financed to maturity, including Belgium, Italy, Spain, Portugal and Ireland. MF Holdings made such announcement on October 25, 2011. These countries have some of the most troubled economies that use the euro. Concerns over euro-zone sovereign debt have caused global market fluctuations in the past months and, in particular, in the past week. These concerns ultimately led last week to downgrades by various ratings agencies of MF Global's ratings to 'junk' status. This sparked an increase in margin calls against MFGI, threatening overall liquidity.

(Forbes Magazine*, 11 September 2011)*

This particular banking collapse highlights a new and emerging dimension to the crisis in financial markets, namely, the deteriorating credit quality of sovereign debt, notably Greek and Italian bonds, which were being discounted heavily with ten-year Greek bonds yielding 26 per cent and Italian bonds over 7 per cent as at the end of November 2011. The assumption in the risk management models that hedged or CDS (credit default swap) backed investments will net out may also start to unravel as counterparties are unable to cover their positions. It is assumed that bonds held and offset with default swaps help to reduce risk, but if the business models of counterparties, often banks and insurance companies, are fragile, it is not safe to assume that the counterparty will be able to cover the debt where the issuer of that debt is in default.

We now turn to consider the specific case of Wachovia Bank in the USA, which was a victim of the financial crisis and became insolvent in a matter of months during 2008, as mortgage defaults combined with goodwill impairments to force its sale to Wells Fargo.

Wachovia and Wells Fargo: a rushed marriage

Wachovia Corporation was the fourth largest bank holding company in the USA, with balance sheet assets totalling £800 billion, but exposure to mortgage charge-offs and provisions for credit losses undermined its reported net income, market valuation and balance sheet equity.

Over the period Q3 2007 to Q3 2008, Wachovia reported increased provisions for credit loss rising from 0.09 per cent to 1.37 per cent of total loans, roughly in line with US banking sector averages (see Table 8.4). Although this is a small percentage of loans under management (1.37 per cent of $482 billion), it translates into a $6.6 billion loss provision which is large when net revenues were just $6 billion in Q3 2008. Overall, this forced Wachovia into a net loss of $7.6 billion in Q3 2008 after covering all non-interest expenses. Significantly, a large proportion of actual and anticipated credit losses originated in the Golden West Financial Corporation of Oakland, California which had been acquired by Wachovia for $25.5 billion in 2006. Specifically Golden West specialized in 'pick a payment' loans, accounting for $119 billion of the $482 billion of mortgages issued on Wachovia's balance sheet as at September 2008. 'Pick a payment' loans allowed the borrower to choose from four payment options: a minimum payment, interest only, a fully amortizing fifteen-year payment term and a fully amortizing thirty-year payment term. Of those taking out pick a payment loans, 85 per cent had applied using the 'quick qualifier' programme, with the result that loans in the 'quick qualifier' programme had varying levels of income and asset verification (Wachovia 10Q, October 2008; see also Keys *et al.*, 2008).

> Substantially all of the Golden West mortgage portfolio has consisted of a product, referred to as 'option ARMs' or adjustable rate mortgages with monthly payment options. The credit quality of this portfolio has deteriorated significantly in the current mortgage crisis.
>
> *(Wachovia Corporation form S4:C3)*

At the end of September 2008 two-thirds of Wachovia's 'pick a payment' loans

TABLE 8.4 Wachovia: loans, credit losses and net income, Q3 2007 to Q3 2008

	Loans net ($ billion)	Provision for credit losses ($ billion)	Provisions as % of net loans	US average (%)	Net income before goodwill impairment ($ billion)
2007 Q3	449.2	0.4	0.09	0.23	2.6
2007 Q4	461.9	1.5	0.32	0.42	0.1
2008 Q1	480.4	2.8	0.58	0.69	−0.7
2008 Q2	488.2	5.7	1.17	1.01	−4.8
2008 Q3	482.3	6.6	1.37	1.50	−7.6

Source: Edgar dataset, SEC Washington, 8Ks and company website,
www.sec.gov/Archives/edgar/data/36995/000095014408007959/g16268qexv19.htm.

were in the form of the 'minimum monthly payment' and so those taking out these loans were building up 'negative amortization', that is, accumulating unpaid interest on top of the original loan. Deferred interest on these loans amounted to $4.1 billion as at the end of Q3 2008. During the period Q3 2007 to Q3 2008, Wachovia increased provisions for credit losses from its 'pick a payment' asset class, and in a presentation of September 2008, company managers revealed that, of the $119 billion of outstanding pick a payment mortgages, they expected that a further $23 billion or 22 per cent would need to be charged off against income.[10] Wachovia's problems were concentrated in a mortgage asset class underwritten by thin documentation on the borrowers' finances and offered two-thirds of these borrowers a minimum payment 'credit card' style mortgage repayment plan. On the downside, this class of mortgages resulted in a substantial write-down in Wachovia's net income and reported net income per share.

As earnings per share (EPS) in the US banking system collapsed, this also triggered a negative response from analysts who marked down Wachovia's share price and hence its aggregate market value, which dropped from $95 billion to $14 billion (a loss of 85 per cent) for the five quarters ending Q3 2008 (see Table 8.5). This drop in market value would force auditors to examine any goodwill accumulated in Wachovia's balance sheet to establish whether this was impaired. Auditors were forced to write down goodwill amounting to $18.8 billion arising from the acquisition of Golden West.

> Goodwill impairment testing as of September 30, 2008, resulted in $18.8 billion pre-tax impairment, $18.7 billion after-tax as only a small percentage of goodwill is tax deductible. Drivers of impairment [included] declining market valuation and terms of the merger with Wells Fargo.
>
> *(Wachovia Corporation, 2008: 37)*

Goodwill impairments totalling $24.9 billion accelerated the deterioration in Wachovia's operating financials. Shareholder equity, already thinned down by a $20.5 billion programme of share buy-backs (1990–2007), was further eroded by the goodwill impairment charge lodged in the accounts in Q3 2008.

At the end of the period covered in Table 8.6 the collapse of Wachovia's financials and reduction of market value coincided with disclosures by the bank's man-

TABLE 8.5 Wachovia: market value Q3 2007 to Q3 2008 ($ billion)

	Market value ($ billion)	*Index*
2007 Q3	95.3	100.0
2007 Q4	75.3	79.0
2008 Q1	53.8	56.4
2008 Q2	33.5	35.2
2008 Q3	14.1	14.7

Source: www.sec.gov/Archives/edgar/data/36995/000095014408007959/g16268qexv19.htm.

agement that liquidity was strained and the bank had limited unencumbered assets upon which it could raise further capital to sustain margin calls. Without a rescue deal, it would go into liquidation and holders of common stock 'would likely receive no material value'. At the start of October 2008 Wells Fargo agreed to purchase Wachovia after hasty negotiations. The advisers to the deal, Perella Weinberg, had little time to conduct due diligence on behalf of investors as this extract from the S-4 (merger) documentation reveals.

> Diligence of Wells Fargo was limited to publicly available information, including publicly available estimates of certain research analysts covering Wells Fargo, and did not include discussions with management or represent-atives of Wells Fargo or other diligence that it would customarily conduct in connection with preparing a fairness opinion (S4:C3).
>
> *(Wachovia Corporation form S4:C3)*

In fact the deal was pushed through so quickly that Perella Weinberg sought advice and reassurance as to the quality of Wells Fargo's balance sheet from Wachovia senior management.

> Perella Weinberg is not an expert in the valuation of loan or mortgage port-folios or securities relating to loan or mortgage portfolios, or allowances for losses with respect thereto, and accordingly, did not evaluate the same with respect to Wachovia or Wells Fargo, and assumed, with the consent of Wachovia's board of directors, that Wells Fargo's allowances for such losses were adequate to cover all such losses.
>
> *((Wachovia Corporation form S4:C3)*
> *https://www.wachovia.com/common_files/*
> *WB_WF_Proxy_Statement_Prospectus.pdf)*

The Wells Fargo S-4 documentation provided to its investors information on the proposed merger between the two companies and it reveals the cost of acquiring Wachovia to be $24.5 billion, that is, the cost of acquiring the market value of

TABLE 8.6 Wachovia: net loss after goodwill impairment ($ billion)

	Income	Net income before goodwill impairment	Goodwill impairment ($ billion)	Net income/loss	Total Equity
2007 Q3	7.5	2.6	—	2.6	70.1
2007 Q4	7.4	0.1	—	0.1	76.9
2008 Q1	7.6	−0.7	—	−0.7	78.0
2008 Q2	7.5	−4.8	6.1	−10.8	75.1
2008 Q3	5.8	−7.6	18.8	−26.4	50.0

Source: www.wachovia.com/inside/page/0,,133_205_300,00.html.

outstanding share capital and preferred stock. The fair value of Wachovia's assets had been assessed at just $10 billion, that is, the book value of equity ($50 billion) now reduced by a further $40 billion in respect of anticipated future charge-offs of non-performing loans. (See Table 8.7.)

In a short space of time Wachovia's financial stability had been compromised by a relatively small deterioration in percentage of assets charged off when households defaulted on their repayments. Wachovia was a victim of a banking business model that relied on thin margin trades and leverage where the compounding effect of a collapse in net earnings, market value and goodwill write-downs undermined shareholder equity (capital adequacy), and in these circumstances the bank was also no longer a going concern as far as the auditors were concerned.

Summary

The US financial sector, which includes banking and financial intermediation, has increased its share of US GDP from 3 per cent to 5 per cent since the 1980s, but it has not transformed financial operating ratios as external costs increased and labour costs held the line as a share of gross output. This lack of financial transformation in terms of share of national income and cost structure can be contrasted with this sector's ability to grow its balance sheet. This decoupling of the value of banking assets from GDP and household savings was the result of regulatory change which permitted banks to sell assets to investors to raise additional funding – a process of asset securitization. The transformation of balance sheet leverage also has a lot to do with the computation of risk embodied in banking assets (loans) made to consumers. In circumstances where a bank can claim a smaller proportion of its assets base as 'at risk', the more it can leverage its assets (loans) relative to shareholder equity. Asset securitization that blends AAA with CCC rated loans involves a diversification of risk, and prior to the US banking crisis had been treated by credit rating agencies favourably in terms of their rating of such assets. With a strong credit rating, banks are then able to justify a larger proportion of their assets as being 'not at risk' and not included in their capital adequacy calculations.

TABLE 8.7 Extract from Wells Fargo S-4 purchase cost of Wachovia ($ billion)

	As at 30 September 2008 ($ billion)
Purchase price of shares	14.7
Preferred stock acquired	9.8
Purchase consideration	24.5
Of which: goodwill	(14.5)
Fair value of assets	10.0

Source: http://www.sec.gov/Archives/edgar/data/36995/000095014406006815/g01713a1sv4za.htm.

Note: Wachovia equity value as at 30 September 2008 was $50 billion and expected future loan losses totalled $40 billion.

As household default rates on mortgages outstanding increased into 2008, a relatively small increase in charge-offs had a significant negative impact on banks' reported net income margins which were thin, at just 1 per cent of assets employed, before the financial crisis. The immediate impact of a collapse in reported profits was a two-thirds reduction in US banks' market valuations and the triggering of goodwill impairments. The combination of loan charge-off and goodwill write-downs severely damaged the value of shareholder equity, forcing many banks to breach their capital adequacy ratios. It might have been possible to find an 'equity' cure, that is, raise additional funds from private equity investors, but given the extent of the collapse in banking share prices, this was a difficult proposition at the time. The outcome of government bailouts to maintain the banking business model has been a series of regulatory and policy adjustments. The recent Dodd–Frank Act (2010) takes a 'macro-prudential' approach to US banking, treating it more like a business model within which there is both inter-connectedness and systemic risk transfer, introducing new forms of corporate governance, limiting the extent to which banks can transfer risk through securi-tization, and imposing restrictions on the use of own funds for trading purposes and external restrictions on banks' corporate policy if this is deemed to unsettle macro-prudential conditions.

> The analysis of risks from a systemic perspective, not just from the perspec-tive of an individual firm, is the hallmark of macro-prudential regulation and supervision. And the remedies that might emerge from such an analysis could well be more far-reaching and more structural in nature than simply requir-ing a few firms to modify their funding patterns.
>
> *(Bernanke, 2011: 2)*

In a presentation to the 47th Annual Conference on Bank Structure and Competi-tion, Bernanke observed how, in practice, this macro-prudential business model framework of analysis is being worked through.

> The recent Comprehensive Capital Analysis and Review, in which the Fed-eral Reserve evaluated the internal capital planning processes and shareholder distribution requests of the 19 largest bank holding companies, is an example of a horizontal assessment with a macro-prudential approach. In the wake of the crisis, banks' capital payouts had been kept to a minimum. As banks' earnings and capital positions continued to improve in 2010, however, some firms sought approval to increase dividends or restart share repurchase pro-grams. The simultaneous assessment of the payout requests in the capital review allowed the Federal Reserve, working through the LISCC, to evalu-ate not only the conditions of individual banks but also the potential implica-tions of capital payouts for aggregate credit extension and the sustainability of the economic recovery.
>
> *(Bernanke, 2011: 5)*

The top nineteen US banks, under annual review and stress tested by the Federal Reserve Board in terms of their capital adequacy, account for two-thirds of the assets and more than half of the loans outstanding in the US banking system.[11] One significant outcome of these stress tests is the Federal Reserve Board's insistence that banks need, as a priority, to strengthen their capital base (equity) rather than distribute dividends or fund share buy-backs that weaken equity. At the start of 2011 the rate at which household loans were being charged off had fallen from 2.8 per cent to 1.65 per cent, reducing annual loan losses charged against income from $185 billion to $36 billion. However, the share of outstanding mortgages in default, that is, those overdue thirty days or more and still accruing interest as well as those in non-accrual status, remains at more than 10 per cent for residential mortgages, almost three times higher than in the previous recession of 1991.

The banking business model is still fundamentally fragile because it feeds off financial leverage to generate a healthy return on equity and market value for shareholders. This is reinforced by regulatory arrangements and risk models surrounding the computation of capital adequacy, firebreaks and loss absorbing cushions. The higher the loss absorbing cushion, the lower will be the financial leverage possible on shareholder equity. Banks will thus seek out new forms of counterparty transaction to take risk off balance sheet or improve risk adjusted capital weightings because this boosts the leverage capacity of shareholder equity. The banking business model which captures the financial interest and wealth allocations of households is precariously balanced against the financial interests and calculations of shareholders and their need for leverage. The recent Turner report on UK banking sums up the tensions and conflicts inherent in the banking business model.

> The essential challenge is therefore that the accounting regime which makes sense from the point of view of idiosyncratic risk and of the shareholders of banks operating in stable conditions is quite different from that which may be optimal when viewed from a regulatory, systemic and macro-prudential viewpoint. These different perspectives have in the past been the cause of some disagreements between accounting bodies and regulators on the appropriate way forward.
>
> *(Financial Services Authority, 2009).*

The difficulty and challenge facing the banking business model is that it is also tied into counterparty arrangements and it is with the quality of these extra-banking business models that we should also be concerned. We have previously argued that the central government business model is highly leveraged and banks are purchasers of sovereign debt which is tradable. The current crisis over quality of Greek and Italian sovereign bonds reflects the difficulty of assuming that counterparties in other business models are risk free. A report issued by Standard and Poor's on BICRAs (Banking Industry Country Risk Assessments) observed in 2011:[12]

The results of our review highlight the increased risks for some banking systems since we first published BICRAs in 2006. In our view, banks in Western Europe and North America are more vulnerable, mainly because of the continued repercussions of financial market turmoil and, in the case of Europe, sovereign distress. From this perspective, the heightening of banking industry risks in GIIPS (Greece, Ireland, Italy, Portugal, and Spain) is important.

The next chapter considers the development of the private equity business model (PEBM), which is also highly leveraged and wired into the banking business model as a recipient of debt finance.

9

THE PRIVATE EQUITY BUSINESS MODEL

Leveraged and fragile

Introduction

In this chapter we explore the extent to which the private equity business model (PEBM) is robust or fragile. The PEBM is driven by financial leverage because it depends upon high levels of debt to equity funding to finance the acquisition of target firms. Once a firm is acquired by a private equity partnership, it is subject to a turnaround strategy to boost return on capital and thereby generate a higher market valuation from analysts. In circumstances where the value of an acquired firm (asset) inflates, it can be sold on so that the debt can be repaid and the remaining surplus returned to the private equity limited and senior partners. During the 1990s the emergence of the private equity business model promised sparkling returns, well above the benchmark internal rate of return (IRRs) for equity investors.

In this chapter we outline the growth and development of the PEBM in terms of its funding and how the business model operates to generate financial leveraged returns for equity investors. We also use the case of Terra Firma, a UK private equity partnership, to reveal how portfolios of firms are acquired and financed, before considering how leverage is generated for private equity investors from mark to market accounting. We employ the acquisition of EMI to illustrate the difficulty in transforming an acquired firm's earnings capacity and realizing inflated exit market values which provide the return for private equity partners. Our argument is that PEBM is inherently unstable because it not only depends upon transforming corporate earnings capacity, but also depends on inflated stock market valuations and a liquid debt market with flexible covenants.

Private equity: it's all about financial leverage

In a leveraged buy-out (LBO), specialist private equity partnerships acquire firms with a large proportion of debt relative to equity finance, taking a controlling interest with a view to divesting at some future point in time. This type of invest-ment differs from venture capital partnerships in that the latter tend to invest in start-ups and take a less than controlling interest in the firms in which they invest. Financial leverage itself depends on how financial markets react to changes in man-agement control and the extent to which new management can transform corpo-rate financial performance. Where the market value of an acquired firm increases and debt finance accounts for a significant share of the original buy-out finance structure, it is possible to leverage returns on equity. During the past decade, before the onset of the financial crisis, the share of debt finance in private equity buy-outs increased to stand at a peak of 72 per cent in 2006 (*EVCJ*, 2007).

> In 2002 the average capital structure in a leveraged deal was 55.2% senior debt, 12.2% junior debts, and 32.6% equity, according to Fitch statistics. By 2006 the equity portion reduced to below 30%, senior debt had increased to around 58% and junior debt to nearly 14%.
>
> *(EVCJ, 2007)*

To illustrate the concept of financial leverage let us assume a firm is acquired by a private equity partnership for a price of $1 billion and this deal is financed with $700 million of debt finance and $300 million of equity. Let us also assume that the financial performance of the acquired firm also transformed is such that the stock market value of the acquired firm increases from $1 billion to $2 billion and it is then sold on. In this specific example, the leveraged return to equity stakeholders will be $2 billion – $0.7 billion (of debt finance), that is, $1.3 billion, representing roughly a three-fold return on the equity partnership's original equity financing of $0.3 billion.

Leveraged buy-outs are not new, emerging in the USA during the early 1980s and prompting Jensen (1986) to structure his agency theory of free cash flow around debt finance and leveraged deals. In this article Jensen argues that managers have a general tendency to invest in sub-optimal investment projects that often do not deliver a positive net present value (NPV). Jensen's argument is that managers should instead be forced to disgorge free cash back to investors who would then be able to find alternative higher return on investment opportunities. Debt-financed leveraged buy-outs force managers to distribute cash generated out of operations because they are under a contractual obligation to pay interest rather than discre-tionary dividends. Jensen (1986) is concerned with how contracts (between the firm and the capital market) modify corporate governance and how appropriate incentives would help direct managers towards maximizing returns to investors. Over the period 1990 to 2011 there was a substantial growth in global leveraged buy-outs, helped along by the expansion in private equity partnership funding (PEPs). The accumulated value of global private equity funding stood at $4 trillion in 2010 (see Figure 9.1) and according to Preqin (2011) 40 per cent of these funds are still to be committed.

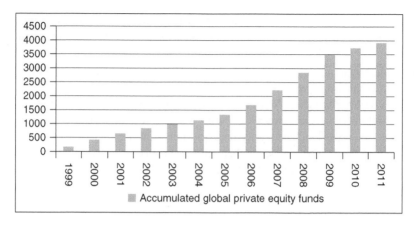

FIGURE 9.1   Accumulated global private equity funds raised, 1999–2011 ($ billion).

Sources: www.pegcc.org/education/pe-by-the-numbers/; www.thecityuk.com/assets/Reports/
Financial-Markets-Series/PrivateEquity2011.pdf.

Private equity: governance for financial transformation

Private equity partnerships modify the governance relationship between investor(s) and firms because the private equity fund managers (or their nominees) take a direct interest in managing firms to (possibly) improve financial performance. Acting on behalf of pension funds, insurance companies and high net worth clients, the private equity partnership, headed by general partners, manages a portfolio of investments (firms) directly on behalf of investors (the limited partners). General partners are paid annual fees (the management fee), usually in the range 2–3 per cent of the market value of funds being managed. They are also able to claim a profit share, often 20 per cent of the difference between the purchase price and the net value of a firm when sold (cash received minus debt repaid). The arithmetic of financial leverage is such that the return to equity stakeholders over and above debt repayments can be high and thus also the (possible) financial rewards to the general partners of a private equity fund that 'buys to sell on'.

In addition to reconfiguring the financial value chain (as between investors and the corporate sector), private equity firms also modify the corporate governance relationship with firms in which they have taken a controlling interest. Private equity partners become *de facto* owner-managers with a substantial implicit financial incentive to improve corporate operating financials because this increases the probability of a higher market value at exit and hence value skim, from both fees and the profit share on sale, for the general partners. This model of corporate governance is supported by Jensen (2002, 2007) because, he argues, it provides a new and more powerful model of general management aligning more closely with the demands of the capital market for shareholder value.

I present in these slides my belief, first argued in my 1989 *Harvard Business Review* paper entitled 'The Eclipse of the Public Corporation' that Private Equity is best thought of as a new and powerful model of General Management. I also summarize some important characteristics of Private Equity that contribute to value creation, how Private Equity generally implements Strategic Value Accountability (what I have labeled the missing concept in corporate governance) much better than the public corporation, and how Private Equity avoids much of the out-of-integrity gaming and lying that dominates the relations between public firms and capital markets.

(Jensen, 2007)

Buyouts help to reduce the number of badly-run companies because such companies are attractive targets for acquisition and transformation into well-run companies. The mere existence of private equity puts the management under constant pressure to perform well in order to avoid becoming a take-over target.

(Mayer, 2006)

The PEBM depends on the extent to which market arbitrage can be deployed to boost the acquired firm's earnings capacity (cash surplus return on capital employed minus cash ROCE) after its balance sheet has been recapitalized following the leveraged buy-out. Leveraged buy-outs inflate balance sheet capitalization ahead of cash earnings, forcing private equity managers to stretch cash extraction out of their acquired portfolio of firms. Transforming corporate financials, after a leveraged buy-out, establishes a basis upon which to construct new positive narratives and numbers for analysts where the expectation is that stock prices will inflate. The current financial crisis is testing the viability of the PEBM such that it is no longer on 'terra firma' but on 'shifting sands'. General partners, for example, now need to pay more attention to the management and governance of their portfolios, choose appropriate limited partners and be more careful about how and where they place investment funds. According to the World Economic Forum report *Globalisation of Alternative Investments 2009*, the current financial crisis has not dampened their enthusiasm for the private equity business model:

Most private equity-owned firms are well managed. The high average levels of management practices in private equity firms are due to the lack of any 'tail' of very badly managed firms under their ownership (that is, very few private equity firms are really badly managed) . . . Private equity-owned firms have strong operational management practices. Private equity-owned firms have strong people management practices in that they adopt merit-based hiring, firing, pay and promotions practices. Relative to other firms, they are even better at target management practices, in that private equity-owned firms tend to have tough evaluation metrics, which are integrated across the short and long run, are well understood by the employees and linked to firm performance. Private equity owned firms are better still at operational management practices. Operational management practices include the adoption of modern lean manufacturing practices, using continuous improvements and a comprehensive performance documentation process. This suggests private equity ownership is associated with broad-based improvements across a wide range of management practices.

(World Economic Forum, 2009)

Private equity investments promise high returns to equity partners because of the nature of financial leverage. Consider the example shown in Table 9.1 where we assume that a private equity partnership invests £1 billion to fund a buy-out where there is a typical 70:30 split between debt finance and equity provided by limited partners. If the acquired firm's market value increases to £2 billion (assuming operational transformation inflates exit stock valuations), then the return on equity after deducting debt finance has been leveraged from £0.3 billion to $1.3 billion, a four-fold increase in the value of the equity.

Private equity partnerships *call down* cash resources paid in by limited partners, deploying this equity blended with debt to buy-out target firms that are then subject to a process of 'transformation' by private equity management. Firms previously acquired are then sold to generate a surplus of cash which can be *distributed* to limited partners, where the cash raised from the sale exceeds debt repayments and the profit share taken by the private equity partnership general partner(s). However, Figure 9.2 reveals that over the period 2000–2011 the value of cash resources called down by private equity partnerships exceeded cash distributions in eight of eleven years. For the same period, we estimate that the value of *called* funds exceeded funds *distributed* by 37 per cent. In the period since 2007 and in the aftermath of the financial crisis from late 2007 to 2010, called funds exceeded cash distributed by a factor of roughly 2:1.

This recent difference between called and distributed private equity funds has been exacerbated by the recent drop in the value of global stock markets in 2008, with the decrease in the S&P 500 being 37 per cent, in MSCI Europe 46.4 per cent and MSCI Emerging Markets 53.2 per cent. This fall in stock market values triggered reductions in the volume and market value of private equity deals, thus limiting cash distributed back to limited equity investors.

TABLE 9.1 Private equity leverage model

Firm market value	£1 billion	£2 billion
Private buy-out		
Debt	0.7	0.7
Equity	0.3	1.3
Return on equity	0	4.3 times

Source: The authors

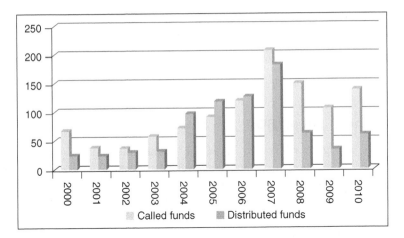

FIGURE 9.2   Global private equity called funds and distributed funds ($ billion).

Source: www.preqin.com/docs/newsletters/PE/Preqin_Private_Equity_Spotlight_October_2011.pdf.

Challenges facing the private equity business model

The growth and consolidation of private equity partnership leveraged buy-outs depends on a plentiful supply of funding in the form of low cost debt with light and flexible covenants attached. For example, loans provided to private equity firms might be 'toggled', that is, interest paid flexibly during the term of the loan. Banks would often provide covenant light debt finance to private equity partnerships for buy-outs and then securitize or collateralize this debt off balance sheet to further increase their liquidity and lending capacity.

> Along with the availability of cheap debt has come a weakening of the terms that accompany that debt. Documentation has become increasingly borrower friendly as covenants have become looser – and in one or two cases so far, non-existent. A whole new lexicon of clauses has emerged, with some of the terms trickling steadily into the mid-market from larger deals. 'Mulligan breaches' allow businesses to breach their covenants at least once without triggering default, for example. 'Toggle notes' have also crept into the market –these enable companies to turn off the cash coupon in mezzanine structures so they pay interest exclusively in notes rather than cash. 'Equity cure' has almost become the standard, in which the private equity firm can inject more equity into the business to prevent default
>
> *(EJVC, 2007)*

Investment banking revenues increased from underwriting private equity debt finance and charging fees for setting up deals. However, deteriorating credit market conditions and lower stock market values left investment banks with poor quality debt finance on their books, and banks quickly became reluctant to lend into private equity partnerships. The banking crisis during 2008 and into 2009 made it more difficult to secure debt finance, and thus private equity partnerships became increasingly reliant on equity drawdown(s) ahead of distributions (see Figure 9.2) to finance acquisitions.

Taking the 'L' out of LBOs

Moreover, as Figure 9.3 reveals, the equity contribution in buy-outs has also adjusted and in 2009 reached a level just over 50 per cent of an average buy-out package, thus reducing the equity investment leverage ratio from 3.3x (assuming debt finance of 70 per cent) to 2x (assuming debt finance of 50 per cent).

> LBO deals required far bigger infusions of equity – 52 per cent of the total purchase price on average in 2009, up from 33 per cent in 2007 and the highest level since at least 1997. In Europe, too, the average debt multiple dropped to 4.1 times EBITDA, from a peak of 6.1 times in 2007. The average equity contribution increased from a low of 34 per cent in 2007 to 56 per cent last year.
>
> *(Bains and Company, 2010: 4)*

Private equity investor returns deteriorate (see also Phalippou and Gottschalg, 2008) when recapitalization requires more equity relative to debt in the financing mix, with the result that internal rate of return (IRR) obtained on more recent vintage funds is progressively lower than earlier vintages (see Figure 9.4). In the mid-1990s spectacular median IRRs of 20 per cent on older vintage funds could be achieved, but progressively the median IRRs for funds of more recent vintage funds have moved towards zero, possibly driven by the fact that cash draw-downs

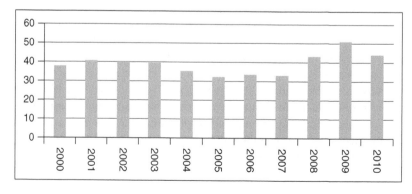

FIGURE 9.3 Equity contribution to private equity leveraged buy-outs, 2000–2010 (%).

Source: www.thecityuk.com/assets/Uploads/Private-Equity-2011-datasheet.xls; Standard and Poor's LCD; Probitas Partners.

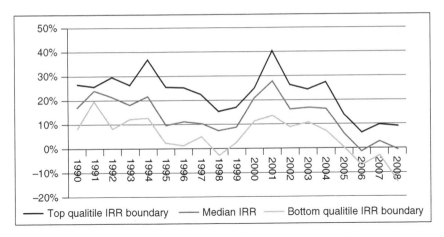

FIGURE 9.4 Private equity funds' IRR by fund vintage, 1990–2008.

Source: www.ocroma.com/tl_files/oc_clipping/ocroma-preqin.pdf.

now also exceed cash distributions in addition to the equity component in financing increasing.

Fair value reporting and negative leverage

Adjusting to and accounting for market values is a major challenge facing private equity partnerships, especially during the recent decline in stock market and asset market values, for example in real estate. The Financial Accounting Standards Board's SFAS 157 (FASB, 2001) in the USA, and its equivalent in Europe,[1] have, since 2001, required firms to adjust the value of their balance sheets to reflect market values. The FASB website summarizes the statement on fair value reporting and notes that 'this Statement emphasizes that fair value is a market-based measurement, not an entity-specific measurement. Therefore, a fair value measurement should be determined based on the assumptions that market participants would use in pricing the asset or liability' (FASB, 2001b).

Fair value reporting requires that private equity partnerships recalibrate their balance sheets to reflect the market value of their investments. As stock market values fell during 2008, the assets held in the balance sheet of private equity partnerships became impaired and holdings losses were charged against income which, in turn, is carried forward into the liabilities accounts of private equity partnerships, reducing the value of limited partner equity funds.

> Fair value is one of the hottest topics facing the alternative investments sector today. The ever-increasing investor, regulatory and accounting pressure for companies to focus more attention on valuation has coincided with the credit crunch and the most difficult economic conditions in years. The combination of a significant decrease in stock market values across most sectors, an increased

focus on debt values and a decrease in the number of transactions promises to make the current valuation process extremely difficult and is likely to mean large write-downs for private equity investments at the year end.

(PriceWaterhouseCoopers, 2008: 2)

Throughout the fourth quarter of 2007 to the first of 2009, the net asset value of private equity partnerships was in negative territory as adjustments were made to market values, increasing the pressure on limited equity partners to stretch the financial performance of firms held in their portfolios and dampening exit possibilities. To explore some of these issues in more detail we consider the case of Terra Firma, a private equity partnership, and its acquisition of EMI, which it included in its investment portfolio in 2007. EMI was an LBO financed to the tune of £4.2 billion in August 2007 by Terra Firma (Maltby Capital Ltd[2]) managed by Guy Hands. Terra Firma immediately set about presenting narratives about the problematic past and promise of a different and better future for EMI.

Terra Firma's buy-out of EMI

The acquisition in August 2007 revealed that despite having dedicated people and pockets of real excellence throughout the division, EMI Music lacked business discipline and effective leadership.

(Maltby Capital, 2008)

The Maltby Capital report and accounts describes the logic of this deal to investors, justifying the EMI LBO because there was significant scope for transforming EMI's financials and market value.

From the outside, EMI was a great brand with world-class assets whose strategy had failed. This report will detail the reasons for that failure, but particular factors are worth noting here. EMI Music had a history of signing great artists but had not adapted sufficiently to the changing consumer market for music. Additionally, it had grown through acquisition and deals into a sprawling organisation with a culture that in many ways had not been brought into line with current business practice.

It was unsurprising, therefore, that prospective buyers could see the significant potential for transforming the business into a professionally-run, modern music services organisation. Given the asset underpinning of the strong Music Publishing business, the world-class catalogue, the potential recovery in Music and an excellent debt package, EMI represented a superb opportunity.

(Maltby Capital, 2008: 14)

Terra Firma in its annual review (2008) reiterates the benefits to investors of placing their investment funds into this private equity partnership, principally their expertise in turning businesses around.

EMI draws on Terra Firma's experience in strategically transforming businesses, repositioning assets, driving operational change and enhancing cash flows. It is an asset-rich business with exceptional publishing and recorded music catalogues.

(Terra Firma, 2008)

It is clear that EMI had been operating in weak product markets, generating erratic profits and low cash earnings from sales (see Table 9.2) as music media shifted from CDs to digital downloads. Profits generated from sales averaged 0.4 per cent, cash generated from sales 9 per cent, cash return on assets 12.2 per cent and, significantly, EMI had accumulated losses of £2.5 billion before its buy-out by Terra Firma. However, even before the buy-out, EMI's management team had been adept at cost cutting, for example, reducing employment by 2,600 (2003–2007) and lowering employment costs by £100 million, although this did not transform earnings capacity. Some observers were clear that the cost-cutting exercises also damaged EMI's cost recovery ability.

Prior to Terra Firma's acquisition, cost-cutting under the previous management had led to market share losses to rivals Universal Music and Sony BMG. Terra Firma have continued along the cost-cutting path reducing staff number by 2,000 in the past 12 months and reportedly on track to make its targeted £200m savings from EMI's £700m cost base.

(http://news.tixdaq.com/2009/03/03/Terra-Firma-writedown-1-15bn-of-EMI-investment/)

As at March 2010, three years after the buy-out, Terra Firma management had not succeeded in arresting EMI's deteriorating financials, with revenues declining by

TABLE 9.2 EMI financials, 2000–2007

Year end (March)	Sales revenue (£ million)	Post-tax profit (£ million)	Net cash flow (£ million)	Total assets (£ million)	Profit to sales (%)	Cash in Sales (%)	Cash return on assets (%)
2000	2,387	158	247	1,806	6.6	10.3	13.7
2001	2,673	79	315	1,959	3.0	11.8	16.1
2002	2,446	−199	212	1,777	−8.1	8.7	11.9
2003	2,175	234	117	1,792	10.8	5.4	6.5
2004	2,120	−72	309	1,499	−3.4	14.6	20.6
2005	2,001	75	189	1,485	3.7	9.4	12.7
2006	2,080	90	188	1,544	4.3	9.0	12.2
2007	1,808	−287	7.3	1,122	−15.9	0.4	0.7
Totals/ average	17,690	78	1584.3	12,984	0.4	9.0	12.2

Source: EMI annual report and accounts, various years.

TABLE 9.3 EMI financials after the Terra Firma buy-out

Year	Sales revenue (£ million)	Post-tax profit (£ million)	Net cash flow (£ million)	Total assets (£ million)	Profit to sales (%)	Cash in sales (%)	Cash return on assets (%)
2008	1,458	−258	−28	6,430	−17.7	−1.9	−0.4
2009	1,569	−1,031	161	6,468	−65.5	10.2	2.5
2010	1,651	−704	250	5,484	−42.6	15.1	4.5

Source: EMI annual report and accounts. See, for example, the 2009/2010 report and account: www. emimusic.com/wp-content/uploads/2010/02/MCL_AR_09101.pdf.

20 per cent and post-tax profits collapsing (see Table 9.3). With revenues stagnant and profits under pressure from the increased cost of servicing debt, there was also a need to write off goodwill impairments and report losses of £1.03 billion in 2009 and £0.7 billion in 2010, reflecting the loss of market value.

In 2009, the value of assets held on the EMI balance sheet had increased by a factor of 3.65 due, in part, to mark to market valuation adjustments associated with the cost of acquiring EMI at its quoted stock market value (see Table 9.4). The difference between book and market value was accounted for by adjustments in the value of music and copyrights and goodwill that 'were required to be stated at their fair value in the financial statements of Maltby. This resulted in the recognition on acquisition of £3,411 million of intangible assets, relating to the catalogues, contractual arrangements with artists and writers, software, brands and other intangible assets' (Maltby Capital, 2008: 35).[3]

Market value absorption inflated EMI's balance sheet capitalization (loans and equity funding) ahead of cash earnings and immediately increased market value added at risk. To renormalize financial performance, Terra Firma's new

TABLE 9.4 EMI balance sheet, 2007–2010 (£ million)

Assets	2007	2008 (£ million)	2009	2010	Change 2007–2010
Music and copyright	306	3,553	3,660	3,086	
Goodwill	29	1,507	1,555	1,186	
Other assets	1,164	1,370	366	1,212	
Total assets	1,499	6,430	5,581	5,484	× 3.65
Liabilities					
Deferred tax	4	930	1,952	1080	
Loans	1,317	3,776	3,623	3514	
Other liabilities	1,329	1,179	798	1526	
Equity	−1,151	545	95	−636	
Total liabilities	1,499	6,430	6,468	5,484	× 3.65

Source: EMI annual report and accounts. See, for example, the 2009/2010 report and account, www. emimusic.com/wp-content/uploads/2010/02/MCL_AR_09101.pdf.

managers at EMI would be under pressure to arbitrage contracts with a range of stakeholder groups to release additional cash resources. In the Maltby Capital report and accounts, Terra Firma's management's strategic initiatives for the financial turnaround of EMI principally involved renegotiating settlements with executives, employees and artists.

> EMI Music executive salaries were historically very high, with some individual executives being paid at the very top of their peer group in UK companies. At the same time, contracts at EMI Music were often fixed over unusually long periods and guaranteed its executives generous benefits.
>
> EMI Music paid some functional roles salaries at double market rates or more, while paying more junior staff closer to average salaries. At the same time, EMI Music was overstaffed at these junior levels and lacked suitably qualified middle management.
>
> *(Maltby Capital, 2008: 24)*
>
> Much of the £200 million of cost cuts identified at acquisition and to be achieved over the initial period of restructuring relate to the salary bill.
>
> *(ibid: 23)*

With EMI now in private hands, it was possible to aggressively manipulate stakeholder contracts to boost corporate financials at the company, but there were good reasons to suppose that, if the future were to be like the past, these actions would only make things worse. Our analysis of corporate financial performance more generally (Andersson *et al.*, 2008b) suggests that boosting the appropriate financial operating ratios is not an easy or straightforward task. In any case matters are further complicated when private equity leveraged buy-outs inflate balance sheet capitalization ahead of cash earnings as they 'load the donkey'. Private equity investment and new management practices could not easily and quickly transform EMI's financials and this, in turn, negatively impacted on EMI's market value, forcing substantial balance sheet impairment charges (for goodwill and intangible assets) in the income statement.

In the 2010 EMI (Maltby Capital Ltd) annual report, the auditors (KPMG) in forming their opinion noted, 'The group incurred a net loss of £512m during the year ended 31st March 2010 and, at that date, the Group's current liabilities exceeded its current assets by £3,255 million.' The auditors also draw attention to the possible underfunding of the EMI pension scheme and possible liabilities that might arise, and observed that the survival of the firm was predicated on maintaining bank covenants on loans and securing additional equity 'cure' funds to maintain solvency and liquidity. The failure to transform EMI's operating financials and secure strong market value appreciation impacted negatively on Terra Firma's consolidated accounts, which have absorbed significant 'mark to market' losses on the value of the investment made into EMI. We now turn to the financial impact on Terra Firma.

Accounting for Terra Firma

> Terra Firma adds value through involving ourselves directly in the companies we buy. Working alongside management, we overhaul the business both strategically and operationally.
>
> *(Terra Firma, 2008)*

The private equity firm Terra Firma has investments in a range of firms including Annington, AWAS, DAIG, EMI, Infinis, Odeon/UCI, PNG and Tank and Rast. It is an independent private equity advisory firm set up in March 2002 by Guy Hands and some of the former employees of the Principal Finance Group of Nomura International plc. It was one of the first private equity firms to publicly report financials and the analysis that follows is taken from these annual reviews. In recent years (2006–2009), Terra Firma has drawn down €6.8 billion of cash resources from its limited equity partner funds and distributed €2.7 billion of cash returns to investors such that draw-downs exceeded distributions by a factor of 3:1 (see Table 9.5). From a position where the equity partnership fund market value exceeded investment by roughly 2:1, this had fallen, in 2009, to 1:1.

In 2008, we estimate that the value of the investment made in EMI was roughly half of the market value of investments made by Terra Firma in its portfolio of bought-out firms. The lack of financial transformation at EMI forced Terra Firma to reduce the book value of the investment made in the company by £1.4 billion over a quarter of the investment made and in line with market expectations about realizable value.

> Terra Firma Capital Partners Ltd. has written down half its £2.3 billion ($3.29 billion) investment in EMI Group Ltd, according to the private-equity firm's annual review, an acknowledgement that the British music company's value isn't likely to recover amid continuing global declines in music sales. Terra Firma took a charge of £1.37 billion, which it attributed to the 'permanent impairment in value' of investments – primarily EMI, which it bought in 2007.
>
> *(Wall Street Journal, 4 March 2009)*

TABLE 9.5   Terra Firma equity investment and market value at year end (€ billion)

	2006	2007	2008	2009
Equity investments	2.520	5.514	5.106	4.598
Fair valuation	5.745	7.794	4.489	4.953
Fair value to equity ratio	2.27	1.40	0.88	1.08

Source: Terra Firma annual reviews, 2007, 2008 and 2009.

Note: Equity investment is calculated as draw-downs plus returns minus impairments.

The regulations governing fair value accounting suggest that firms should reflect the market value of assets (including goodwill) and where asset values change they should then be adjusted within the financial statements to 'mark to market'. In the accounts of EMI (Maltby Capital Ltd), the value of assets written down would then also be shown as a holding loss in the income statements and adjustment in the value of equity funds invested by Terra Firma to recognize the reduced market value of investments made in EMI. In Table 9.6 we have extracted the profit and loss statement from Terra Firma's accounts and this reveals a €1.7 billion write-down 'provision for impairment' arising from the revaluation of the investment in EMI.

In an earlier year (2007) Terra Firma recorded a capital gain on its investments (assets held) of €1.039 million which is then carried forward into the balance sheet, boosting shareholder equity. This would signal to limited equity partners that their investments were accruing additional realizable market value over and above the book value of investments made. However, the health warning is that capital markets can go up as well as down, and in 2008 and 2009 holding losses from the investment made in EMI are recognized as a 'provision for impairment' (see Table 9.6). By 2009, Terra Firma had reported an accumulated net loss due to impairments arising out of the EMI investment of €1.64 billion, thereby reducing the value of equity partners' funds in the balance (see Table 9.7).

Terra Firma was not alone in writing down a significant level of its investment portfolio at this time. Candover, one of the first private equity firms established, reduced the value of its limited partner investments by 57 per cent in 2008, and the 3i Group incurred a 33 per cent reduction in investment valuations in 2008. Since that time the 3i Group has consistently underperformed the FTSE 250 group and has been under pressure to distribute more cash to its investors as dividends and share buy-backs to enhance distributions and offset its draw-downs. Employment levels have been cut by 40 per cent since 2008 and dividends in 2011 doubled to provide a 4 per cent yield to equity shareholders. According to Bloomberg, chief

TABLE 9.6 Profit and loss account, Terra Firma, 2008 and 2009

Income and expenditure	Aggregate 2009 (€ thousand)	Aggregate 2008 (€ thousand)
Bank interest	4,982	980
Foreign exchange gain	74	(9,142)
Equalization adjustment	(248)	—
Partnership expenses	(12,811)	(13,655)
Foreign exchange loss	(25)	—
Auditors' remuneration	(175)	(189)
Bank charges	(13)	(17)
Net income	(8,216)	(22,023)
Provision for impairment	(255,649)	(1,365,396)
Net result for year	(263,865)	(1,387,419)

Source: www.terrafirma.com/annual-reviews.html.

TABLE 9.7 Terra Firma balance sheet summary, 2009 and 2008

Investments	Aggregate 2009 (€ thousand)	Aggregate 2008 (€ thousand)
As at 1 January	4,598,641	5,514,289
Additions during year	762,290	454,469
Disposals during year	—	—
Equalization adjustment	222	—
Provision for impairments	(255,649)	(1,365,396)
Foreign exchange impact	1,327	4,721
Cost of investments 31 December	5,106,831	4,598,641
Estimated fair value	4,953,020	4,489,826

Source: www.terrafirma.com/annual-reviews.html.

executive officer Michael Queen 'doesn't anticipate significant asset sales in the next six months as the Europe sovereign debt crisis affects the ability of banks to lend to fund purchases and casts clouds on the European economies, Queen said today. He said deal making fell to a level comparable to 2003 and 2004' (*Business-week*, 10 November 2011).

In the current financial climate where capital markets are volatile and debt financing so uncertain, funding partners will become less willing to provide additional finance because they are focused on recovering return on existing investments and significantly trying to sell off investments and take the cash. The private equity business model depends upon capital market liquidity for the supply of funds to execute leveraged buy-outs. It was not clear, for example, with EMI how the cash margin could have increased by a factor of four in line with the increase in balance sheet capitalization when market conditions were deteriorating and where the previous management's significant cost cutting to boost cash (EBITDA) had also failed. As the financial condition of EMI deteriorated during 2008 and into 2010, the mechanics of debt to equity leverage slipped into reverse gear as the company ran up against debt covenants and the timing of loan repayments. Of significance were loans provided to Terra Firma (Maltby Capital Ltd) from Citigroup that were due for repayment in 2010/2011 and covenants attached to these loans that required EMI to maintain certain financial ratios such as the ratio of debt to earnings before interest, tax, depreciation and amortization (EBITDA). A Reuters communication in August 2009 observed:

> Now the recorded music unit, EMI Music — once home to Rolling Stones and Radiohead, needs more cash injections over the next eight months to avoid a loan default as the unit is not generating enough profit to comply with the requirements for a 950 million pounds loan from Citigroup, according to the report, which cites unnamed people familiar with the situation. The loan from Citigroup includes certain requirements for the ratio of debt to earnings before interest, tax, depreciation, and amortization.

> (*Reuters, 14 August 2009*)

In 2011, after a further desperate attempt to reduce the debt owing to Citigroup, Guy Hands accused the investment bank of inflating the price paid by Terra Firma for EMI. The lawsuit went against Hands and Citigroup took control of EMI, immediately writing off a further tranche of its debt owing from £3.4 billion to £1.2 billion, which means that Citigroup had incurred a total loss of £2.2 billion. But EMI is up for sale again. Possible buyers include Sony Corp., BMG Chrysalis, Universal Music Group and Warner Music Group, all of which have an interest in capturing EMI's music catalogue.

Summary

The PEBM depends on the supply of debt finance, loose covenants and inflating stock markets to facilitate exit (selling on) at higher valuations to leverage the financial return for limited equity partners. Mark to market financial reporting forces private equity partnerships like Terra Firma to recognize both holding gains and (significantly) losses for their limited equity partners as the market value of similar publicly listed firms improves or deteriorates. As stock market values fell during 2008, private equity partnerships were forced to mark down the value of their equity investments, increasing the debt to equity ratio and reducing return on investment for limited equity partners.

In the case of EMI, the leveraged buy-out by Terra Firma inflated balance sheet capitalization ahead of cash earnings, undermining shareholder value. It might have been possible for the 'new management' at EMI to more aggressively arbitrage product, procurement and labour markets to boost earnings capacity. However, financial transformation is less tractable than the sales pitch of the PEBM would suggest (see Andersson et al., 2010). The challenges facing the PEBM relate to aligning corporate financial transformation with capital market conditions: a plentiful supply of debt financing at low cost and opportunity for financial leverage because asset prices (stock market valuations) are inflating. It is a business model that is both fragile and volatile because productive transformation for a competitive economy runs in at second place to that of generating financial leverage from capital market gambles. It is a business model that is founded upon shifting sands not terra firma.

10

BIO-PHARMA

A maturing business model?

Introduction

Investment in the creation of knowledge-based assets through innovation and a high level of R&D spending generates both academic and political support because it is viewed as a significant element in maintaining relative corporate and national competitiveness, often summarized as closing the 'innovation gap'. Government policy documents and the academic literature identify the potential of the creative and innovative sectors to transform economic growth and national competitiveness (Barney, 1991; DCMS, 1998, 2001; Lazonick and O'Sullivan, 2000; Lazonick, 2008; Mazzucato and Dosi, 2006; Prahalad and Hamel, 1990). The general argument is that investment in innovation can strengthen corporate financial performance and transform industry and national economic competitiveness. Investment in knowledge development and commitment to high levels of R&D spending is key to maintaining competitiveness and closing the 'innovation gap'.

> In terms of private R&D, pharmaceutical companies in the United States also invest more resources than EU companies. Proportionally, companies based in the United States invest almost twice as much in R&D as their European counterparts. As a result, these high-technology enterprises can benefit both from their own higher R&D investments and the higher public R&D investments that generate a broader knowledge base from which they can capitalise and develop new innovative products and processes.
>
> *(European Commission, 2011: 422)*

In the USA an International Trade Commission report issued in 1999 observed that:

> As we enter the twenty-first century, the US pharmaceutical industry appears to be in a strong competitive position. Over half of the top 10

pharmaceutical companies of 1997 . . . are headquartered in the United States, which indicates that US firms are highly competitive with foreign companies. Additionally, NCE [new chemical entities] approvals are on the rise in the United States . . . pointing to a regulatory environment that is particularly conducive to innovation.

(US International Trade Commission, 1999)

A more critically reflective literature is concerned with how the demands of the capital market are modifying strategic priorities and corporate governance in an era of shareholder value where management and shareholder interests align (Froud *et al.*, 2002; Andersson *et al.*, 2007b; Lazonick, 2008). This literature exposes tensions and contradictions between the 'expectation' that innovation can transform corporate, industry and national economic performance and 'outcomes' that tend to be more disappointing. Lazonick (2008) argues that in a financialized economy the priorities of the capital market hold sway over the productive, because firms are encouraged to maximize their returns to shareholders rather than reinvest in innovative new product for the future financial health of their firms and the US corporate sector. Froud *et al.* (2006) are concerned with how, in a financialized economy, the role of management becomes that of structuring narratives that flatter the outcomes of research and development and corporate performance to maintain the confidence of analysts who, in turn, influence market valuations of firms on the stock market.

Lazonick and Tulum (2009) develop their general financialized account of 'downsize and distribute' more specifically in their paper on the US bio–pharma industry.

Since the 1980s the US business community, the BP *(Bio-pharma)* industry included, has embraced the ideology that the performance of their companies and the economy are best served by the 'maximization of shareholder value' . . .

It is an ideology that, among other things, says that any attempt by the government to interfere in the allocation of resources can only undermine economic performance. In practice, what shareholder ideology has meant for corporate resource allocation is that when companies reap more profits they spend a substantial proportion of them on stock repurchases in an effort to boost their stock prices, thus enriching first and foremost the corporate executives who make these allocative decisions.

(Lazonick and Tulum 2009: 4)

Froud *et al.* (2006), in their financialized account of GlaxoSmithKline, observe that the pharma business model has less to do with R&D and product innovation and more to do with defensive mergers, corporate restructuring and narratives promising research productivity that 'has not yet come through in the numbers' (Froud *et al.*, 2006: 11; see also Gleadle and Haslam, 2009).

In this chapter our purpose to construct an alternative account of the bio-pharma business model where we argue that this business model is degrading because focal firms are struggling to maintain earnings capacity (return on capital employed). The big-pharma business model depends upon the development and renewal of drugs under development and maintaining a supply of blockbusters that generate a significant share of revenues and strong cash margins. The big-pharma business model is driven by a significant financial commitment to research and development (R&D) and there is no doubt that the share of sales revenue allocated into the R&D function is large relative to other types of business model. This said, we argue that marketing and distribution expenses are also necessary to this business model when there is a need to sustain sales along extended distribution chains that feed into individual health centres and doctors' surgeries geographically dispersed. In recent years the big-pharma business model has come under financial threat from out-of-patent 'generic' copies sold at significantly lower prices than the previous 'in patent' drug. Cost recovery conditions have become increasingly unstable as price structures erode whilst at the same time big-pharma is under pressure to sustain the flow of regulatory approved products into the ethical drugs and over the counter (OTC) market. What we find is that to sustain financial performance, the big-pharma business model has entered a phase of intensive restructuring through corporate acquisitions and a process of outsourcing as the business model evolves and adapts.

The evolving big-pharma business model

The global bio-pharma business model is dominated by big-pharma that have the financial and resource-based capacity to develop new ethical pharmaceutical products that can also meet with regulatory approval from the US Food and Drugs Administration Agency (FDA). It is estimated that one in a thousand products that enter the testing process at the pre-clinical stage of development progress to human testing. Of this group, one in five is expected to obtain final approval from the FDA[1] (see Figure 10.1), and Pfizer's 2009 annual report notes:

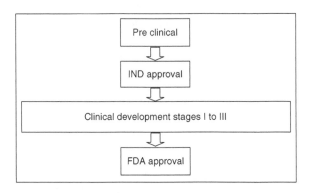

Figure 10.1 Drug testing process.

Source: The authors.

Drug discovery and development is time consuming, expensive and unpredictable. On average, only one out of many thousands of chemical compounds discovered by researchers proves to be both medically effective and safe enough to become an approved medicine. The process from early discovery to development to regulatory approval can take more than ten years. Drug candidates can fail at any stage of the process. Candidates may not receive regulatory approval even after many years of research.

(Pfizer, 2008)

Estimates suggest that the current total investment required to clinically develop, obtain regulatory approval and distribute to market a new drug such as Lipitor are $1.3–1.7 billion. In the past the financial rewards from investment in research and development (R&D) led to the coining of the phrase 'blockbuster' for a successful product and it is still the case that single products can command massive global sales, for example Pfizer's Lipitor, a cholesterol inhibitor, had sales of $12.4 billion in 2008, although they had softened by 2010 to $10.7 billion.

The global market for pharmaceutical products is dominated by the US, Japanese and European markets which account for roughly 70 per cent of total global pharmaceutical sales (see Table 10.1). The US market alone accounts for just over one-third of the market and it is with US firms that we are primarily concerned in the financial analysis and review of the big-pharma business model.

In 2009 five of the top ten global pharmaceutical companies were also domiciled in the USA with global overseas operations: Pfizer, Merck and Co., Johnson & Johnson, Eli Lilly and Abbott Laboratories. In the top half of Table 10.2 we disclose the income and expenditure profiles for the top five major US pharma companies and show these as a share of total sales revenue in the bottom half of the table. On average, in 2010, the share of total revenue deployed as R&D expense was 15.3 per cent, with some companies like Merck and Eli Lilly spending more than 20 per cent of total income.

TABLE 10.1 Major markets for pharmaceutical products

Country	2009 Rank	($ million)	% share
United States	1	300,748	37
Japan	2	89,865	11
France	4	40,575	5
Germany	3	41,275	5
Italy	6	26,857	3
United Kingdom	8	19,843	2
Spain	7	22,818	3
China	5	31,688	4
Canada	9	18,705	2
Brazil	10	17,403	2
Sub-total			75
Total market		808,300	

Source: www.imshealth.com/.

TABLE 10.2 US big-pharma financial profiles

$ billion	Sales	R&D	Selling and distribution	Cash EBITDA	Capital employed
Pfizer	67.8	9.4	19.6	17.8	126.7
Merck	45.9	10.9	13.2	8.9	72.2
Johnson & Johnson	61.5	6.8	19.4	19.8	65.6
Eli Lilly	23.1	4.9	7.1	7.8	19.2
Abbott Laboratories	35.2	3.7	10.4	7.3	34.9
Total/average	233.5	35.7	69.7	61.6	318.6
Share of sales (%)					
Pfizer	100	13.9	28.9	26.3	186.9
Merck	100	23.7	28.8	19.4	157.3
Johnson & Johnson	100	11.1	31.5	32.2	106.7
Eli Lilly	100	21.2	30.7	33.8	83.1
Abbott Laboratories	100	10.5	29.5	20.7	99.1
Total/average	100	15.3	29.9	26.4	136.4

Source: Company 10K accounts, Edgar SEC datasets, www.sec.gov/edgar.shtml.

However, we find that, on average, twice as much is spent on selling, marketing and distribution as is spent on R&D by the big five US firms. Big-pharma companies require intensive marketing and investment to maintain complex long and fragmented distribution channels to deliver sales volume in a competitive market. Although the big-pharma business model is R&D driven, it is also a business model that is market and distribution intensive. After paying out all expenses, the cash margin (EBITDA, cash surplus form operations) as a share of total income averaged 26 per cent of total income, with two firms, Johnson & Johnson and Eli Lilly, generating more than 30 per cent of total income as cash (see Table 10.2).

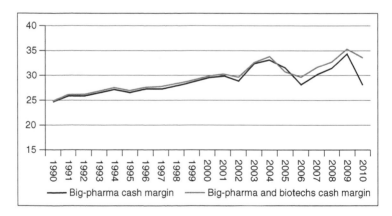

Figure 10.2 US S&P 500 pharma business model cash margin (%). Cash margin is earnings before interest, taxes, depreciation and amortization (EBITDA) divided into total sales.

Source: ThomsonOneBanker.

Throughout the period 1990–2010, the US pharma business model secured a stronger cash operating margin in sales, up from 25 per cent to 33 per cent at its peak in 2004 before reaching a cyclical 'plateau' at around 30 per cent (see Figure 10.2). Although cash margins have been strengthened from downward adjustments to cost structure, the underlying revenue trajectory of the US S&P 500 bio-pharma business model has deteriorated. For the period 1990–2000 the compound average growth rate (CAGR) of total sales was 8.8 per cent, but in the second period, 2000–2010, this had fallen to a CAGR of 3.4 per cent.

The slowdown in revenue growth (see Figure 10.3) could partly be explained by the financial damage caused when drugs are out of patent and the price floor collapses as 'generic' substitutes enter the market at discounts that can be as much as 80 per cent of the previous in-patent price level. For example, Pfizer's Lipitor accounts for $12 billion of sales, of which $7 billion is from US patients, but this particular drug ran out of patent protection towards the end of 2011. This prompted the following note in Pfizer's 2010 annual report:

> We expect that we will lose exclusivity for Lipitor in the US in November 2011 and, as a result, will lose the substantial portion of our US revenues from Lipitor shortly thereafter. We have granted Watson Laboratories, Inc. (Watson) the exclusive right to sell the authorized generic version of Lipitor in the US for a period of five years, which is expected to commence in November 2011. As Watson's exclusive supplier, we will manufacture and sell generic atorvastatin tablets to Watson. In markets outside the US, Lipitor has lost exclusivity in certain countries and will lose exclusivity at various times in certain other countries.
>
> *(Pfizer, 2010: App. A)*

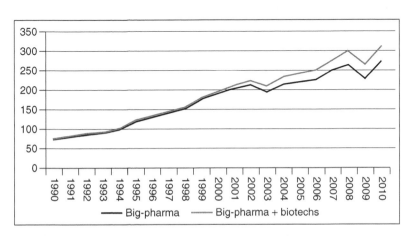

Figure 10.3 US S&P 500 big-pharma and biotech business model sales revenue ($ billion).

Source: ThomsonOneBanker.

Currently the Indian generic drug manufacturer Ranbaxy Laboratories (and up to ten other manufacturers) are awaiting FDA approval for a generic copy of Lipitor and a delay would help Pfizer maintain price structures for a little while longer. According to Michael Kleinrock, director of research at IMS Institute for Health Care Informatics, a generic copy of Lipitor could cut the costs to US patients by $6 billion (an 85 per cent revenue drop for Pfizer). He further observes:

> Over the next five years, the largest ever group of products will face generic competition, that's $102Bn of current drug sales over the next five years. Typically patients switch to generics very quickly and generic prices are typically 90% cheaper than the brand. This represents an unprecedented level of savings for American consumers.
>
> *(Chicago Tribune, 9 June 2011)*

The need to replenish the flow of drugs under development and also rationalize the spread of R&D across therapeutic areas is forcing significant restructuring in the big-pharma business model. It is a business model that is consolidating and reconfiguring as firms merge or are acquired, whilst big-pharma is also out-sourcing new drug development into SME bio-pharmas to spread the financial risk associated with creating and developing New Chemical Entities (NCEs).

Restructuring US big-pharma

The traditional R&D, manufacture and marketing driven big-pharma business model is degrading as NCEs are delivering only incremental health management improvements, for example reducing the side effects of previously approved patented drugs, whilst out-of-patent generics spoil existing price structures, putting additional financial pressure on big-pharma companies that must still continue to recover their heavy investments in product development and marketing networks. This is forcing big-pharma to adapt, restructure and consolidate within their business model. As John L. La Mattina, Pfizer's former head of R&D, observes:

> In major mergers today, not only are R&D cuts made, but entire research sites are eliminated. Nowhere is this more evident than with Pfizer. Before 1999, Pfizer had never made a major acquisition. Over the next decade, it acquired three large companies – Warner-Lambert (in 2000), Pharmacia (in 2003) and Wyeth (in 2009) – and multiple smaller companies, such as Vicuron, Rinat and Esperion. Over this time frame, to meet its business objectives (a euphemism for raising its stock price) Pfizer closed numerous research sites in the United States, including those at Kalamazoo, Michigan (formerly a site for Upjohn), Ann Arbor, Michigan (formerly a site for Warner-Lambert) and Skokie, Illinois (formerly a site for Searle). It has also recently announced the closure of the Sandwich site in the UK.
>
> *(Forbes Magazine, 8 January 2011)*

In 2000 Pfizer paid $90 billion for Warner Lambert and then in 2003 $60 billion for Pharmacia (a 36 per cent premium above market value). In January 2009 Pfizer made another significant acquisition, of Wyeth, for $68 billion and the expectation again was that the acquisition would cut costs through synergies in the consolidated company.

> Analysts expect Pfizer to be able to cut as much as 25% of costs to get 'synergies' in a Wyeth deal. Pfizer has to find a way to cut more than the $5 billion of costs in its own operations that it already has identified in order to maintain its dividend, say Deutsche Bank analysts.
>
> (Wall Street Journal, 23 January 2009)

Pfizer's major acquisitions, excluding smaller deals, have cost the company $220 billion, a sum roughly double its spend on R&D over the period 1990–2010 ($92 billion). The significance of these acquisitions relates to both their scale in terms of financial commitment and how cash resources are deployed to help structure and leverage these deals. On the one hand, some $52 billion of cash resources were deployed to fund acquisitions and a further $60 billion of cash used to repurchase shares for treasury stock which could also be used as part of the financing package for acquisitions. During the period 2000–2010, Pfizer's spend on corporate mergers was more significant than the funds deployed to finance R&D as the firm's strategy became increasingly financialized.

It is significant that Pfizer's acquisition of Warner Lambert was accounted for under the so-called pooling method of accounting, where the income, expenditure and book values (not market values) of the two entities are blended together subject to some minor accounting adjustments. After 2000 the accounting regulations in the USA required firms to account for their acquisitions at 'fair value' according to SFAS 157, that is, absorb the market value of deals on to the balance sheet. In cases where the market value exceeds the recorded book value of the acquired company, this is shown in the acquirer's accounts as 'goodwill on acquisition'. Recording the market value of business combinations increased Pfizer's balance sheet capitalization faster than its cash earned from sales, even after synergies and cost reduction.

To illustrate how the absorption of market value damages Pfizer's financial profile, we show in Figures 10.4 and 10.5 a range of financial indicators where a score of 4 is strong performance relative to all other firms listed in the S&P 500. In 2003 Pfizer's financial profile was generally strong with a majority of scores locating the firm in the top 20 per cent of the US S&P 500. Figure 10.5 reveals the extent of Pfizer's deteriorating 'relative' position with a number of scores now in the bottom 40 per cent of firms listed in the S&P 500 in 2009. The most significant deterioration relates to the expansion of capital employed (CII in these figures) as the market value of acquisitions is absorbed on to the balance sheet. We can also observe that there has been some loss of relative position in terms of cost structure and cash margin.

Over the period 1990–2000, US big pharma generated a cash ROCE that averaged a relatively steady 40 per cent, and during the same time period Pfizer's own cash ROCE was on an upward trajectory, reaching a peak of nearly 60 per cent in

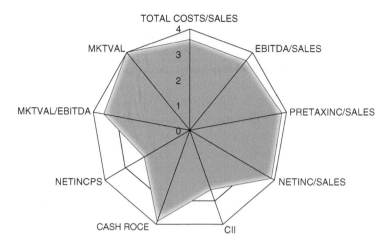

Figure 10.4   Pfizer Inc.: financial profile, 2001. MKTVAL is market value at year end; EBITDA is earnings before interest, taxes, depreciation and amortization; CII is capital intensity (sales/capital employed as long-term debt plus equity); net income is after tax and dividends; NETINCPS is net income per share.

Source: Authors' datasets.

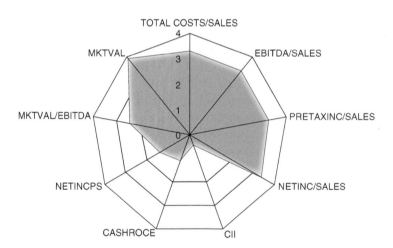

Figure 10.5   Pfizer Inc.: financial profile, 2009. For key see Figure 10.4.

Source: Authors' datasets.

2000 after the acquisition of Warner Lambert. Thereafter, the change in accounting regulation to fair value reporting inflated Pfizer's and, more generally, US big-pharma balance sheets ahead of their cash earnings, forcing the ROCE on a downwards trajectory after 2000 to 2010. In the year 2000 the average cash ROCE generated by the US big-pharma business model stood at 45 per cent and by 2010 this had halved to 20 per cent (see Figure 10.6). This deterioration in the business model's capacity to generate higher returns on capital employed has impacted negatively on the share of S&P market value accounted by the US big-pharma business model, which is down from 11 to 5 per cent (see Figure 10.7).

The US big-pharma business model is degrading as restructuring, forced by patent exposure, consolidates and reduces the number of firms whilst also forcing balance sheet capitalizations of those that remain ahead of cash earnings. Although the big-pharma business model may be degrading, we have to add into the framework analysis US biotechs (Pisano, 2006) as this group of firms have also emerged to modify the composition of the US pharma business model and are now listed in

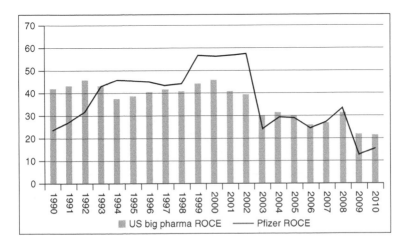

Figure 10.6 US big-pharma cash ROCE (%).

Source: ThomsonOneBanker.

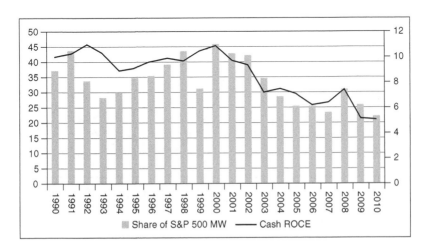

Figure 10.7 US big-pharma share of S&P 500 market value and cash ROCE (%).

Source: ThomsonOneBanker.

the S&P 500 group of firms. In 1990 US biotechs listed in the S&P 500 represented just 2 and 5 per cent of big-pharma sales and market value, but by 2010 these shares had risen to 16 and 23 per cent respectively (see Figure 10.8).

The biotech component of the US bio-pharma business model has itself matured relatively quickly, and whilst it now accounts for a larger share of sales and market value in the US bio-pharma business model, it has not helped to transform the return on capital employed. Biotech, in an intermittent fashion, tracks big-pharma cash return on capital employed (see Figure 10.9)

We have noted that another dimension to the evolution of the big-pharma business model is the decision, by large firms, to out-source R&D, product development and

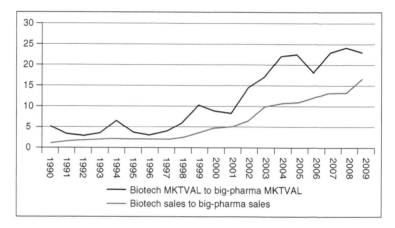

Figure 10.8 Biotech sales and market value relative to big-pharma (%).
Source: ThomsonOneBanker.

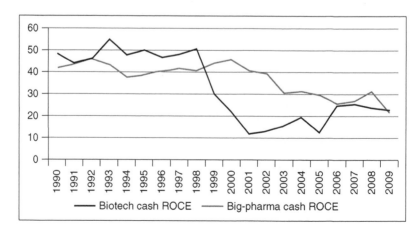

Figure 10.9 US S&P 500 biotech and big-pharma cash ROCE (%).
Source: ThomsonOneBanker.

financial risk into small and medium-sized enterprise (SME) bio-pharma networks. In the next section we consider how this has facilitated the evolution and adaption of the bio-pharma business model and establishment of new listed SMEs in the UK.

Out-sourcing and the rise of AIM listed SME bio-pharma

We have argued that the big-pharma business model has restructured through a process of consolidation and business combinations, but it has also recalibrated by out-sourcing R&D and the associated financial risk into a network of SMEs. These SMEs (or their NCEs) are acquired by big-pharma when they are considered to be an attractive proposition.

> Large pharmaceutical companies seek that next successful business model which supports both scientific innovation and speed to market. The recent economic downturn has hastened these efforts. Dwindling development pipelines, increased regulatory pressures and spiralling healthcare costs have put extra strain on an old and once-successful corporate model that supported the development of blockbuster drugs.
>
> The emerging business model combines continued acquisition of smaller companies with constant reorganization of the parent, to preserve shareholder value and provide the flexibility to capitalize on rapidly-evolving science, global expansion of markets and changing regulations.
>
> *(Nerac, 2009: 1)*

This reconfiguration of the pharma business model presented an opportunity for SME bio-pharmas which also receive direct and indirect funding from government, for example, with R&D tax breaks and funding via universities (McMillan *et al.*, 2000) to promote knowledge transfer and company spin-outs. In some cases, the commercial ventures established retain links to medical research centres and universities through a strategic alliance or else contractual arrangements that out-source the research and development work back to the university (Standing *et al.*, 2008; Robinson and Stuart, 2001). Venture capital (VC) partnerships and private investors, sensing financial opportunity, have channelled significant funding into SME bio-pharma. SME bio-pharmas are a gamble because financial returns depend on their capacity to produce NCEs that can progress towards regulatory approval in a world where regulatory approval is like winning the lottery. However, the financial returns to equity investors can be substantially leveraged if, for example, NCEs do progress along the clinical testing pipeline and achieve strong milestone reports.

The emergence of this new dimension to the big-pharma business model could simply be viewed as an extension of the productive purpose of the bio-pharma business model where R&D, innovation and knowledge development are put in the service of creating NCEs. From this productionist perspective the SME bio-pharma business model is adding to the pool of NCEs through a combination of technical ingenuity and patient capital (see Hopkins *et al.*, 2007) for long-run financial returns.

Alternatively, it is possible to construct a complementary financialized business model of SME bio-pharma, one that places emphasis on the tension between innovative possibilities, cash hungry firms, capital market liquidity and market value. In SME bio-pharmas, narratives about the development of new chemical entities take on added importance because it is often the case that these firms burn cash provided by equity investors. Narratives, for example, about drug development, trials and testing outcomes (milestones) act as a substitute for sensible financial numbers, such as cash earnings, in establishing a market value for equity (shareholder) capital. SME bio-pharma is thus a speculative business model that shares many of the characteristics of firms involved in oil, gas and mineral exploration where narratives about possible discovery operate as a substitute for actual discovery.

Achieving development milestones for products in the pipeline provides the opportunity to generate income from out-licensing to partners where the partner also takes a share of potential final realizable commercial income, royalties and licence fees. A specific product may have a number of partners financing its development, increasing the possibility that there will be a number of buyers wishing to make an acquisition further down the development pipeline. The problem facing individual SMEs is that they may have a range of potentially viable NCEs in their development pipelines, but they are not able to cross-subsidize because funds provided by partners are for specific product(s) in the pipeline. Firms may have cash reserves in their balance sheet, but these effectively become a type of restricted fund. The productionist model of SME bio-pharma attributes importance to patient investors willing to stay with product development over significant periods of time. The alternative financialized business model is not about equity investors in a marathon, but rather equity investors in a relay race looking to hand on ownership (Haslam *et al.*, 2011). The challenge for equity investors is one of securing an exit where this all depends upon capital market conditions: the availability of credit, liquidity and stock market valuations.

We have already noted that the bio-pharma business model is one which depends on a flow of funding along a chain from conception to final approval where ownership and contractual claims are modified. This funding, as we have noted, flows in from different sources: venture capital firms, investment banks, hedge funds, private equity and big-pharma (as partners or acquiring firms) are all required to oil the financial linkages to keep it all going. Sustaining this flow of funding is problematic when the financial value chain is fragmented, the calculations and motivations of investors variable, and where additional follow-on funding might also dilute existing equity stakes. Moreover, the average bio-pharma firm is a collection of products at various phases of development where financial deals often, as we have noted, attach to individual products. Obtaining financial support for specific products in the pipeline may not secure the SMEs financial viability when it is investing in a portfolio of products at various stages of development to spread financial risk.

Figure 10.10 illustrates the complexity of the SME bio-pharma business model which depends upon progressing product along the pipeline from concept stage and into clinical testing. Milestone narratives matter because these encourage analysts to

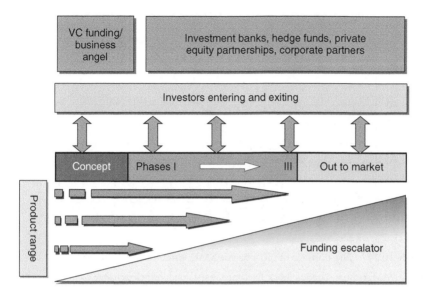

Figure 10.10   The SME bio-pharma business model.
Source: Anderssen *et al.*, 2010.

adjust their market valuations, thereby attracting additional cash funding from equity investors. The identities of these equity investors change over time and as product development moves up a funding escalator. The SME bio-pharma business model is essentially a speculative activity where investors are entering and exiting at various points along the product development pipeline. It is a lottery when, as Ernst and Young (2008: 38) observe: 'the success rate of companies that are truly commercially successful and sustainable is well below 10%' (see also Ernst and Young, 2009).

AIM listed SME bio-pharma

Bearing in mind the complexity of the SME bio-pharma business model, the number of such firms listing on the UK Alternative Investment Market (AIM) totaled 106 over the period 1998–2010. The total investment funding received by this group of firms amounted to £2 billion. Some of the firms remain listed on the market and some have exited. The number listed reached a peak of 76, but by the end of 2010 this had fallen back to 40 firms (Figure 10.11).

SME bio-pharmas listing on the AIM can be split into those which survive and those which exit, where some firms that do exit generate a strong market value return for equity investors and others may not. Over the period 1998–2011 a total of 11 per cent of funds invested into SME bio-pharmas (£200 million) had been in weak exits that generated little or no market value. Fifty per cent of total investment into SME AIM listed bio-pharmas delivered a strong market value for investors upon exit. Haslam *et al.* (2011) reveal that investment totalling £1.1 billion

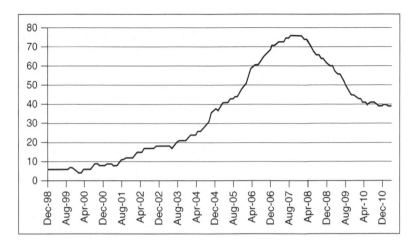

Figure 10.11   The number of bio-pharma SMEs listed on the London AIM.

Source: AIM statistics, London Stock Exchange, www.londonstockexchange.com/statistics/historic/aim/aim.htm.

in strong exits generated a market value of $3.3 billion, whilst the survivor group of firms still listed in the AIM received investment totalling £700 million and had quoted market values of £2.5 billion at the end of 2010, on average generating a 2.5 times return on funds invested.

Whilst capital at risk in the SME bio-pharma might be relatively low (Haslam *et al.*, 2011), the stakeholder network that constitutes the SME bio-pharma business model is complex and fragile.

> The bio-pharma business model is highly dependent upon refinancing because firms consume externally sourced cash resources in order to advance product development in their pipelines. In the recent financial crisis many

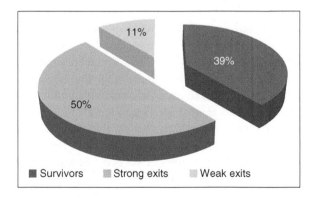

Figure 10.12   AIM SME bio-pharma total investment.

Source: www.icas.org.uk/site/cms/download/res/Gleadle_Haslam_Report_July_11.pdf.

firms have been (and still are) close to running out of cash and so are freezing product development and/or rationalizing products in pipeline. Analysis reveals an important distinction between the 'risk' attached to sustaining a complex bio-pharma stakeholder network, which is relatively high, and risk connected with return on capital which is relatively low.

(Haslam et al., 2011: 21)

The SME bio-pharma business model relies on a complex network of stakeholders to maintain its viability: universities, medical schools, charitable organizations, regulatory and government authorities, a variety of investor types and a viable relationship with big-pharma for licensing and partnership arrangements. The viability of out-sourcing R&D into SMEs depends also upon complex financial arrangements, liquid equity markets for financing and inflated asset values to provide exit possibilities for equity investors.

11

BUSINESS MODELS FOR A DIGITAL LIFESTYLE

Introduction

This chapter is about the emergence of a digital lifestyle business model (DLBM) which for consumers, households and corporate business has revolutionized the way in which information, hardware, software (applications) and communications technologies combine to affect our everyday lives. The age of personal computing, mobile telephony and software applications is transforming the way work is done and leisure time spent.

> We have lived with the PC paradigm for around 30 years now, since IBM introduced its first personal computers and pushed them into businesses in the early 80s. Until the launch of the iPad last year the only comparable change in the market had been the laptop, which led to the emergence of an army of travelling salespeople whose most urgent need was always to find a power point where they could charge their machine's fading battery.
>
> The iPad seems to be different – a third stage of computing. Horace Dediu, a former analyst with the mobile phone company Nokia who now runs his own consultancy, Asymco, argues that 'the definition of a new generation of computing is that the new products rely on new input and output methods, and allow a new population of non-expert users to use the product more cheaply and simply'.
>
> (The Observer, *27 March 2011*)

This is the technology that allows us to work from home, on the train, in the local coffee shop with a Wi-Fi, watch TV, listen to downloads, shop on the internet, order the food and get it delivered, pay household bills and make phone calls. This technology is 'adaptive to today's digital age' and is portable and easy to use. In

1990 100 million personal computers were 'in use' and by 2010 1.4 billion (see Table 11.1), and in 1990 there were 10 million mobile phone subscribers in the OECD countries and in 2009, 1.3 billion (see Figure 11.1).

For the economists the digital world presents new opportunities to effect technological change and drive up productivity:

> One may distinguish at least three major effects of the introduction of novel information and communication technologies (IT). First, it may have a direct positive effect on the technology of production at given firms because it improves the technology of information processing within the firm. Secondly, it may affect the search process by way of which agents in the market meet. Thirdly, it may introduce a new type of firms (and a new IT sector) in the economy.
>
> *Van Den Berg (2005: 1)*

TABLE 11.1 Worldwide personal computers in use, 1975–2020

	PCs in use (millions)
1975	0.05
1980	2.1
1990	100
2000	529
2010	1,425
2015 (projected)	2,165
2020 (projected)	2,480–2,520

Source: www.etforecasts.com/products/ES_pcww1203.htm.

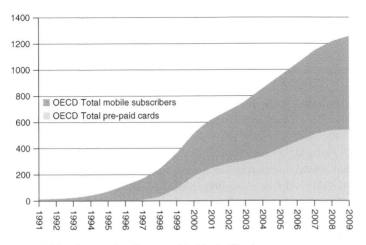

Figure 11.1 Mobile phone subscribers worldwide (million).

Source: OECD Communications Outlook 2011.

In terms of improving productivity the evidence is uncertain and economists have struggled with explaining the so-called productivity paradox. In Chapter 5 we have observed how GDP growth in recent times has slowed in the advanced economies relative to the developing economies of China and India even though, of course, these advanced economies, and especially the USA, have been the beneficiaries of the digital age.

> Economists have been engaged in a debate over the so-called 'productivity paradox,' which asks how productivity growth could have slowed during the 1970s and 1980s in the face of phenomenal technological improvements, price declines, and real growth in computers and related IT equipment. Much of this debate has revolved around the question of measurement, for example, are the output and growth of industries that use IT equipment being adequately measured?
>
> *(Moulton, 1999: 1)*

There is then the issue of how agents (buyers and sellers) meet in the 'market' which has been 'revolutionized' in the age of internet communications and how it is possible to modify the relationship between agents that constitute the market for goods and services. There is no doubt that in the digital age the culture of consumption has been modified to create new business opportunities, but our concern is with the extent to which the digital age business model is itself robust and viable.

> The availability of inexpensive IT equipment and services has enabled businesses to do their work in new ways and has led to the creation of new firms and even entire industries. Are these new forms of business and production being adequately counted in our gross domestic product (GDP)? Have our economic statistics kept up with electronic commerce, new kinds of financial services, and new methods of inventory and product distribution?
>
> *(Moulton 1999: 2)*

In this chapter our focus is again on the USA, because it still accounts for a dominant share of global hardware, software, internet services and communications systems development. In 1990 US firms accounted for 57 per cent of the global software market[1]. If we include smart phones as being equivalent to PCs, this share was still roughly 50 per cent in 2011, (as regards computer PCs alone, US firms account for roughly 30 per cent of global production).[2] An alternative perspective is provided when considering the Forbes top 200 firms in information services, software development and computer technology and hardware where the group of US firms listed account for 40 per cent of sales revenue, 48 per cent of total assets employed and 65 per cent of market value.

In the USA we observe the emergence of a new digital lifestyle business model (DLBM) in the S&P 500 group of listed firms constellating around four 'industry' defined elements: computer hardware and peripherals, software and applications, internet and software services, and communications technologies. In this chapter we consolidate these activities into a single broader 'digital lifestyle business model' rather than treat firms as belonging to an industry such 'software' or 'hardware'. Our logic for doing so is that the products of these 'industries' share many similar stakeholder network characteristics and thus it is sensible to combine their financials. In any case as firms evolve and adapt they may organically migrate or be absorbed (by acquisition) into other industry sectors or provide outputs which are used as inputs by other sectors, such that a 'business model' might best be described as a loose matrix of activities that share relatively similar stakeholder and information networks. The adoption of this broader concept of what constitutes the DLBM can then be used to reveal how the blended mix of activities and financial outcomes of hardware, software applications and cellular communications are variably evolving and adapting in the business model.

> By the mid-1980s the PC became the driving force for the whole computer industry, and it retained this crown for over 10 years. PC industry dynamics changed by the late-1990s when PCs became the means to get to the Internet. Since the late 1990s the Internet has become more important than the PC industry. Today the Internet applications are the main driving force for the PC and the whole computer industry. But it is important to understand that the foundation of the Internet is mainly based on the PC industry and a vast land-based packet communication network. In the next decade a cellular-based packet communications network and broadband will further grow the Internet applications and the Internet access devices.
>
> Over the next 10 years the PC industry will prosper and thrive with two additional driving forces – consumer electronics devices built with computing platforms and mobile devices such as Smartphone's and multi-function cell phones.
>
> *(eTForecasts, 2011: 1)*

We then turn to consider the contribution to the evolution of this business model of focal firms within this matrix: CISCO, Apple, IBM, Microsoft and Intel. Focusing on key players, we argue, does not in itself reveal how the business model is evolving and adapting, and so in the following section of this chapter we construct a financial framework of analysis that charts the expansion of the DLBM in the USA that includes software and hardware, internet services and communications technology based firms.

Firms within the US DLBM

The business leaders of CISCO, Apple, IBM, Microsoft and Intel have drawn plaudits in their time as they have contributed to the development and evolution of the DLBM with their products: hardware, software and communications systems. The academic and business literature is intoxicated by new technology firms, their way of doing things and how they are managed. Academic journals and the business press focus attention on managerial leadership, corporate behaviour and culture, technical innovation in product development, strategy and the mobilization of organization functions and resources.

> The magazine measured the financial performance of each CEO, using very detailed, specific metrics, notably stock prices adjusted for a variety of factors, such as for industry and for country. The change in market capitalisation over the CEO's tenure was calculated and adjusted for inflation in each country. Other types of control and analysis was done as well. Then the results were compiled and reported . . . Jobs' value was rated as the most significant of any CEO in the world. He has increased Apple market value by approximately $150 billion since he took over, and the magazine says that he delivered to Apple a 3,188 per cent industry-adjusted return – quite astounding.
> (Computer World, *22 December 2009*)

> Consider Ed Zander, who's been hailed as 'Motorola's modernizer.' When Zander took over as CEO of Motorola in January 2004, the company was in steep decline. After being in the high-velocity world of Silicon Valley, Zander found himself at the helm of a company that seemed to be running, in his words, 'on autopilot.' In taking on the challenge of turning Motorola around, Zander described his guiding philosophy as, 'Whack yourself before somebody whacks you.' He observed, 'A lot of companies have clogged arteries.'
> (Harvard Business Review, *February 2006: 1*)

It is difficult to keep focused on what precisely is going on when the analysis of firms is focused on either broad or narrow issues and where folklore blends with a selective use of statistics and perspectives. All of which adds up to a 'bricolage' about what Microsoft, CISCO, EBay and Apple are up to, but where we do not have a view of the general financial landscape. Our starting point is to construct alternative focal firm narratives around the financial trajectory and development of a few key firms located within the DLBM. Our narratives deliberately avoid establishing connections between financial performance and corporate leadership, branding, marketing, open or closed systems where connections are difficult to make and because the patterns are ever changing and malleable. Our analysis presents the financial numbers reported by CISCO, Apple, IBM, Microsoft and Intel, all focal firms in the DLBM, to reveal similarities and differences; describe trajectory and change. Our purpose is to consider firm-level financial performance, construct an amalgam of firm financial data to describe the DLBM and contrast this business model's financial profile with the S&P 500 group of firms.

In an earlier period Microsoft and Intel operated with very high cash margins in sales (see Figure 11.2), peaking at 40–50 per cent in the year 2000 but thereafter falling to 40 per cent, which is still exceptional when we consider that the average S&P 500 firm had an average cash margin of 20 per cent during this period. CISCO systems declined from a high of 40 per cent to 30 per cent by 2010 and IBM is an

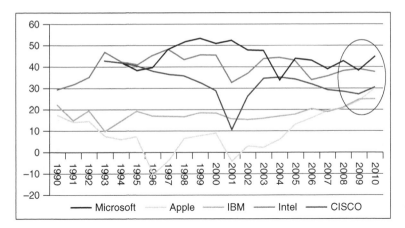

FIGURE 11.2   DLBM focal firms' cash margin (%).

Source: ThomsonOneBanker.

average firm, running a 20 per cent cash surplus margin 1990–2010. Apple Inc. recovered from a period of decline in 1990–1996 to deliver a 30 per cent cash margin in 2010, in the ball park with the rest of its peers.

With regards to the reported cash ROCE (see Figure 11.3), there is a general downwards trajectory over the period 1990–2001, taking the cash return on capital to roughly 25 per cent which at that time was the average for the S&P 500 group of firms. Thereafter the cash ROCE recovers, with Microsoft and IBM both delivering a 50 per cent return on capital. Note again how Apple's cash return on capital at first deteriorates before recovering after 2000, reaching more than 30 per cent by 2010. Apart from CISCO, the major focal firms in the DLBM were delivering exceptional financial performance in 2010 when compared with the S&P 500

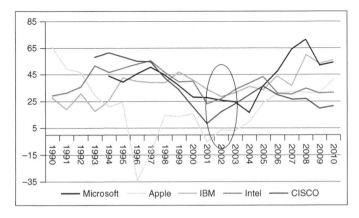

FIGURE 11.3   DLBM focal firms' cash ROCE (%).

Source: ThomsonOneBanker.

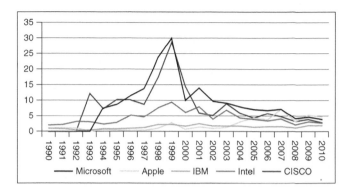

FIGURE 11.4   DLBM focal firms' market value to sales ratio.

Source: ThomsonOneBanker.

average. Figure 11.4 reveals the market value to sales ratio for this group of focal firms and reveals that, after registering a very high market value to sales ratios in 1999, Microsoft and CISCO drifted down to a ratio of 4–5:1. Likewise Intel drifted down from a 10:1 market value to sales ratio towards the range 2–3:1. IBM maintained its average 2:1 market value to sales profile and Apple Inc. transformed from less than 1:1 to more than 4:1 by 2010. The market value return on sales for this group of firms was two to three times higher than the average S&P 500 firm in 2010.

The DLBM does contain a number of exceptionally high performance firms which have emerged over the past two decades in the S&P 500 list of firms. To illustrate the level of performance, we have profiled three firms, Intel, Microsoft and Apple, and their key operating financials.

Figures 11.5 to 11.7 position each financial ratio or value relative to all other

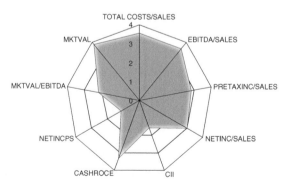

FIGURE 11.5   Intel, financial profile, 2009. MKTVAL is market value at year end; EBITDA is earnings before interest, taxes, depreciation and amortization; CII is capital intensity (sales/capital employed as long-term debt plus equity); net income is after tax and dividends; NETINCPS is net income per share.

Source: Authors' datasets.

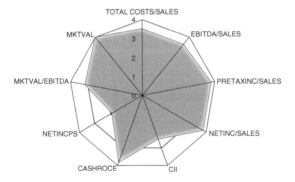

FIGURE 11.6   Microsoft, financial profile, 2009. For key see Figure 11.5.

Source: Authors' datasets.

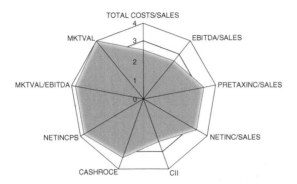

FIGURE 11.7   Apple, financial profile, 2009. For key see Figure 11.5.

Source: Authors' datasets.

firms in the S&P 500 group of firms. The more of the 'web area' that is shaded the stronger is the firm relative to the S&P 500. In general Apple, Microsoft and Intel are positioned within the top 20 per cent of the S&P 500 group of firms.

In the next section we aggregate reported financials for all firms listed in the S&P 500 and which are located within the following sectors: internet and software services, communications equipment, computers and peripherals, software and semiconductors. This financial information is used to broadly describe the DLBM, where our purpose is to outline how this business model evolved and adapted financially over the period 1990 to 2010.

The US digital lifestyle business model

Our analysis tracks the evolution of the US S&P 500 DLBM and to do this we composite together financial data for internet and software services, communications equipment, computers and peripherals, software and semiconductors. We then consider the financial performance of the S&P 500 DLBM from a number of perspectives: composition of activity, cost structure, returns on capital and finally trajectory of this business model relative to the S&P 500 as a whole. We start with the changes in the composition of activities subsumed within the DLBM.

Composition of activity within the S&P 500 DLBM

Figures 11.8 and 11.9 reveal the changing composition of sales and cash generated within the DLBM, illustrating the ebb and flow of these adjustments as software development and packaging increases its revenue share, internet and software providers enter the index in 1996, and communications technology systems have a reduced share as new wireless systems are incorporated into hardware product.

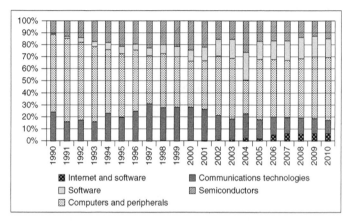

FIGURE 11.8 Evolution of sales revenue in the S&P 500 digital lifestyle business model.

Source: ThomsonOneBanker.

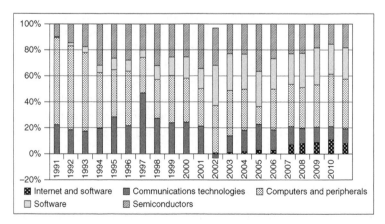

FIGURE 11.9 Evolution of cash generated in the S&P 500 digital lifestyle business model.

Source: ThomsonOneBanker.

The pattern of cash surplus from operations generated by firms within the DLBM also fluctuates over time, with computers and peripherals ceding cash share to software development, and internet and software services and communications technologies again suffering a loss of cash share as the business model evolves. We appreciate that the process of compositional adjustment will be driven not just by product market forces, but that some firms operating in one industry may evolve and migrate into another or be acquired by a firm which is located within another industry sector. Thus the analysis is a general overview of the changing composition and may reflect also how technology changes absorb one activity into another, for example, communications technology is absorbed into computers and peripherals and mobile devices like smart phones.

Within the DLBM there are focal firms with familiar famous brand identities, including such companies as eBay, Yahoo and Google classified within internet and software providers; Apple, Hewlett Packard, IBM and Dell located in computers and peripherals; Sun Systems, Microsoft and Adobe within software; and Intel and Texas Instruments in semiconductors. Our objective is now to track the key financial operating characteristics of this DLBM as it evolves over the period 1990 to 2010 and use this to establish the extent to which the business model is robust.

Cost structure and return on capital in the DLBM

In Chapter 2 we outlined how by subtracting external costs and internal labour costs we arrive at the residual of cash surplus generated from operations. Our analysis focuses on the cash surplus and cash return on capital employed (cash ROCE). The cash margin reflects the extent to which cash is extracted from sales revenue as technology, resources and spatial manipulation of the value chain modify stakeholder relations and work their way through into the financial numbers, whilst the inclusion of the cash ROCE introduces balance sheet capitalization which reveals the extent to which cash resources are being generated with more or less debt and equity funding. The first thing to note from Figure 11.10 is that the cash surplus margin is gently increasing for the S&P 500 DLBM over the period 1990–2010 from 15 to 25 per cent of sales and reflects a combination of factors: off-shoring, process technology, and brand lock-in that deliver both cost reduction and secure strong cost recovery conditions within a global financial value chain. The cash ROCE is more erratic, reflecting two distinct periods, the first being 1990–1997 when the ratio improves from 25 to 35 per cent before deteriorating to a low of just 15 per cent at the height of the US recession in 2001. Thereafter the cash ROCE is restored to a higher level of 30 per cent, but it is below the previous peak of 35 per cent in the mid-1990s.

Over the period 1990–2000 market value runs ahead of cash earnings (EBITDA) in the S&P 500 DLBM, reaching 33:1 in 1999 and a very high valuation multiple relative to the average for the S&P 500 at 10:1. From the late 1990s the market value to cash earnings multiple progressively falls back to level of 10:1 by 2010 compared with the S&P 500 average of 7:1 (see Figure 11.11). This is a business

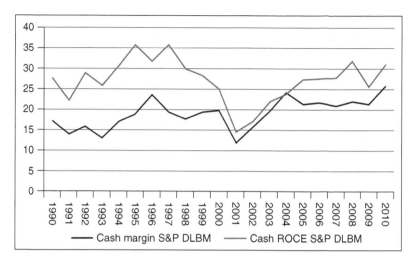

FIGURE 11.10   S&P 500 DLBM cash margin and cash ROCE (%.)

Source: ThomsonOneBanker.

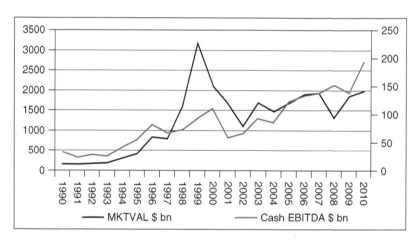

FIGURE 11.11   S&P 500 DLBM market value to EBITDA ratio.

Source: ThomsonOneBanker.

model which has secured higher cash margins relative to the S&P 500 average, but has not transformed the return on capital to the same extent.

Our analysis of the evolution, trajectory and financial development of the DLBM generates a complementary level of analysis and alternative insight out of which we can generate critically informed narratives. However, we now consider the extent to which the DLBM has, in aggregate, generated a more significant financial presence within the S&P 500 group of firms and how, relative to the S&P 500 group, the DLBM has itself migrated.

Performance relative to the S&P 500 constituents

In this section we compare the performance of the S&P 500 DLBM with that of the aggregate performance of S&P 500 constituents as a benchmark to explore the extent to which, relative to the S&P 500, this business model is expanding, maturing or degrading. The DLBM subsumed within the S&P 500 has operated with a strong revenue trajectory, starting with roughly $200 billion of sales in 1990 and delivering nearly $800 billion in 2010. The compound annual growth rate (CAGR) in sales 6.8 per cent can be compared with that of the S&P 500 group of 4.8 per cent over this same period. This time period (1990–2010) can be split into two distinct sub-periods: 1990–2000 and 2001–2010. During the earlier period sales revenues grew at a CAGR of 10.3 per cent up to the recession in the USA in 2001, and in the follow-on period, 2001–2010, the CAGR was just 2.8 per cent, now slightly below the S&P 500 average. During this second period, the share of S&P 500 sales revenue accounted for by the digital lifestyle business model remained steady in the range 7–8 per cent (see Figure 11.12 and Table 11.2).

Over the period 1990–2010 the S&P 500 digital lifestyle business model accounts for 6–8 per cent of S&P 500 sales revenues, and the share of cash (EBITDA) also tracks the share of sales revenue until 2007 when there is a significant jump that takes the share of cash to 12 per cent of the S&P 500 (Figure 11.13). This jump has

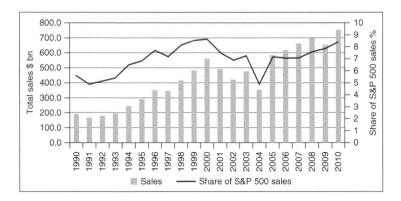

FIGURE 11.12   S&P 500 DLBM sales growth and share of S&P 500 sales revenue.

Source: ThomsonOneBanker.

TABLE 11.2 Nominal sales growth rates in S&P 500 and S&P 500 digital lifestyle business model (%)

	S&P 500 sales CAGR	*S&P 500 DLBM sales CAGR*
1990–2010	4.8	6.8
1990–2000	6.0	10.3
2001–2010	3.1	2.8

Source: ThomsonOneBanker.

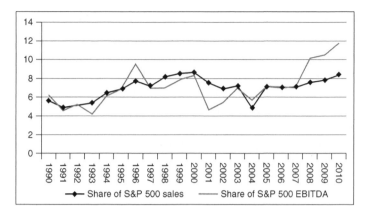

FIGURE 11.13 S&P 500 DLBM share of S&P 500 sales and cash (EBITDA).

Source: ThomsonOneBanker.

less to do with what was happening in the DLBM than with what was not happening in the rest of the S&P 500 group of companies, that is, restoring cash earnings back to 2007 levels. In contrast to the previous 2001 recession in the USA, the DLBM, this time around, is far more resilient, with cash earnings in 2010 up on 2007 by 40 per cent.

As the DLBM consolidates its position within the S&P 500 constituent list throughout the 1990s, there is a gentle increase in its share of sales and cash earnings from 5 per cent to nearer 10 per cent by 2010 (Figure 11.13). This was accompanied by a strong increase in the DLBM's share of SP500 market value which peaked in 1999 at 25 per cent before falling and stabilizing at a 15 per cent share throughout the period 2000–2010 (see Figure 11.14).

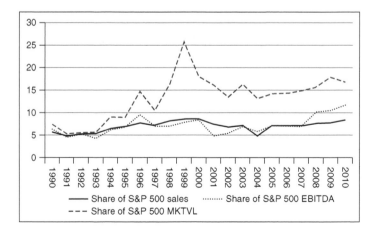

FIGURE 11.14 S&P 500 DLBM share of S&P 500: sales, cash and market value (%).

Source: ThomsonOneBanker.

The financial profile of the DLBM subtended within the S&P 500 reveals that it very quickly establishes itself on a strong growth trajectory relative to the S&P 500 group as a whole. However, there are some signs that trajectories, in terms of income, cash and market value, are slowing and this may be a sign that focal firms within this business model are entering a more mature phase of development where consolidation and restructuring is now a distinct possibility.

Summary

The literature and business press reports surrounding the technology and firms located in the DLBM often focus on the role of the chief executive officer (CEO) or founder of the company, exploring their motivations and what drives them to get up in the morning to shape and reshape the strategic fortunes of firms within their industry. It is a literature that is often focused on headline financial information such as sales growth, profits and market value added this year compared with last year. It is also about the nature of the technologies supporting new applications, hardware and communications and how these are transforming workplace productivity and the way we, as individual consumers and households, use this technology within our leisure time. In this chapter we have not concentrated on the nature of corporate leadership, innovation, core competences, and how the competitive positions of firms within the industry might contribute towards transforming financial performance for value creation.

The purpose of this chapter has been to try and reconceptualize the DLBM by grouping together firms which share similar stakeholder networks, regulatory frameworks and general purpose. Although we admit that this is subject to variable interpretation and judgement, our analysis consolidates firm-level financial information into more aggregated formats that can then be employed to describe the evolution, composition and adaptability of focal firms within their business model. Furthermore we argue that narratives about the development of a business model should be set within the context of a more broadly defined econosphere of business models. Thus we argue that critically engaged narratives about performance, evolution and adaptability should be drawn out from different levels of analysis:

1) Focal firm
   Analysis that follows the progress of a focal firms over a period of time to reveal its rate of growth, changes in cost structure, earnings capacity and balance sheet capitalization.
2) Focal firm within its business model
   Analysis comparing the focal firm with all firms consolidated within its business model, in this specific case software development, internet information services, computer technology and hardware.
3) Business model relative to the broader econosphere of business models
   Analysis of a specific business model relative to that of a broader set of business models (in this case captured by consolidating all firms listed in the S&P 500).

There is no doubt that individual firms (Microsoft, Intel, Apple) are, within this business model, delivering spectacular cash margins and return on capital, and that whilst the ratios of market value to sales revenue have fallen, they are still double that achieved on average by the S&P 500 group of firms. In terms of the evolution of this business model, software (applications) and internet service providers are taking an increased share of sales revenues and cash generated. And, after a period of expansion (1990–2001), the DLBM share of S&P 500 revenues, cash earnings and market value has matured and has remained relatively stable over the period 2001–2010. Thus we suggest that focal firms within the business model will migrate into applications and services, but also that consolidation (business combinations) will accelerate the process of restructuring, with the health warning, however, that this will inflate capitalizations (see the Pharma case in previous chapter) ahead of cash earnings as the DLBM business model evolves and matures.

12

ACCOUNTING FOR THE UK HOSPICE BUSINESS MODEL

Introduction

Our final case reveals that it is possible to employ a business model framework of analysis to review the nature of non-corporate activities and in this case we employ voluntary hospices. Our reason for choosing this case is that it reveals how the hospice business model has evolved from simply taking in donations which are then used to provide palliative case for terminally ill patients. The activities and stakeholder interactions that constitute the hospice business model are more complex now compared with an earlier period. At the same time UK government policy towards the so-called third sector is also changing as funding constraints encourage governments to seek the support of the voluntary sector within national health-care provision.

Since the opening of the first hospice, St Christopher's, in 1967, the hospice movement has grown rapidly in Britain and the voluntary sector is still at the forefront of developments in the country's palliative care. More than 70 per cent of the available palliative care units are voluntary sector initiatives (Help the Hospices, 2005) and the majority of hospices are independent, service delivery voluntary organizations, governed by trustees who report to the Charity Commission and comply with the relevant Health and Social Care regulations (Finlay, 2001; Help the Hospices, 2006). Charitable status allowed hospices to independently raise funds and organize their services based on the needs of local communities, but this reliance on non-government funding and the fragmented nature of the hospice movement means that there is often a lack of national planning for the provision of palliative care. This resulted in an ad hoc development of services, depending mainly on the vision of the founders (Finlay, 2001). Hence, palliative care services in the UK are mainly funded through charitable activities and fundraising, with the government covering around one-quarter to one-third of the voluntary hospices' expenditure (Help the Hospices, 2008).

The provision of palliative care forty years after the opening of St Christopher's Hospice has changed considerably. Initial focus was on providing terminal care to cancer patients, but this has progressively shifted to a more holistic model that reflects the influence of domestic and international developments. The current approach anticipates the need to provide palliative care to a diverse group of patients, for example, children, teenagers and elderly patients, those infected with HIV/AIDS and with neurological problems (Hospice Information, 2005; Finlay 2001; Saunders, 2001). The importance of the patient's family and their specific needs attracts attention in the literature on palliative care, especially services required to support the family both before a person's death and during the grieving period.

National statistics project the population in England and Wales combined to increase from 54 million to 60 million by 2031, roughly a 10 per cent increase. In addition, a structural shift in the age distribution of the population means that more people are living longer. Currently, 16 per cent of the UK population is aged 65 and over and this will reach 23 per cent by 2031. This means that an additional 7.8 million people will be living over the age of 65.[1] The share of the population living past 80 is also expected to grow from its current level of 2.5 million to 4.9 million by 2031. By 2031 the population aged over 65 will have doubled and if we assume that the incidence of cancer per 100,000 of the population remains at current trends, then the demand for palliative care from hospices would almost certainly double.

In the next section we construct a descriptive hospice 'business model' which first reveals the variety of sources of income before turning to consider the costs structure of this business model and its balance sheet capitalization.

Constructing the hospice business model

The Help the Hospices report on the accounts of hospices reveals the income of this sector in the UK to have been £626 million in 2007 (see Help the Hospices, 2008). Our business model framework is constructed from the financial information we have consolidated for the top twenty-five hospices in England ranked by their total income, and we estimate that this group accounts for roughly one-half of hospice income. At the top of the list we have St Christopher's Hospice, receiving £18 million of income in 2009, and at the bottom of our group, we have the Marlets hospice with an income of £5.4 million. This means that the majority of hospices have total incomes of less than £4 million to provide palliative in-care facilities and home visits within their locality

Hospices generate their income from a range of sources: donations, legacies, fundraising, trading income, lotteries, and income on invested funds, all of which have varying characteristics. For example, legacy income can be volatile because it depends on both a specific set of conditions governing the pattern of giving and also capital market valuations, for example, of property or financial assets promised within a legacy. Income from investments will also tend to be volatile and equally depends on interest rates and the condition of capital markets when hospices also make investments.

Table 12.1 reveals the aggregate share of income received by our group of hospices for the period 2003–2009. This reveals a high level of aggregate stability, but this disguises higher levels of volatility within specific hospices as Table 12.2 shows.

Table 12.2 reveals high levels of income volatility. For example, at peak, legacies accounted for one-third of total income in 2006 and just 19 per cent in 2011. The financial crisis emerging in 2008 and continuing throughout 2009 impacted adversely on this hospice, reducing total income from £9.5 million to £7.9 million, a drop of 17 per cent, and by 2011 total income was back to £11 million, but only 14 per cent up on 2007. In Figure 12.1 we show the total income for our group of twenty-five hospices which account for roughly one-third of all hospice income. This figure reveals that whilst the growth in total hospice income has slowed down in recent years, expenditures are inflating ahead of income as hospice managers try to maintain the provision of palliative care services.

The current financial crisis is impacting negatively on hospices which are struggling to maintain their cash reserves as expenses run ahead of income.

TABLE 12.1 Top twenty-five hospices' income breakdown (%)

	Donations	Legacies	Fundraising	Trading income	Investment income	Grants received	Fees received	Total income
2003	19.2	21.5	9.7	20.1	3.0	25.0	1.6	100
2004	19.2	21.5	9.7	20.1	3.0	25.0	1.6	100
2005	17.0	20.2	8.9	21.1	3.5	27.2	2.1	100
2006	16.3	22.4	10.1	20.2	3.4	26.1	1.5	100
2007	17.8	20.9	10.1	20.7	3.6	25.4	1.4	100
2008	17.6	20.0	10.3	19.6	4.2	26.8	1.5	100
2009	17.0	19.5	10.4	21.3	4.0	26.2	1.7	100
2010	17.2	21.1	9.2	21.0	2.0	28.0	1.5	100

Source: Charity Commission.

TABLE 12.2 Income breakdown: Pilgrims Hospice

	Donations	Legacies	Fundraising	Trading income	Investment income	Grants received	Fees received	Total income
2003	13	27	7	27	6	19	1	100
2004	12	18	11	31	4	23	1	100
2005	12	28	9	26	3	21	1	100
2006	11	34	7	23	3	20	1	100
2007	12	37	7	21	4	19	1	100
2008	13	23	9	24	4	25	3	100
2009	13	18	9	27	5	26	3	100
2010	11	27	7	24	3	25	3	100
2011	9	19	8	25	3	32	4	100

Source: Charity Commission.

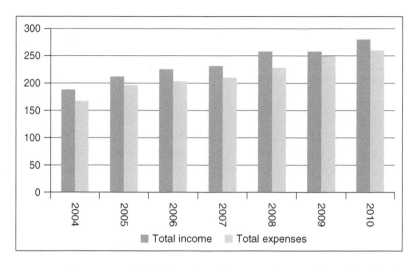

FIGURE 12.1   Top twenty-five UK hospices: income and expenditure (£ million).

Source: Charity Commission.

Hospice managers are motivated to extend their income-generating activities, for example, investing in more shops to boost trading income and employees whose job is to increase funding so as to maintain palliative care services. However, in recent years employment expenses and external contracted service costs have run ahead of income, and for many hospices this has forced them to draw down cash reserves and rethink their reserves strategy. In 2010 our group of twenty-five hospices reduced balance sheet cash reserves by £17 million or 20 per cent. The Pilgrims Hospice's latest report and accounts notes:

> The free reserves at 31 March 2011 stood at £11.9 million, including the investment properties (£1.7 million), quoted investments (£8.3 million) and cash and its equivalent (£1.7 million). This is less than the long term target level of holding the equivalent of 18 months' running costs in reserve but the trustees consider that, in light of the current economic situation, this is adequate.
>
> *(Pilgrims Hospice, 2011: 6)*

Hospices are charities and report their financials according to the Charity Statement of Recommended Practice (SORP), maintaining reserves (as cash and invested funds) as a contingency against uncertainty. Many hospices maintain investments in the hope that holding gains can be extracted from capital market appreciation and this employed to modernize and renew hospice facilities going forward. But hospices have been exposed to the vagaries of the capital market just like those of us who have our pension funds invested in global stock markets.

Figure 12.2 reveals how hospices have suffered from a reduction in cash reserves which peaked in 2008 and also in terms of the value of investments that are only, in

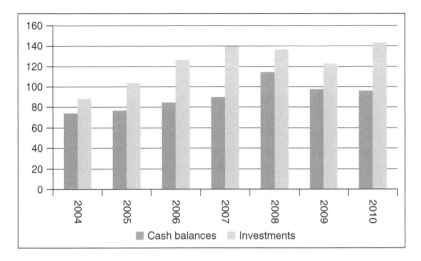

FIGURE 12.2 Hospice cash burn balances and investments ($£$ million).

Source: Charity Commission.

2011, back to the 2007 peak before the onset of the financial crisis. Our analysis of the hospice financial business model reveals that income has come off a growth trajectory and that expenses tend to run ahead to maintain capacity to generate income (fundraising, lotteries and shops) and sustain palliative care for their communities. As expenses run ahead of income, this has forced hospices to re-evaluate their reserves policy, more often than not reducing the months of financial coverage. They are also experiencing a reduction in reserves affected by capital market fluctuations which not only impact negatively on the value of legacies granted to hospices but also on the value of capital invested in investment banks.

Sustaining palliative care

The Calman–Hine report, published in 1995, attempted to set out a policy framework for the commissioning of cancer services, highlighting the need for planning in order to direct resources to areas of greatest need. Although this report focused on services for cancer patients, the subsequent government executive letter revealed that its principles applied equally to those for patients with other life-threatening conditions, including AIDS, neurological conditions, cardiac and respiratory failure. More recently the 'End of Life Care Strategy' published by the Department of Health in the UK attempts to develop the strategic framework on both commissioning and delivery of palliative care services. Aiming to widen access, standardize quality and co-ordinate provision, this is a document that emphasizes the role of primary care trusts (PCTs) as central co-ordinating facilities for the commissioning of palliative care at locality level (see Department of Health, 2008). The UK government 'End of Life Care Strategy' is a response to a growing need for palliative care.

On the one hand, the demand for the provision of palliative care to patients suffering from acquired immunodeficiency syndrome (AIDS) has increased and Saunders (1993) notes that the focus on cancer palliative care delayed the development of hospice provision in other areas of need, specifically AIDS as a case in point. The demand and scope for palliative care is also increasing because children who once would not have reached early adulthood are surviving longer as new treatments and effective therapies are introduced. Relief care to the patient and practical support to parents must be provided after diagnosis and continue even after the child's death in the form of bereavement care for the family (Worswick, 1995; Dominica, 1987). In addition to the widening patient base in need of palliative care services, demographic factors are imposing additional challenges on the hospice sector. The population of the UK is ageing such that over the past twenty-five years the percentage of the population aged 65 and over increased from 15 per cent in 1983 to 16 per cent in 2008, an increase of 1.5 million people in this age group.[2] Considering the fact that cancer is predominantly a disease of the elderly, only 0.5 per cent of cases registered in 2003 were in children (aged under 15) and 26 per cent were in people aged under 60.[3] We can safely predict that demand for palliative care services will increase accordingly as both the population and numbers of people living beyond the age of 65 increase. In addition, the survival rates for most common cancers have also improved in England, and this is an additional challenge stretching hospices' resources as the average length of care per patient increases.[4]

Summary

In this chapter we have considered the nature of the UK hospice business model in the aftermath of a financial crisis and our analysis reveals that through 2008 and into 2010 the level of income flowing into this voluntary sector has come off its peak. We have also highlighted the vulnerability of hospices to income volatility and also to deteriorating capital market conditions which have reduced holdings gains and leverage on invested funds. Hospices share many of the financial characteristics of a private sector business model, especially their exposure to uncertain and volatile income streams. Hospice executives are keen to maintain their capacity to generate income and also maintain services, and so expenses (internal and external) have run ahead of income. In the first instance trustees are drawing down cash and invested reserves to maintain their services and extend capacity, but the extent to which this can continue depends on financial recovery.

The UK government's 'End of Life Care Strategy' envisages the voluntary sector supporting the increased need for palliative care and the government does provide hospices with a quarter of their income in the form of grants, but for our group of twenty-five hospices this source of income also levelled off in 2010. There is an opportunity for government (as a major stakeholder) to intervene in the business model to reduce income uncertainties and exposure to capital market risk exposure, for example, offering hospice bonds that pay a coupon above treasury rate or sponsoring a 'matched' insurance/contingency fund against which hospices could borrow. These interventions are required to reconfigure the UK hospice business model but must now be set in the context of deteriorating public sector finances and expected cut-backs in funding of 25–30 per cent in UK public sector services. Given the extent of these cut-backs it is not clear whether the hospice business model is robust enough to provide additional palliative care going forward.

The hospice business model depends on sustaining a complex network of stakeholder relations that underwrite a varied range of income streams and expenditures which are deployed to extend palliative care services and also sustain funding from shops, lotteries, donations and legacies. The current financial crisis is stressing this business model at the same time as the central and local government public sector business model is also in crisis. It is not clear how voluntary hospices will sustain their capacity to deliver palliative care going forward as both the scope and demand for their care increase.

NOTES

1 Introduction

1 Credit default swaps (insurance).
2 http://www.bankofengland.co.uk/publications/fsr/fs_paper08.pdf.
3 As at 29 November 2011.

2 Accounting for the firm as a business model

1 Where NPV is the difference between the discounted value of future cash flows and initial investment outlay.
2 Available at http://www.iasplus.com/iasplus/0709ias1revised.pdf.
3 See http://www.fasb.org/pdf/fas157.pdf; http://www.iasb.org/NR/rdonlyres/1D9CBD62-F0A8-4401-A90D-483C63800CAA/0/IAS39.pdf.
4 See http://4.bp.blogspot.com/_m3CQF7whYY4/SQI-Ko558zI/AAAAAAAAA68/2XRczpkUVeA/s1600-h/spy.JPG.

3 Strategy: arbitrage for financial leverage

1 Quasi-rent is such excess return in the short run.
2 John Kay (1993) provides a critical and extended discussion of many such assets and capabilities.
3 See http://www.sternstewart.com/?content=proprietary&p=eva.

4 Business models: reworked for a financialized world

1 Capital employed is here shareholder equity plus long-term debt.
2 Software, computers and peripherals, internet services, telecommunications, semi-conductors.

5 Business models: global context

1 Office for National Statistics, UK real earnings up 8 per cent and employment increase negligible, 2001–2010.

2 GOS is similar to cash from operations or earnings before interest, taxes, depreciation and amortization (EBITDA).
3 This study covers the thirteen largest private pension fund markets: www.towerswatson.com/assets/pdf/3761/Global-Pensions-Asset-Study-2011.pdf.

6 Accounting for national business models

1 In 2009, USA 47 per cent, UK 55 per cent and Germany 62 per cent.
2 Germany 74 per cent, UK 65 per cent, USA 61 per cent and Japan 65 per cent.
3 www.census.gov/compendia/statab/cats/income_expenditures_poverty_wealth/household_income.html.
4 Quarterly equity withdrawal by individuals as a percentage of their post-tax income, data series LPQB3VH, Bank of England.
5 http://blogs.wikinvest.com/dailyangle/2009/10/the-sps-price-to-book/.
6 www2.fdic.gov/SDI/main4.asp.
7 www.iasplus.com/standard/ias36.htm.
8 http://data.worldbank.org/indicator/FB.AST.NPER.ZS.
9 Delinquent loans are those past thirty days or more and accruing interest as well as those in non-accrual status as a per cent of end of period loans outstanding.
10 www.guardian.co.uk/news/datablog/2011/jun/17/greece-debt-crisis-bank-exposed.
11 Agency debt is government off balance sheet in Fannie Mae and Freddie Mac home loans.
12 The acquisition in 2007 of ABN Amro was a consortium purchase that included RBS, Santander and Fortis.

7 Business models: adaptation and restructuring

1 MSCI Global Equities Index, www.msci.com/products/indices/size/standard/performance.html.
2 www.raymondjames.com.uy/ecm/rjmergersandacquisitions/pdfs/2010_spring_national.pdf.
3 Although it needs to be noted that a proportion of this cash is in overseas subsidiaries and is difficult to repatriate.
4 Earnings before tax plus depreciation and amortization minus capital expenditure.
5 www.globalagro.com.ar/upload/EqStrat.11.23.09.pdf.
6 www.jpmorgan.com/cm/BlobServer?blobcol=urldata&blobtable=MungoBlobs&blobkey=id&blobwhere=1158632602152&blobheader=application%2Fpdf.
7 www.gasb.org/pdf/fas141r.pdf.
8 During the year goodwill acquired is tested against cash inflows (discounted) or market value of assets acquired.
9 www.bea.gov/international/di1usdop.htm.
10 Cash surplus flow is value retained minus employment costs. Total assets calculated for parent and foreign affiliates excludes finance and insurance companies.
11 www.molex.com/documents/William_Blair_Conf.pdf.

8 US banking: a viable business model?

1 See chapter 2 on derivative accounting in banks which in the USA net off derivatives rather than account for these at gross value.
2 http://research.stlouisfed.orfred2seriesUSROA?rid=55&soid=6.
3 Following SFAS 157 'Fair Value Measurements' and more specifically SFAS 144 'Accounting by Creditors for Impairment of a Loan' and SFAS 133 'Accounting for Derivative Instruments and Hedging Activities', charge-offs of irrecoverable loans and

discounted asset backed securities should be made with reference to the loans' carrying value and 'estimated fair value' of collateral securing the loan.

4 www.wsws.org/articles/2010/jan2010/home-j16.shtml.
5 This is total of all real estate loans outstanding for FDIC-insured commercial banks in the USA.
6 http://media.corporate-ir.net/media_files/irol/71/71595/reports/2007_AR.pdf.
7 S&P 500 financial institutions index (SSBANKX:IND).
8 www.iasb.org/nr/rdonlyres/a288c781-7d39-4988-ba71-9ab77a263ba0/0/ias36.pdf.
9 www.bloomberg.com/apps/news?pid=newsarchive&sid=aZchK__XUF84.
10 www.wachovia.com/file/WB3Q08_Presentation.pdf.
11 www.bloomberg.com/apps/news?pid=newsarchive&sid=aVlgKH_MT_mo&refer =home.
12 http://img.en25.com/Web/StandardandPoors/S%26Ps_BICRAs_HighlightShifting-Balance_110911.pdf.

9 The private equity business model: leveraged and fragile

1 www.iasplus.com/resource/ec0105.pdf.
2 Maltby Capital Ltd was a newly incorporated company formed at the direction of Terra Firma for the purpose of making the offer for EMI.
3 www.emimusic.com/wp-content/uploads/migration/0,,12641~140527,00.pdf.

10 Bio-pharma: a maturing business model?

1 www.medicinenet.com/script/main/art.asp?articlekey=9877.

11 Business models for a digital lifestyle

1 www.unctad.org/en/docs/psitetebd12.en.pdf.
2 www.brightsideofnews.com/news/2011/2/24/top-10-worlds-biggest-computer-makers-revealed-surprised.aspx.

12 Accounting for the UK hospice business model

1 Population aged over 65, 7.8 million to 13.8 million, www.statistics.gov.uk/pdfdir/proj0704.pdf.
2 www.statistics.gov.uk/cci/nugget.asp?ID=949.
3 www.statistics.gov.uk/CCI/nugget.asp?ID=1332andPos=1andColRank=1andRank= 310.
4 www.statistics.gov.uk/CCI/nugget.asp?ID=861andPos=4andColRank=1andRank=1 60.

REFERENCES

Abernathy, M.A., J. Bouwens, and L. Van Lent. (2004) 'Determinants of control system design in divisionalised firms', *Accounting Review*, 79(3): 545–570.

Accenture. (2010) *You're Off-shoring. Now What?*, London: Accenture, www.accenture.com/us-en/Pages/insight-application-outsourcing-offshoring-reduce-cost-summary.aspx.

Allen, F. and E. Carletti. (2009) 'The roles of banks in financial systems', in A. Berger, P. Molyneux and J. Wilson (eds), *Oxford Handbook of Banking*. Oxford: Oxford University Press, 37–57.

Almor, T. and N. Hashai. (2004) 'The competitive advantage and strategic configuration of knowledge-intensive, small- and medium-sized multinationals: A modified resource-based view', *Journal of International Management*, 10: 479–500.

Altunbas, Y., L. Gambacorta and D. Marqués. (2007) *Securitisation and the Bank Lending Channel*, European Central Bank Working Paper 838, www.ecb.int/pub/pdf/scpwps/ecbwp838.pdf.

American Securitization Forum. (2003) Hearing on Protecting Homeowners: Preventing Abusive Lending while Preserving Access to Credit, 5 November, Subcommittee on Housing and Community Opportunity Subcommittee on Financial Institutions and Consumer Credit, United States House of Representatives.

Amit, R. and P. Schoemaker. (1993) 'Strategic assets and organizational rent', *Strategic Management Journal*, 14: 33–46.

Andersson, T., C. Haslam, E. Lee and N. Tsitsianis. (2007a) 'Financialised accounts: Share buy-backs, mark to market and holding the financial line in the S&P 500', *Accounting Forum*, 31 (2): 165–178.

Andersson, T., C. Haslam, E. Lee and N.Tsitsianis. (2007b) 'Financialised accounts: A stakeholder account of cash distribution in the S&P 500 (1990–2005)', *Accounting Forum*, 3: 217–232.

Andersson, T., C. Haslam, E. Lee and N. Tsitsianis. (2008a) 'Financialisation directing strategy', *Accounting Forum*, 32(4): 261–275.

Andersson, T., C. Haslam, E. Lee and N. Tsitsianis. (2008b) 'A financialised account of corporate governance', in R. Strange and G. Jackson (eds), *Corporate Governance and International Business: Strategy, Performance and Institutional Change*. Basingstoke: Palgrave Macmillan, 226–241.

Andersson, T., C. Haslam and E. Heilpern. (2009) 'When it comes to the crunch: What are the drivers of the US banking crises?', *Accounting Forum*, 33 (2): 99–113.

Andersson, T., C. Haslam, E. Lee, G. Katechos and N. Tsitsianis. (2010) 'Corporate strategy financialised: Conjuncture, arbitrage and earnings capacity in the S&P 500', *Accounting Forum*, 34 (3–4): 211–221.

Asher, C.C., J.M. Mahoney and J.T. Mahoney. (2005) 'Towards a property rights foundation for a stakeholder theory of the firm', *Journal of Management and Governance*, 9: 5–32.

ASSC. (1975) *The Corporate Report*, Accounting Standards Steering Committee, Institute of Charted Accountants in England and Wales, London, www.ion.icaew.com/ClientFiles/6f45ef7e-1eff-41ff-909e-24eeb6e9ed15//The%20Corporate%20Report2.pdf .

Bain and Company. (2010) *Global Private Equity Report 2010*, www.bain.com.

Bank of England. (2010) *Understanding International Bank Capital Flows during the Recent Financial Crisis*, Financial Stability Paper no. 8, Bank of England, London, www.bankofengland.co.uk/publications/fsr/fs_paper08.pdf.

Bank of England. (2011) *Financial Stability Report*, no. 30, Bank of England, London, www.bankofengland.co.uk/publications/fsr/2011/fsrfull1112.pdf.

Bank for International Settlements. (2008) 'How might the current financial crisis shape financial sector regulation and structure?' Keynote address by Mr Már Gudmundsson, Deputy Head of the Monetary and Economic Department of the BIS, September, www.bis.org/speeches/sp081119.htm.

Bank for International Settlements (BIS). (2011a) *Global Liquidity Concept Measurement and Policy Implications*, CGFS paper no. 45, Basel, Switzerland, www.bis.org/publ/cgfs45.pdf.

Bank for International Settlements (BIS). (2011b) *Rescue Packages and Bank Lending*, Monetary and Economic Department, Basel, Switzerland, www.bis.org/publ/work357.pdf.

Barnard, C. (1938) *The Functions of the Executive*. Cambridge, MA: Harvard University Press.

Barney, J.B. (1986) 'Strategic factor markets: Expectations, luck and business strategy', *Management Science*, 32(10): 1231–1241.

Barney, J.B. (1991) 'Firm resources and sustained competitive advantage', *Journal of Management*, 17: 99–120.

Barney, J.B. (2001) 'Is the resource-based "view" a useful perspective for strategic management research? Yes', *Academy of Management Review*, 26(1): 41–56.

Belsky, E. and J. Prakken. (2004) *Housing Wealth Effects: Housing's Impact on Wealth Accumulation, Wealth Distribution and Consumer Spending*. W04-13, www.jchs.harvard.edu/sites/jchs.harvard.edu/files/w04-13.pdf.

Berle, A. and G. Means. (1932) *The Modern Corporation and Private Property*. London: Macmillan.

Bernanke, B.S. (2011) 'Implementing a macro-prudential approach to supervision and regulation', Paper presented to the 47th Annual Conference on Bank Structure and Competition, Chicago, Illinois, 5 May 2011, www.bis.org/review/r110509b.pdf.

Bernard, V.L., R.C. Merton and G.P. Krishna. (1995) 'Mark-to-market accounting for banks and thrifts: Lessons from the Danish experience', *Journal of Accounting Research*, 33(1): 1–32.

Besanko, D., D. Dranove and M. Shanley. (2000) *Economics of Strategy*. New York: John Wiley & Sons.

Bezemer, D.J. (2010) 'Understanding financial crisis through accounting models', *Accounting Organisations and Society*, 35(7): 676–688.

Blair, M. (2005) 'Closing the theory gap: How the economic theory of property rights can help bring "stakeholders" back into theories of the firm', *Journal of Management and Governance*, 9: 33–39.

Bryant, J. (1989) 'Assessing company strength using added value', *Long Range Planning*, 22(3): 34–44.

Business Insight. (2009) *Key Trends in Offshoring Pharmaceutical R&D: Company Strategies, Emerging Markets and Impact on ROI*, Business Insights Texas, March, www.researchand-markets.com/.../key_trends_in_offshoring_pharmaceutical.pdf.

Carroll, A.B. (1989) *Business and Society: Ethics and Stakeholder Management*. Cincinnati, OH: South-Western.

CFA Institute. (2005) *A Comprehensive Business Reporting Model: Financial Reporting for Investors*. Charlottesville, VA: CFA Institute.

Chandler, A. (1962) *Strategy and Structure: Chapters in the History of the Industrial Enterprise*. Cambridge, MA: MIT Press.

Chandler, A. (1966) *Strategy and Structure*. New York: Doubleday & Company.

Chandler, A. (1977) *The Visible Hand: The Managerial Revolution in American Business*. Cambridge, MA: Harvard University Press.

Chesbrough, H. (2006) *Open Business Models: How to Thrive in the New Innovation Landscape*. Boston, MA: Harvard Business School Press.

Cheung, S.N.S. (1983) 'The contractual nature of the firm', *Journal of Law and Economics*, 26: 1–21.

Christophers, B. (2011) 'Making finance productive', *Economy and Society*, 40: (1): 112–140.

Clarkson, M.B.E. (1995) 'A stakeholder framework for analysing and evaluating corporate social performance', *Academy of Management Review*, 20(1): 92–117.

Coase, R.H. (1937) 'The nature of the firm', *Economica*, 4(16): 386–405.

Coase, R.H. (1961) 'The problem of social cost', *Journal of Law and Economics*, 3: 1–44.

Coase, R.H. (1988) 'The nature of the firm: Influence', *Journal of Law, Economics, and Organizations*, 4(1): 33–47.

Coase, R.H. (1990) 'Accounting and the theory of the firm', *Journal of Accounting and Economics*, 12: 3–13.

Coase, R.H. (1992) 'The institutional structure of production', *American Economic Review*, 82(4): 713–719

Conner, K.R. (1991) 'A historical comparison of resource based theory and five schools of thought within industrial organization economics: Do we have a new theory of the firm?' *Journal of Management*, 17(1): 121–154.

Conner, K.R. and C.K. Prahalad. (1996) 'A resource-based theory of the firm: Knowledge versus opportunism', *Organization Science*, 7(5): 477–501.

Copeland, T., T. Koller and J. Murrin. (1990) *Valuation: Measuring and Managing the Value of Companies*, 1st edn. New York: John Wiley & Sons.

Copeland, T., T. Koller and J. Murrin. (2000) *Valuation: Measuring and Managing the Value of Companies*, 3rd edn. New York: John Wiley & Sons.

Cordell. L., K. Dynan, A. Lehnert, N. Liang and E. Mauskopf. (2009) *Designing Loan Modifications to Address the Mortgage Crisis and the Making Home Affordable Program*, Federal Reserve Board, Finance and Economics Discussion Series: 2009 (43).

Cornell, B. and A. Shapiro. (1987) 'Corporate stakeholders and corporate finance', *Financial Management*, 16: 5–14.

Cox, B. (1979) *Value Added: An Application for the Accountant Concerned with Industry*. London: Heinemann.

Deliotte. (2005) *Global Financial Services Offshoring: Scaling the Heights*. London: Deliotte, www.arengufond.ee/upload/Editor/.../offshoring_trends_Deloitte.pdf.

Department for Culture, Media and Sport (DCMS). (1988) *Creative Industries Mapping Document*. Creative Task Force. London, http://webarchive.nationalarchives.gov.uk/+/http://www.culture.gov.uk/reference_library/publications/4740.aspx.

Department for Culture, Media and Sport (DCMS). (2001) *Creative Industries Mapping Document*. Creative Task Force. London, www.creativitycultureeducation.org/research-impact/exploreresearch/creative-industries-mapping-document-2001,11,PAR.html.

Department of Health. (1995) *A Policy Framework for Commissioning Cancer Services: A Report by the Expert Advisory Group on Cancer to the Chief Medical Officers of England and Wales*. London: Department of Health.

Department of Health. (2008) *End of Life Care Strategy: Promoting High Quality Care for all Adults at the End of Life*. London: Department of Health.

Dominica, F. (1987) 'Guest editorial', *Journal of Advanced Nursing*, 12(2): 3.

Donaldson, T. and L. Preston. (1995) 'The stakeholder theory of the Corporation: Concepts, evidence and implications', *Academy of Management Review*, 20(1): 65–91.

Drucker, P.F. (1995) 'The information executives truly need', *Harvard Business Review* (January/February): 54–62.

Duffie, D. (2008) *Innovation in Credit Risk Transfer: Implications for Financial Stability*, Bank for International Settlements, Working Paper 255, www.bis.org/publ/work255.pdf.

Easterby-Smith, M. and I.M. Prieto. (2008) 'Dynamic capabilities and knowledge management: An integrative role for learning?', *British Journal of Management*, 19: 235–249.

EMI Annual Report. (2004) www.shareholder.com/visitors/dynamicdoc/document.cfm?documentid=672&companyid=EMIL.

EMI Annual Report. (2005) www.shareholder.com/visitors/dynamicdoc/document.cfm?documentid=1232&companyid=EMIL&Pin=569682107.

EMI Annual Report. (2006) www.shareholder.com/visitors/dynamicdoc/document.cfm?documentid=1232&companyid=EMIL&Pin=569682107.

EMI Annual Report. (2007) www.shareholder.com/visitors/dynamicdoc/document.cfm?documentid=1798&companyid=EMIL.

Epstein, G. (2005) 'Financialization and the world economy', in G. Epstein (ed.), *Financialization and the World Economy*. Cheltenham and Northampton: Edward Elgar.

Ernst and Young. (2008) 'Beyond borders: Global biotechnology report 2008', www.ey.com/Publication/vwLUAssets/Industry_Biotechnology_Beyond_Borders_2008/$FILE/Biotechnology_Beyond_Borders_2008.pdf.

Ernst and Young. (2009) 'Beyond borders: Global biotechnology report 2009', www.ey.com/Publication/vwLUAssets/Beyond_borders_2009/$FILE/Beyond_borders_2009.pdf.

Erturk, I., J. Froud, S. Johal, A. Lever and K. Williams. (forthcoming) 'Financialisation across the Pacific: Manufacturing cost ratios, supply chains and power'. Paper submitted to *Critical Perspectives on Accounting*.

eTForecasts. (2011) *Worldwide PC Market*. Arlington Heights, IL: eTForecasts.

European Commission. (2011) *Innovation Union Competitiveness Report 2011. Analysis Part III: Towards an Innovative Europe Contributing to the Innovation Union*. Brussels: European Commission.

European Venture Capital Journal (EVCJ). (2007) Special issue, 'Deep in debt', April.

Evan, W.M. and R.E. Freeman. (1993) 'A stakeholder theory of the modern corporation: Kantian capitalism', in T. Beauchamp and N. Bowie (eds), *Ethical Theory and Business* Englwood Cliffs, NJ: Prentice Hall, 75–84.

Feng, H., J. Froud, S. Johal, C. Haslam and K. Williams. (2001) 'A new business model? The capital market and the new economy', *Economy and Society*, 30(4): 467–503.

Finance Accounting Standards Board (FASB). (2006) *Statement no 157: Fair Value Measurements*, www.fasb.org/summary/stsum157.shtml.

Financial Accounting Standards Board (FASB). (1998) SFAS 133, www.fasb.org/st/summary/stsum133.shtml.

Financial Accounting Standards Board (FASB). (2001a) SFAS 144, www.fasb.org/st/summary/stsum144.shtml.

Financial Accounting Standards Board (FASB). (2001b) SFAS 157, www.fasb.org/st/summary/stsum157.shtml.

Financial Accounting Standards Board (FASB). (2001c) Summary of Statement no. 142, *Goodwill and Other Intangible Assets*, June, www.fasb.org/summary/stsum142.shtml.

Financial Accounting Standards Board (FASB). (2007) SFAS 14, www.gasb.org/pdf/fas141r.pdf.

Financial Services Authority (2009) *The Turner Review: A Regulatory Response to the Global Banking Crisis*, www.fsa.gov.uk/pubs/other/turner_review.pdf.

Finlay, I. (2001) 'UK strategies for palliative care', *Journal of the Royal Society of Medicine*, 94: 437–441.

Frankel, A. (2006) 'Prime or not so prime? An exploration of US housing finance in the new century', *BIS Quarterly Review*, 67–78, www.bis.org/publ/qtrpdf/r_qt0603f.pdf.

Freeman, E. (1984) *Strategic Management: A Stakeholder Approach*. London: Pitman.

Freeman, E. (2000) 'Business ethics at the millennium', *Business Ethics Quarterly*, 10(1): 169–180.

Freeman, R.E. and W.M. Evan. (1990) 'Corporate governance: A stakeholder interpretation', *Journal of Behavioral Economics*, 19(4): 337–359.

Freeman, R.E., A. Wicks and B. Parmar. (2004) 'Stakeholder theory and "The Corporate Objective" revisited', *Organizational Science*, 15(3): 364–369.

Froud, J., S. Johal and K. Williams. (2002) 'Financialisation and the coupon pool', *Capital and Class*, 78: 119–151.

Froud, J., S. Johal, A. Leaver and Williams, K. (2006). *Financialisation and Strategy: Narrative and Numbers*. London: Routledge.

General Motors. (1937), Annual report.

Gereffi, G. (1994) 'The organisation of buyer-driven global commodity chains: How US retailers shape overseas production networks', in G. Gereffi and M. Korzeniewicz (eds), *Commodity Chains and Global Capitalism*. Westport, CT: Praeger, 95–122.

Ghoshal, S. and P. Moran. (1996) 'Bad for practice: A critique of the transaction cost theory', *Academy of Management Review*, 21(1): 13–47.

Gillchrist, R. (1971) *Managing for Profit: The Value Added Concept*. London: Allen and Unwin.

Gleadle, P. and C. Haslam. (2009) 'Medco: An exploratory study of an early stage R&D-intensive firm under financialisation', *Accounting Forum*, 34(1): 54–65.

Gordon, I., C. Haslam, I. McCann and B. Scott-Quinn. (2009) 'Off-shoring of work and London's sustainability as an international financial centre', in C. Karlsson, A.E. Andersson, P.C. Cheshire and R.R. Stough. (eds), *New Directions in Regional Economic Development*. Berlin: Springer.

Grant, R.M. (1991) 'The resource based theory of competitive advantage: Implications for strategy formulation', *California Management Review*, 33(3): 114–135.

Gupta, S. (2006) 'Financial services factory', *Journal of Financial Transformation*, 45–52.

Hamel, G. and C.K. Prahalad. (1994) *Competing for the Future*. Boston: Harvard Business School Press.

Haslam, C., P. Gleadle and N. Tsitsianis. (2011) *UK Bio-pharma: Innovation, Reinvention and Capital at Risk*. Institute of Chartered Accountants Scotland (ICAS), www.icas.org.uk/site/cms/download/res/Gleadle_Haslam_Report_July_11.pdf.

Hayek, F.A. (1945) 'The use of knowledge in society', *American Economic Review*, 25(4): 519–530.

Help the Hospices. (2005) *Hospice and Palliative Care Facts and Figures 2005*. London: Help the Hospices.

Help the Hospices. (2006), *Hospice and Palliative Care: Access For All*. London: Help the Hospices.

Help the Hospices. (2008) *Who we are*, www.helpthehospices.org.uk/whoweare/index.asp.

Hill, C. and T. Jones. (1992) 'Stakeholder-agency theory', *Journal of Management Studies*, 29(2): 131–154.

Hopkins, M.M., P. Martin, P. Nightingale, A. Kraft, S. Mahdi. (2007) 'The myth of the biotech revolution: An assessment of technological, clinical and organisational change', *Research Policy*, 36(4): 566–589.

International Accounting Standard 8 (Accounting Policies, Changes in Accounting Estimates and Errors) (2005), www.iasplus.com/standard/ias08.htm.

International Accounting Standard 2 (Inventories) (2005), www.iasplus.com/standard/ias02.htm.

International Accounting Standard 16 (Property, Plant and Equipment) (2009), www.iasplus.com/standard/ias16.htm.

International Accounting Standard 19 (Employee Benefits) (2011), www.iasplus.com/standard/ias19.htm.

International Accounting Standard 39 (Financial Instruments: Recognition and Measurement) (2009), www.iasb.org/NR/rdonlyres/1D9CBD62-F0A8-4401-A90D-483C63800CAA/0/IAS39.pdf.

International Monetary Fund (IMF). (2009) 'Restarting securitization markets: Policy proposals and pitfalls', in *Global Financial Stability Report*, IMF, www.imf.org/external/pubs/ft/gfsr/2009/02/pdf/chap2.pdf.

International Monetary Fund (IMF). (2010) 'Europe and IMF agree €110 billon financing plan with Greece', *Survey Magazine*, May, www.imf.org/external/np/exr/faq/greecefaqs.htm.

International Monetary Fund (IMF). (2011) *Bank Behavior in Response to Basle III: A Cross-Country Analysis*. Working paper no. 119, Washington, DC, www.imf.org/external/pubs/ft/wp/2011/wp11119.pdf.

Jacobides, M. (2003) *How Do Markets Emerge: Organizational Unbundling and Vertical Disintegration in Mortgage Banking?* Centre for the Networked Economy Working Paper, London Business School.

Jensen, M.C. (1986) 'Agency costs of free cash flow, corporate finance, and takeovers', *American Economic Review*, 76(2): 323–329.

Jensen, M.C. (2002) 'Value maximization, stakeholder theory and the corporate objective function', *Business Ethics Quarterly*, 20(2): 235–256.

Jensen, M.C. (2007). 'The economic case for private equity (and some concerns)', keynote slides, www.scribd.com/doc/18741883/The-Economic-Case-for-Private-Equity.

Jensen, M.C. and W.H. Meckling. (1976) 'Theory of the firm: Managerial behaviour, agency costs and ownership structure', *Journal of Financial Economics*, 3 (4): 305–360.

Jensen, M.C. and W.H. Meckling. (1990) 'Specific and general knowledge and organizational structure', http://business.illinois.edu/aibrahim/readings/Specific%20and%20General%20Knowledge.pdf.

Johanson, J. and L.G. Mattsson. (1987) 'Interorganizational relations in industrial systems: A network approach compared with the transaction-cost approach', *International Studies of Management and Organization*, 17(1): 64–74.

Kaler, J. (2006) 'Evaluating stakeholder theory', *Journal of Business Ethics*, 69: 249–268.

Kaplan, D. and R. Kaplinsky. (1998) 'Trade and industrial policy on an uneven playing field: The case of the deciduous fruit canning industry in South Africa', *World Development*, 27(10): 1787–1802.

Kaplan, R. and D. Norton. (1996) *The Balanced Scorecard: Translating Strategy into Action*. Boston: Harvard Business School Press.

Kaplan, S.N. and P. Strömberg. (2009) *Leveraged Buyouts and Private Equity*. Stockholm: Institute for Financial Research.

Kaplan, R. (1988) 'One cost system isn't enough', *Harvard Business Review* (January–February): 61–66.

Kay, J. (1993) *Foundations of Corporate Success*. Oxford: Oxford University Press.

Keynes, J.M. (1972) *Essays in Persuasion*, in *The Collected Writings of John Maynard Keynes*, Volume IX. London and Basingstoke: MacMillan and St Martin's Press, for the Royal Economic Society.

Keys, B.J., T. Mukherjee, A. Seru and V. Vig. (2008) 'Did securitization lead to lax screening? Evidence from subprime loans', www.moodyskmv.com/conf08/papers/secur_lax_ screening.pdf.

Klein, B., R. Crawford and A. Alchian. (1978) 'Vertical integration, appropriable rents, and the competitive contracting process', *Journal of Law and Economics*, 21: 297–326.

Kogut, B. (1984) 'Normative observations on the international value-added chain and strategic groups', *Journal of International Business Studies*, 15(2): 151–167.

Kogut, B. (1985) 'Designing global strategies: Comparative and competitive value-added chains', *Sloan Management Review*, 26(4): 15–28.

KPMG. (1999) *Unlocking Shareholder Value: The Key to Success*. London: KPMG.

Krinsman, A.N. (2007) 'Subprime mortgage meltdown: How did it happen and how will it end?', *Journal of Structured Finance*, 13(2): 13–19.

Krippner, G. (2005) 'The financialisation of the American economy', *Soci-Economic Review*, 3: 173–208.

Laplume, A., K. Sonpar and R. Litx. (2008) 'Stakeholder theory: Reviewing a theory that moves us', *Journal of Management*, 34: 1152–1189.

Lazonick, W. (2007) 'The US stock market and the governance of innovative enterprise', *Industrial and Corporate Change*, 16(6): 983–1035.

Lazonick, W. (2008) 'The quest for shareholder value: Stock repurchases in the US economy', *Louvain Economic Review*, 74 (4): 479–540.

Lazonick, W. (2010) 'Marketization, globalization, financialisation: The fragility of the US economy in an era of global change', University of Massachusetts and University of Bordeaux, www.york.ac.uk/media/tyms/documents/cegbi/WLazonick_paper.pdf.

Lazonick, W. and M. O'Sullivan. (2000) 'Maximizing shareholder value: A new ideology for corporate governance', *Economy and Society*, 29(1): 13–35.

Lazonick, W. and Ö. Tulum. (2009) *US Biopharmaceutical Finance and the Sustainability of the Biotech Boom*. Lowell: Centre for Industrial Competitiveness, University of Massachusetts, www.industrystudies.pitt.edu/chicago09/docs/Lazonick%204.1.pdf.

McMillan, G.S., F. Narin and D.L. Deeds. (2000) 'An analysis of the critical role of public science in innovation-capital market: The case of biotechnology', *Research Policy*, 29(1): 1–8.

Madhok, A. (2002) 'Reassessing the fundamentals and beyond: Ronald Coase, the transaction cost and resource-based theories of the firm and the institutional structure of production', *Strategic Management Journal*, 23: 535–550.

Magnan, M. (2009) *Fair Value Accounting and the Financial Crisis: Messenger or Contributor?*, CIRANO, Montreal, www.cirano.qc.ca/pdf/publication/2009s-27.pdf.

Magretta, J. (2002) 'Why business models matter', *Harvard Business Review*, (May): 3–8.

Mahadevan, B. (2000) 'Business models for internet-based e-commerce: An anatomy', *California Management Review*, 42(4): 55–69.

Mahoney, M., W. Milberg, M. Schneider and R. Von Arnim. (2006). *Distribution, Growth and Governance in US Services Off-shoring*. Schwartz Center for Economic Policy Analysis, New School for Social Research, www.lse.ac.uk/collections/DESTIN/pdf/GlobalisationAmericasConference/Milberg.pdf.

Maltby Capital Annual Report. (2008), www.emimusic.com/wp-content/uploads/. . ./ 0,,12641 ~140527,00.pdf.

Maltby Capital Annual Report. (2009), www.emimusic.com/wp-content/uplo-ads/2010/02/MCL_AR_09101.pdf.

Marshall, A. (1920) *Principles of Economics*. London: Macmillan.

Mazzucato, M. and G. Dosi (eds). (2006) *Knowledge Accumulation and Industry Evolution: Pharma-biotech*. Cambridge: Cambridge University Press.

Mayer, T. (2006) 'Private equity: Spice for European economies', *Journal of Financial Trans-formation*, www.capco.com/files/pdf/66/02_FACTORY/10_Private%20equity,%20spi ce%20for%20European%20economies.pdf .

Milberg, W. (2008) 'Shifting sources and uses of profit: Sustaining US financialization with global value chains', *Economy and Society*, 37(3): 420–451.

Milberg, W. and D. Winkler. (2010) 'Financialisation and the dynamics of off-shoring in the US', *Cambridge Journal of Economics*, 34(2): 275–293.

Minsky, H.P. (1993) *The Financial Instability Hypothesis*. Jerome Levy Economics Institute of Bard College Working Paper no. 74, www.levyinstitute.org/pubs/wp74.pdf.

Moulton, B.R. (1999) *GDP and the Digital Economy: Keeping up With the Changes*, Bureau of Economic Analysis, US Department of Commerce Washington, DC.

Mouritsen, J., H.H. Larsen and P. Bukh. (2005) 'Dealing with the knowledge econo-my: Intellectual capital versus balanced scorecard', *Journal of Intellectual Capital*, 6(1): 8–27.

Nerac. (2009) *Finding the Prime Target: Acquisition Ideas for the New Pharma Business Model*. Tolland, CT: Nerac.

Norreklit, H. (2000) 'The balance on the balanced scorecard: A critical analysis of some of its assumptions', *Management Accounting Research*, 11: 65–88.

OECD. (2007) 'Moving up the (global) value chain', *Policy Brief* (July), www.oecd.org/ dataoecd/45/56/38979795.pdf.

Osterwalder, A., Y. Pigneur and C.L. Tucci. (2005) *Clarifying Business Models: Origins, Present and Future of the Concept*. University of Lausanne and BusinessModelDesign.com, http:// scholar.google.co.uk/scholar?start=10&q=business+model&hl=en&as_sdt=2000.

Petersen, M.A. and R.G. Rajan. (2002) 'Does distance still matter? The information revolu-tion in small business lending', *Journal of Finance*, 57(6): 2533–2570.

Pfizer. (2008) Annual Report, www.sec.gov/Archives/edgar/data/78003/0001193125090 40568/d10k.htm#toc67429_27.

Pfizer. (2010) Annual Report, www.pfizer.com/files/annualreport/2010/financial/finan-cial2010.pdf.

Phalippou, L. and O. Gottschalg. (2008) 'The performance of private equity funds', *Review of Financial Studies* 22(4): 1747–1776.

Pilgrims Hospice. (2011) Annual Report, www.charitycommission.gov.uk/Accounts/ Ends68/0000293968_ac_20110331_e_c.pdf.

Pisano, G. (2006) *Science Business: The Promise, the Reality, and the Future of Biotech*. Boston: Harvard Business School Press.

Pisano, G. and W.C. Shih. (2009) 'Restoring American competitiveness', *Harvard Business Review* (July–August): 1–23.

Porter, M.E. (1980) *Competitive Strategy: Techniques for Analysing Industries and Competitors*. New York: The Free Press.

Porter, M.E. (1985) *Competitive Advantage: Creating and Sustaining Superior Performance*. New York: The Free Press.

Prahalad, C.K. and G. Hamel. (1990) 'The core competence of the corporation', *Harvard Business Review* (May–June): 79–91.

Preqin. (2011) *The Preqin Quarterly*, Preqin, London, July.

Preston, L.E. (1990) 'Stakeholder management and corporate performance', *Journal of Behavioural Economics*, 19(4): 361–375.

PriceWaterhouseCoopers. (2008) 'Fair value challenges in the current environment: A review of the current valuation requirements and practices in the private equity industry', PWC, London.

PricewaterhouseCoopers. (2009) 'Getting serious about offshoring in a struggling economy', Shared Services News PWC, London, https://offshoring.fuqua.duke.edu/pdfs/Shared%20Services%20News_ORN.pdf.

Rappaport, A. (1979) 'Strategic analysis for more profitable acquisitions: A seller's market demands more careful evaluation than ever before', *Harvard Business Review* (July–August): 99–110.

Rappaport, A. (1987) 'Linking competitive strategy and shareholder value analysis', *Journal of Business Strategy*, 7(4): 58–67.

Reuters. (2011) 'S&P 500 stock buybacks up 117% in 2010; Share repurchases increase for the 6th quarter in a row', 23 March, www.reuters.com/article/2011/03/23/idUS139424+23-Mar-2011+PRN20110323.

Riahi-Belkaoui, A. (1992) *Value Added Reporting: Lessons for the US*. New York: Quorum Books.

Robinson, D.T. and T. Stuart. (2001) 'Just how incomplete are incomplete contracts? Evidence from biotech strategic alliances', http://w4.stern.nyu.edu/emplibrary/Robinson01.pdf.

Roslender, R. and S. Hart. (2003) 'In search of strategic management accounting: Theoretical and field study perspectives', *Management Accounting Research*, 14(3): 255–279.

Ross, S. (1973) 'The economic theory of agency: The principal's problem', *American Economic Review*, 63: 134–139.

Rumelt, R. P. (1974) *Strategy, Structure and Economic Performance*. Cambridge, MA: Harvard University Press.

Saunders, C. (1993) *Oxford Textbook of Palliative Medicine*, in C.S. Denice and B.F. Saunders, (2001) 'The evolution of palliative care', *Journal of the Royal Society of Medicine*, 94(9): 430–432.

Walter (1996) *Hospice and Palliative Care Concepts and Practice*. Sudbury, MA: Jones and Bartlett.

Schnure, C. (2005) *Boom-Bust Cycles in Housing: The Changing Role of Financial Structure*. IMF Working Paper (WP/05/200), www.imf.org/external/pubs/ft/wp/2005/wp05200.pdf.

Selznick, P. (1957) *Leadership in Administration*. New York: Harper and Row.

Shankman, N.A. (1999) 'Reframing the debate between agency and stakeholder theories of the firm', *Journal of Business Ethics*, 19: 319–334.

Shiller, R.J. (2006a) 'Asset prices, monetary policy, and bank regulation', www.tc.pbs.org/nbr/site/images/shillerbankStructureChicagoFed03.pdf.

Shiller, R.J. (2006b) 'Long-term perspectives on the current boom in home prices', *Economists' Voice* 3(4:4), www.bepress.com/ev/vol3/iss4/art4.

Sloan, A.P. (1963) *My Years with General Motors*. New York: Doubleday.

Solomons, D. (1965) *Divisional Performance Measurement and Control*. New York: Financial Executives Research Foundation.

Standard and Poor's Case Shiller Index House Price Values, www2.standardandpoors.com/portal/site/sp/en/us/page.topic/indices_csmahp/0,0,0,0,0,0,0,0,0,1,1,0,0,0,0,0.html.

Standard and Poor's. (2006). 'Global graying: Aging societies and sovereign ratings', Standard and Poor's ratings direct 27 June, www.savings-bond-advisor.com/Global-Graying.pdf.

Standard and Poor's. (2011) *S&P 500 2010: Pensions and Other Post-employment Benefits (OPEBs)*, 26 May, McGraw-Hill, www.spindices.com/assets/files/sp500/pdf/SP_500_OPEB-Pensions-May26-2011.pdf.

Standing, S., C. Standing and C. Lin. (2008) 'A framework for managing knowledge in strategic alliances in the biotechnology sector', *Systems Research and Behavioral Science*, 25(6): 783–796.

Stockhammer, E. (2004) 'Financialization and the slowdown of accumulation', *Cambridge Journal of Economics*, 28: 719–741.

Strange, R. (2009) 'The outsourcing of primary activities: Theoretical analysis and propositions', *Journal of Management and Governance*, 15(2): 249–269.

Sturgeon, T. (1997) *Turn-Key Production Networks: A New Model of Industrial Organization?* BRIE Working Paper no. 92A, Berkeley Roundtable on the International Economy, Berkeley, CA: University of California at Berkeley.

Tapscott, D. (2001) 'Rethinking strategy in a networked world: Or why Michael Porter is wrong about the internet', *Strategy and Business*, 24: 1–8, www.strategy-business.com/archives/?issue=19818.

Tapscott, D., D. Ticoll and A. Lowy. (2000) *Digital Capital: Harnessing the Power of Business Webs*. Boston, MA: Harvard Business School Press.

Teasdale, A. (2003) *The Process of Securitisation*, www.yieldcurve.com/Mktresearch/files/Teasdale_SecuritisationJan03.pdf.

Terra Firma. (2007) Annual Review, www.terrafirma.com/ar07.pdf.

Terra Firma. (2008) Annual Review, www.terrafirma.com/ar08/ar08.pdf.

Thomson Financial. (2007) 'Deep in debt'; reproduced from *European Venture Capital Journal*, 141, europeancapital.com/news/pdfs/pc20070401.pdf.

Timmers, P. (1998) 'Business models for electronic markets', *Electronic Markets*, 8(2): 3–8.

Tollison, R.D. (1982) 'Rent seeking: A survey', *Kyklos*, 35(4): 575–602.

UNCTAD. (2004) 'Service off-shoring takes off in Europe: In search of improved competitiveness'. Geneva: UNCTAD, www.rolandberger.com/media/pdf/rb_press/RB_Service_offshoring_20040616.pdf.

US Bureau of Economic Analysis. (2000) *An Examination of the Low Rates of Return of Foreign Owned US Companies in Survey of Current Business*, Washington DC, www.bea.gov/scb/pdf/internat/fdinvest/2000/0300rr.pdf.

US Department of Labor. (2011) *Monthly Labor Review*, April, www.bls.gov/opub/mlr/2011/04/art1full.pdf.

US Federal Reserve Board. (2009) Designing Loan Modifications to Address the Mortgage Crisis and the Making Home Affordable Program, Finance and Economics Discussion Series Divisions of Research & Statistics and Monetary Affairs, Washington, DC, www.federalreserve.gov/pubs/feds/2009/200943/200943pap.pdf.

US Government Accountability Office. (2010) Bureau of the Public Debt's Fiscal Years 2010 and 2009 Schedules of Federal Debt, November, www.treasurydirect.gov/govt/reports/pd/feddebt/feddebt_ann2010.pdf.

U.S. International Trade Commission (1999) *Review of Global Competitiveness in the Pharmaceutical Industry*, Publication 3172, April, Washington, DC.

US Treasury Department. (1997) US Comptroller of the Currency Administrator of National Banks, Asset Securitization, Washington DC, www.occ.treas.gov/publications/publications-by-type/.../assetsec.pdf.

Van Den Berg, G. (2005) 'Revolutionary effects of new information technologies', Institute for Study of Labor, IZA Bonn, Working Paper 1655, http://ftp.iza.org/dp1655.pdf.

Veblen, T. (1904) *The Theory of Business Enterprise*. Repr. 1978, New Brunswick, NJ: Transaction.

Vilen, L. (1991) 'The value-added chain approach as a method of assessing business strategies: Case: The Finnish food-processing industry', Helsinki: School of Economics and Business Administration.

Wachovia Corporation. (2008) Third Quarter Highlights, www.wachovia.com/inside/page/0,,133_205_300,00.html.

Weill, P. and M.R. Vitale. (2001) *Place to Space: Migrating to E-business Models*. Boston, MA: Harvard Business School Press.

Williams, K., C. Haslam and J. Williams. (1992) 'Ford versus "Fordism": The beginning of mass production?', *Work, Employment and Society*, 6(4): 517–555.

Williams, K., C. Haslam, S. Johal and J. Williams. (1994), *Cars: Analysis, History, Cases*. Oxford: Berghahn.

Williamson, O.E. (1971) 'The vertical integration of production: Market failure considerations', *American Economic Review*, 61: 112–123.

Williamson, O.E. (1975) *Markets and Hierarchies: Analysis and Antitrust Implications*. New York: The Free Press.

Williamson, O.E. (1985) *The Economic Institutions of Capitalism: Firms, Markets, Relational Contracting*. New York: The Free Press.

Williamson, O.E. (1991) 'Comparative economic organisation: The analysis of discrete structural alternatives', *Administrative Science Quarterly*, 36: 269–296.

Womack, J.P., D.T. Jones and D. Roos. (1990) *The Machine that Changed the World*. New York: Harper Perennial.

World Bank. (2009) 'The leverage ratio', *Crisis Response*, December, www.worldbank.org/financialcrisis/pdf/levrage-ratio-web.pdf.

World Economic Forum. (2009) *Globalization of Alternative Investments*. Working Papers Volume II: The Global Economic Impact of Private Equity Report 2009, www.weforum.org/pdf/cgi/pe/Full_Report2.pdf.

Worswick, J. (1995) 'Helen House: a model of children's hospice care', *European Journal of Palliative Care*, 2(1): 17–21.

Worthington, A.C. and T. West. (2001) 'Economic value-added: A review of the theoretical and empirical literature', *Asian Review of Accounting*, 9(1): 67–86.

Yu, S.C. (1966) 'Micro accounting and macro accounting', *Accounting Review*, 41(1): 8–20.

INDEX